Lecture Notes in Computer Science   11738

Sjouke Mauw · Mauro Conti (Eds.)

Security
and Trust Management

15th International Workshop, STM 2019
Luxembourg City, Luxembourg, September 26–27, 2019
Proceedings

 Springer

Editors
Sjouke Mauw 🆔
University of Luxembourg
Esch-sur-Alzette, Luxembourg

Mauro Conti 🆔
University of Padua
Padua, Italy

ISSN 0302-9743   ISSN 1611-3349 (electronic)
Lecture Notes in Computer Science
ISBN 978-3-030-31510-8   ISBN 978-3-030-31511-5 (eBook)
https://doi.org/10.1007/978-3-030-31511-5

LNCS Sublibrary: SL4 – Security and Cryptology

This Springer imprint is published by the registered company Springer Nature Switzerland AG
The registered company address is: Gewerbestrasse 11, 6330 Cham, Switzerland

Preface

The Security and Trust Management (STM) group is a Working Group of the European Research Consortium in Informatics and Mathematics (ERCIM) established in 2005 to provide a platform for researchers to present and discuss their ideas and foster cooperation. One of the means to achieve these goals is the organization of a yearly workshop.

These proceedings contain the papers selected for presentation at the 15th International Workshop on Security and Trust Management (STM 2019), held during September 26–27, 2019, in conjunction with the 24th European Symposium on Research in Computer Security (ESORICS 2019) in Luxembourg City, Luxembourg. The STM 2019 workshop received 23 submissions that were evaluated on the basis of their significance, novelty, technical quality, and appropriateness to the STM audience. After intensive reviewing and electronic discussions, nine full papers were selected for presentation at the workshop, giving an acceptance rate of 39%. In addition, the Program Committee selected one short paper for presentation at the workshop.

The workshop program included two invited talks by Alberto Fittarelli (Facebook) and Arthur Gervais (Imperial College London). As in previous editions, the program of the STM 2019 workshop also featured a talk by the recipient of the 2019 ERCIM STM Best PhD Award. The laureate of this year was Felix Günther for his thesis "Modeling Advanced Security Aspects of Key Exchange and Secure Channel Protocols," written at the Technische Universität Darmstadt.

We would like to thank all the people who volunteered their time and energy to make this year's workshop happen. In particular, we thank the authors for submitting their manuscripts to the workshop and all the attendees for contributing to the workshop discussions. We are also grateful to the members of the Program Committee and the external reviewers for their work in reviewing and discussing the submissions, and their commitment to meeting the strict deadlines. Our thanks also go to all the people who played a role in the organization of the event: Pierangela Samarati (chair of the STM working group), Joaquin Garcia-Alfaro (publication chair), Eleonora Losiouk (publicity chair), Olga Gadyatskaya (organization chair), and Aleksandr Pilgun (Web chair). Finally, we would like to thank the Computer Science department of the University of Luxembourg for sponsoring our event.

August 2019

Mauro Conti
Sjouke Mauw

Organization

Program Committee

Cristina Alcaraz	University of Malaga, Spain
Gildas Avoine	INSA Rennes, France
Lejla Batina	Radboud University, The Netherlands
Giuseppe Bernieri	University of Padua, Italy
Stefano Calzavara	Università Ca' Foscari Venezia, Italy
Mauro Conti	University of Padua, Italy
Cas Cremers	CISPA Helmholtz Center for Information Security, Germany
Jorge Cuellar	Siemens AG, Germany
Sabrina De Capitani di Vimercati	Università degli Studi di Milano, Italy
Zekeriya Erkin	Delft University of Technology, The Netherlands
Sara Foresti	Università degli Studi di Milano, Italy
Olga Gadyatskaya	University of Luxembourg, Luxembourg
Manoj Gaur	Malaviya National Institute of Technology, India
Ghassan Karame	NEC Laboratories Europe, Germany
Riccardo Lazzeretti	Sapienza University of Rome, Italy
Giovanni Livraga	Università degli Studi di Milano, Italy
Eleonora Losiouk	University of Padua, Italy
Luigi Mancini	Sapienza University of Rome, Italy
Fabio Martinelli	IIT-CNR, Italy
Sjouke Mauw	University of Luxembourg, Luxembourg
Catherine Meadows	Naval Research Laboratory, USA
Veelasha Moonsamy	Radboud University, The Netherlands
Stjepan Picek	Delft University of Technology, The Netherlands
Georgios Portokalidis	Stevens Institute of Technology, USA
Michael Rusinowitch	Loria, Inria Nancy, France
Giovanni Russello	University of Auckland, New Zealand
Riccardo Spolaor	University of Oxford, UK
Mark Strembeck	Vienna University of Economics and Business, Austria
Juan Tapiador	Universidad Carlos III de Madrid, Spain
Tom Van Goethem	Katholieke Universiteit Leuven, Belgium
Mathy Vanhoef	New York University, Abu Dhabi
Chia-Mu Yu	National Chung Hsing University, Taiwan

Additional Reviewers

Andreina, Sébastien
Chen, Xihui
Dushku, Edlira
Ersoy, Oguzhan
Hitaj, Dorjan
Mekdad, Yassine

Paul, Soumya
Smith, Zach
Truong, Hien
Turrin, Federico
Ullrich, Johanna

Contents

Improving Identity and Authentication Assurance in Research & Education Federations

Jule Anna Ziegler[1(✉)], Michael Schmidt[1(✉)], and Mikael Linden[2]

[1] Leibniz Supercomputing Centre, Garching near Munich, Germany
{ziegler,schmidt}@lrz.de
[2] CSC - IT Center for Science Ltd., Espoo, Finland
mikael.linden@csc.fi

Abstract. In this paper we present a lightweight identity and authentication assurance framework tailored to the needs of the research & education (R&E) sector. A comprehensive requirements analysis has been carried out with its findings being compared with existing assurance frameworks such as NIST 800-63-3, IGTF and Kantara. Due to the special requirements in a federated environment that spans multiple countries, none of the existing frameworks seems to scale in this environment. In this context, conditions such as the independence of organizations, the different organizational cultures and technical capabilities prevent the definition of strict security requirements as they are required in most policies. The REFEDS assurance suite presented here, defines a set of identity and authentication assurance criteria also including two assurance profiles differentiating between low-risk and high-risk research use cases. The presented approach still incorporates relevant criteria from existing frameworks and has been evaluated by means of a public consultation and a technical pilot. The evaluation has shown successful configuration and testing with Shibboleth and SimpleSAMLphp software, but also positive feedback from the R&E community members.

Keywords: Federated Identity Management · Trust framework · Identity and authentication assurance

1 Introduction

Higher research and education organizations, typically universities or research centers, operate a variety of ICT services for their employees and members (e.g. students). Such services include, for example, collaboration tools like video conferencing or wikis, computing environments, cloud storage and research resources such as data archives, but also organizations' internal services such as human resources and exam management. To provide users with intuitive and convenient access to all of these services, typically some kind of identifier, such as an user name, combined with a credential (e.g. password) is used. At today's state of the

© Springer Nature Switzerland AG 2019
S. Mauw and M. Conti (Eds.): STM 2019, LNCS 11738, pp. 1–18, 2019.
https://doi.org/10.1007/978-3-030-31511-5_1

art, a central organization-wide identity and access management (IAM) manages these accounts and performs user authentication.

As soon as it becomes necessary to access external services or resources of another organization, for example due to a common research collaboration, *Federated Identity Management* (FIM) is one concept to achieve this. In FIM, authentication and authorization are typically decoupled from each other. The management of the user identity as well as user authentication are still performed by the organizational IAM of the user whereas the authorization decision is carried out by the corresponding external service. Technically the organizational IAM communicates with external services by means of the Security Assertion Markup Language (SAML) [2], where the home organization (e.g. university) of the user is subsumed under the term "Identity Provider" (IdP) and the corresponding counterpart under the term "Service Provider" (SP).

An identity federation is an association of organizations that come together to exchange information as appropriate about their users and resources to enable collaborations and transactions. In research & education (R&E), on national level, these identity federations are managed by so called *National Research and Education Networks* (NRENs).

As national identity federations cannot solve the problem of cross-national research collaborations, and a single worldwide R&E federation would be utopian, GÉANT has provided a possible solution to the problem. The service is based on the concept of *Inter-Federated Identity Management* (Inter-FIM). Since 2011, the operational service eduGAIN [1] connects participating national R&E identity federations and thus enables a researcher of an organization of federation A to access a service registered in federation B as well.

However, within this environment a common language to exchange information on identity and authentication quality is still missing. It is, for instance, not specified whether a technical identifier is always assigned to the same person during its lifetime or whether this identifier can at some point of time be re-assigned, e.g. when the person is leaving the organization. Furthermore, the strength of the authentication factor and how identity proofing has been performed are not communicated. Especially for research services, which often provide access to highly sensitive data or expensive and delicate research equipment, reliable identity and authentication information is particularly critical. Consequently, in R&E, a uniform definition of such information is necessary to enable any service provider to interpret the information it receives from the user's home organization. Qualitative information on identity and authentication is typically accomplished by means of communicating *assurance information*, its strength being expressed by different levels of assurance (LoAs).

A general problem with the creation of any specifications is the lack of a hierarchical organizational structure, which is necessary for generally valid top-down specifications. Although the GÉANT Association exists as an umbrella organization, it has a more service-oriented than a legislative role. In terms of the participants, this is merely an association of independent organizations which collaborate in a spirit of partnership. Thus there are hardly any possibilities to enforce regulations against the will of the participants or to force individual organizations to implement specifications. In addition, the service providers are largely independent of the identity providers. However, the implementation of security requirements results in a mutual dependency. An identity provider (a user's home organization) will probably only implement requirements if this is required by the services of its users. A service provider, on the other hand, can't make any demands on identities without at least in the meantime excluding large parts of users. For this reason, any specifications must be designed in such a way that they meet with widespread acceptance in the community. These requirements result in a balancing act between adequate security and effort.

Although there are already various assurance frameworks in place, such as ITU-T X.1254 [7], NIST SP 800-63-3 [9] or Kantara IAF SAC [14], these are often perceived as complex with high requirements and consequently are hardly used in R&E identity federations. Therefore, a lightweight, modular approach for identity and authentication assurance is needed, which does not dispense with relevant criteria from existing assurance frameworks and thus provides an assurance baseline that can be implemented in the given scope with justifiable effort. Hence, the following questions will be answered in this paper:

- What are the use cases and requirements of the R&E sector (Sect. 2)?
- Which assurance frameworks exist so far and can they be reused (Sect. 3)?
- How could a lightweight identity and authentication assurance framework look like (Sect. 4)?
- Is the approach feasible and are there obstacles to its implementation (Sect. 5)?

Ultimately, the last section concludes the paper and provides and outlook to further work.

2 Use Cases and Requirements

The scenario considered in this paper is focused on identity federations in the R&E sector. The interfederation service eduGAIN is spanning an umbrella federation across participating national federations and thus facilitates cross-national research collaboration. The architectural concept is depicted in Fig. 1. An IdP ellipse exemplary represents an Identity Provider within a federation, a SP ellipse a Service Provider respectively.

2.1 Use Cases

There are many SPs withing a federation and each of them offers a different type of service. While some of them simply provide access to relatively low security services like survey tools, others provide access to highly sensitive data. These SPs rely on an IdP capability to appropriately check the identity of its users and perform secure authentication. Due to the fact that these IdPs are managed by individual organizations using various security measures themself they offer a

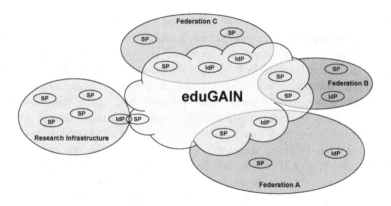

Fig. 1. eduGAIN overview

different security level for their users. But the security level of an IdP and their users is not transparent or communicated, thus SPs have to trust that identities and authentications are handled securely. However, SPs want to ensure that the identity and authentication assurance of a given user matches the security requirements of their service offering. For this reason SPs and IdPs need a common international framework that does not only define shared security levels to handle identities and authentication events but also a way to communicate them in a standardized way.

Besides federations, a research infrastructure can provide IAM services for researchers or organizations to enable them to collaborate with the objective of a common research project, regardless of national boundaries, and usually over a longer period of time. Such IAM services may be connected to the interfederation via a central hub, which is in fact an IdP-SP-proxy. ELIXIR, for instance, is a research infrastructure for biological data and includes over 180 distributed research organizations spread across Europe. However, many research infrastructures provide access to highly expensive equipment or sensitive data, such as human samples (e.g. sequenced genome data), which is why the identity and authentication assurance is considered urgent. It is important to know, for example, who exactly the user is, what their current affiliation is or how user authentication was performed.

2.2   Functional Requirements

In order to be able to tailor an assurance framework - as lightweight and easy to implement as possible - to the environment described above, functional requirements from an interview [8] are taken into account. In this interview, several research and e-infrastructures were interviewed with the aim of determining the minimum level of assurance information required.

Thus, the following six requirements form the basis for the further proceeding:

F1 **Each account must belong to a known individual person**: Accounts must not be shared and must be traceable to its holder. Allowing the use of shared accounts would thwart accountability, making it impossible to trace the actions done using the account back to a single natural person.

F2 **Persistent user identifier**: User identifiers must not be re-assigned. Some organizations have chosen to reassign user identifiers i.e. allow recycling them to different persons when their first holder departs. This practice may risk information security as the new holder of the identifier may get access to the previous holder's service profiles.

F3 **Documented identity vetting procedures**: The identity vetting process (independent of the method used, e.g. postal, in person) must be identified and documented for transparency.

F4 **Password authentication**: For services with limited risk profile, password authentication is sufficient but a minimum security baseline for password authentication must be in place (e.g. password length, complexity).

F5 **Departing user's affiliation must change promptly**: Access to services is often not given to researchers personally but as a representative of their home organization and if they depart their access rights must be closed. The relying service can do this by observing the user's affiliation attribute as released by the home organization but the relying service needs to be able to rely on the accuracy and freshness of that information. This is a balance between the maximum latency the relying services can tolerate and the agility that the home organization's IAM system can deliver. As a compromise, the freshness of the user affiliation must be one month at the latest.

F6 **Self-assessment**: A regular self-assessment of the identity management practices must be performed. This is a balance between having no assessment at all and requiring external audits or peer audits which can hinder adoption.

2.3 Non-functional Requirements

In addition to the functional requirements mentioned above, the environment itself and the intended use of the framework also creates additional conditions. These are mainly based on experiences from similar projects in a comparable context. Although these are not mandatory requirements but rather soft factors, they influence the later acceptance of the framework in the community, which is a critical success factor. Therefore, the following non-functional requirements apply:

NF1 **Adoptability**: The standards must be easily adoptable by the majority of organizations. Due to the lack of authority to require adoption of standards, a critical mass must instead voluntarily adopt them to motivate the rest of the community.

NF2 **Implementability**: The implementation of the specifications must be possible with the widely used standard software tools (out-of-the-box).

Due to the already existing infrastructure, many IdPs are based on a set of standard software. A standard that cannot be implemented with the already established tools would require a major change, which most IdPs would not be willing to do.

NF3 **Understandability**: Most IdPs are hosted by universities and research institutions themselves. Depending on the size and location of the institution, the size of the IT department may vary, if it exists at all. It is therefore not possible to anticipate the presence of an IT security specialist or persons with the appropriate knowledge. For this reason, all requirements must be understandable and usable also for an administrator without dedicated security knowledge.

NF4 **Self-contained**: As far as possible, the implementation of the requirements should not depend on further reference documents. As with understandability, it cannot be assumed that the organization of an IdP has enough resources and knowledge to read and implement several different standards at the same time.

Based on the use cases presented and the requirements determined, it can be seen that a general framework is needed in the context of eduGAIN in order to establish uniform standards. This must contain both technical and organizational requirements for identity and authentication assurance, which are still lightweight enough to be used in a diversified federated environment. The term "lightweight" is used in this context to express the abstraction of negligible criteria and the ability to fulfill requirements based on the presence of different means. As specified in Sect. 2.2, some of the functional requirements are clearly defined and can easily be mapped to specifications. Others, like password security, are very abstract and have to be tailored to the need of the R&E community first. It remains to be checked to what extent these framework conditions can be translated into a concrete specification and whether they can be covered by existing standards.

3   Existing Assurance Frameworks

Subsequently, we analyzed existing assurance frameworks based on the requirements of Sect. 2 in terms of their suitability and applicability. Due to the large number of assurance frameworks in place, we will only discuss a selected subset of our findings in this section. This includes the Special Publication 800-63-3 Digital Identity Guidelines from the National Institute of Standards and Technology (NIST) and the Kantara Identity Assurance Framework. Ultimately, we will also discuss the Levels of Authentication Assurance established by the Interoperable Global Trust Foundation (IGTF).

In order to evaluate existing frameworks and standards, interviews and discussions with NREN representatives and working group members, which represent the research and education community, took place. Within these discussions it turned out, that a uniform, consistent and not too restrictive framework is needed which still complies with existing national policies. Furthermore, it was pointed out at multiple occasions that there is limited willingness in the community to adopt a framework that requires many changes to their existing infrastructure or software. This disqualifies already many guidelines that define high technical obstacles, even if they can be seen as justified.

3.1   NIST SP 800-63-3 Digital Identity Guidelines

NIST SP 800-63-3 [9] provides a comprehensive assurance framework including assurance levels for a set of three different categories. Each category is described in a separate document. The *Identity Assurance Levels* refer to the strength of the identity proofing process. The *Authenticator Assurance Levels* deal with the authentication process whereas the *Federation Assurance Levels* describes technical requirements to secure assertions transmitted within a federation. Three IALs are defined in NIST 800-63A. Each of them requires a specific set of evidence to proof an identity, which are categorized as Weak, Fair, Strong or Superior. IAL 2 and 3 already define a security level that meets the requirement (F1). Furthermore, the approved methods for performing identity proofing are specified for all IALs in combination with evidence (F3). Unfortunately, the requirements for the IALs and the evidence used are very strict, making it difficult to use them within the scope. For example, IAL 3 does not only require several, at least strong evidence, but the process shall also include address verification and the collection of biometric information.

By means of AAL, NIST provides criteria for digital authentication, such as authenticator requirements (e.g. passwords, OTP Devices, Cryptographic Devices/Software). NIST AAL thus covers F4, in particular regarding password-based authentication, which is predominantly used in the considered scope.

However, due to the variety of "SHALL" requirements, for example in terms of password salting and hashing, the framework is considered too heavy and wouldn't find adoption in the given environment. Furthermore, NIST AAL relies on other standards like FIPS 140, which for example requires certificated verifiers and thus defines a very high technical boundary. It turned out in conversations with representatives from various NRENs that they see themselves incapable of implementing various technical and organizational requirements defined by NIST. Especially smaller organizations rely on standard software suites, which are not capable to fulfill these technical requirements, for example password checking and filtering, without manual adjustment of the underlying infrastructure. NISTs requirements for memorized secrets verifiers forces the Credential Service Provider (CSP) to compare authentication secrets with secrets already known as insecure and enforce a new secret if matched, something that is not possible with LDAP or Active Directory out of the box.

3.2   Kantara Identity Assurance Framework

Kantara Classic which was the first implementation of the Kantara Identity Assurance Framework (IAF) [14] is an abstract framework providing high level security requirements, which relies on the guidelines of other identity frameworks. IAF consists of a summary of Identity Assurance Levels (IALs), an Assurance Assessment Scheme (AAS) and additional criteria by which a service can be assessed. The IAL's are based on the level structure defined in NIST SP 800-63-2. Although IAF defines a set of strict criteria for each IAL, it provides some flexibility to the user due to the abstraction of the given requirements. However, to understand the meaning and boundaries of these high level statements correctly, a deep knowledge of (identity) security is required. Additionally, the framework has strong relationships to other guidelines and therefore requires awareness of these frameworks as well. So many requirements state just to use an approved (e.g national authority or other generally-recognized authoritative body) or suitable solution without exactly defining which measures would be appropriate to mitigate the described risk. Especially relying on a national authoritative body for a multinational collaboration is cumbersome. In contrast to that, others or parts of requirements are highly granular and no real balance between the requirements are given. This was identified as an issue by NREN's as well, which demand flexible but still consistent set of requirements over organizational and national boundaries.

Even though IAF qualifies to most of the functional requirements described in Sect. 2, the framework can be considered too demanding for the target audience, at least to be used as a whole. For example, strong requirements for rate limiting or session timeout can not be easily applied to different organizations in multiple countries, due to their environment specific requirements or policies. A much more open approach instead of the definition of hard coded values was demanded. However, some of the identity proofing requirements might be effectively implemented within the scope, as they allow slightly more flexibility regarding methodology than comparable NIST requirements.

3.3   IGTF Levels of Authentication Assurance

The IGTF Levels of Authentication Assurance (IGTF LoA) [4] consist of a set of four technology-agnostic authentication assurance levels (i.e. ASPEN, BIRCH, CEDAR and DOGWOOD) which refer as well to other well-known documentation such as from Kantara or NIST. Besides the identity-related requirements, IGTF LoA defines operational requirements (e.g. credential management) but also IT service management related requirements like for example to have a disaster recovery in place and the recommendation to perform internal audits regularly. In general, the framework has a strong focus on infrastructure providers instead of CSPs providing identities to end users. The described requirements are limited to high level statements without specific guidance on authenticator or identity security. Still, some requirements regarding identity proofing are well defined and might be suitable for use in the desired scope.

3.4   Requirements Comparison

Each of the described frameworks defines a sound set of requirements that
define a state of the art identity and authentication assurance environment.
All functional requirements (Sect. 2.2) are mentioned to some extent and might
easily fullfill them. This is no surprise especially for NIST and Kantara, two
large sophisticated frameworks that cover almost every aspect of identity and
authentication assurance. However, even IGTF, which could be considered more
lightweight, defines criteria to match the functional requirements. This is probably because these requirements are not R&E specific but more general security
aspects.

Nevertheless, these frameworks lack multiple of the non-functional requirements defined, as depicted in Table 1. However, these requirements, even though
they seem to be common sense, are crucial to establish such a framework in the
target environment. Anyway, one can't just extract some matching functional
requirements from the existing frameworks and merge them. This is not easily
possible since the requirements of a framework depend on each other from a
security point of view and just extracting individual ones would render them
useless.

Table 1. Non-functional requirements comparison

Requirement	NIST	Kantara	IGTF	REFEDS
NF1	✗	✗	(✓)	✓
NF2	✗	✗	(✓)	✓
NF3	✗	✗	✓	✓
NF4	(✓)	✗	(✓)	(✓)

✓: requirement fulfilled
(✓): requirement partly fulfilled
✗: requirement not fulfilled

4   Identity and Authentication Assurance

Given that none of the existing assurance frameworks, as shown in Sect. 3, completely meets the needs of the R&E sector, a new lightweight approach for identity and authentication assurance has been developed. The approach is inspired
by the concept described in [13], which was also adopted by NIST, where multiple
independent values are used to express assurance in an identity and authentication transaction. In accordance with the mathematical concept, each value is
called an *orthogonal component*. Orthogonality tries to achieve that each component is defined and expressed in an non-overlapping way. This enables the
approach to be extensible and composable.

The *REFEDS*[1] *assurance suite* we present here defines an identity assurance framework (in short RAF) including three orthogonal components: identifier uniqueness, identity proofing, and an attribute-related component. The authentication assurance is decoupled from RAF and is represented by means of two separate profiles: the first profile establishes a security baseline for authentication and covers single factor authentication scenarios (Single Factor Authentication Profile). The second profile [11] is derived from former work done by REFEDS and the InCommon Multi-Factor Authentication Interoperability Profile Working Group who already specified a Multi Factor Authentication Profile for high-risk authentication use cases.

Hence, the scope of this paper will be on RAF and the Single Factor Authentication Profile (SFA). All components are designed in an independent way, to allow flexibility and to cover different risk-dependent use cases. The assurance suite is intended to be used in the scenario described above but could potentially be used in any scenario, where appropriate. The assurance suite also defines how to communicate each component using SAML and the newer OpenID Connect (OIDC) protocols, respectively.

A fundamental aspect between the presented approach and existing R&E standards is the difference in the use of SAML attributes. Normally, SAML attributes are defined whose value gives an inherent message about the identity they belong to, such as the name or organization of a person. The REFEDS assurance suite, on the other hand, does not add new personal information to an identity, but make a claim about the quality of existing attributes or, in the case of MFA/SFA, about the entire SAML assertion itself. Therefore, the assurance suite doesn't describe properties of the user itself, but metadata of the user identity, i.e. how reliably the authenticated identity represents its holder.

4.1   REFEDS Assurance Framework

As already introduced, the REFEDS assurance framework [11] is split in three orthogonal components, which can be asserted independently: Identifier uniqueness, identity proofing, attribute quality and freshness. Each component reflects at least one requirement of Sect. 2. In the following subsections all components will be presented.

Identifier Uniqueness: In order to distinguish between users of a service and thus identify returning users, a unique identifier (ID) is required (see also F2). In general, three types of identifiers can be distinguished: transaction, session and permanent. The former only identifies a user within a single transaction. This procedure best describes the anonymous use of a service. If a user is recognized over the course of several transactions, this is referred to as a session-based identifier. After the session has ended, the ID is no longer unique; it can be issued directly to another user. Ultimately, a user can be identified by using a permanent identifier over the entire lifespan of the user account.

---

[1] **R**esearch and **E**ducation **FED**erations group.

For most services where a permanent user account is to be used, a permanent identifier is required. This identifier can be either service scoped (i.e. pair-wise between the IdP and SP) or global. The former is unique only in the context of a single service, i.e. the user has a different ID for different services. The latter uniquely identifies a user across service boundaries, allowing mapping of the user between multiple services. In eduGAIN different identifiers are available for the IdPs and SPs. In the eduPerson specification [6], the permanent identifiers eduPersonPrincipalName (global), eduPersonUniqueId (global) and eduPerson-TargetedID (service) were introduced. Furthermore, SAML 2.0 itself defines a permanent identifier [3] which is called persistent nameID (service).

In this context, the RAF aims not to create another ID type, but to flag a reassignment of an already assigned ID. Therefore, it does not compulsorily specify which type of ID or attribute must be used. With the attribute *unique* it mostly specifies which properties the used identifier must have. Four unique properties are defined that all need to be satisfied at the same time. [11]

This procedure gives both IdPs and SPs the flexibility necessary for eduGAIN. On the one hand, the IdP is not forced to support or release a specific identifier. On the other hand, the SP can still define its ID attribute requirements. Regardless of which identifier the IdP provides, it is ensured that the described requirements are met.

Identity Proofing: A digital identity represents a person and their characteristics in the digital world. In order to prove one's identity when applying for example for a new bank account, the person would show an identity card in the real world. By the general acceptance of the issuer, our identity can easily be proven. This procedure of verifying one's identity is called identity proofing. In the digital world, this procedure is far more difficult because we cannot easily prove our identity by providing physical evidence. Therefore, it is necessary to prove it in the real world to a trustworthy body and then transfer it to the digital world. Depending on how a person has been verified, the certified identity is more or less secure [5, 7].

Based on the presented frameworks, RAF also defines three incremental levels: low, medium and high (F3). However, no new requirements are specified, instead each of these levels can be derived from one or more existing LoA. This allows great flexibility and allows IdPs to continue using existing procedures as long as the criteria of an approved framework are met. This mapping is necessary because a single framework could not reflect the constraints in different federations and organizations that arise in the context of an international use.

Attribute Quality and Freshness: In addition to merely providing an identity, the primary task of an IdP is to manage the corresponding properties, i.e. attributes. In the eduGAIN context, these are primarily the attributes defined in eduPerson. One of the most important attributes in the context of R&E describes the type of affiliation of a person to their home institution. The affiliation information is then used to manage authorisations in the relying services; for instance, only researchers (faculty members) can access sensitive research resources. The affiliation is defined by the Home organization and expressed by assigning one of the following values: faculty, student, staff, alum, member, affiliate, employee, library-walk-in. This affiliation attribute can then be used by SPs to assign roles and permissions in the application. Many SPs thus rely on the IdP's statement about a person's status to provide the service. It is obvious that SPs are therefore interested in a reliable statement. For example, dismissed employees should no longer have access to research data, nor should former students have access to student offers. To enable the SPs to better assess the affiliation provided, RAF defines a value that provides information about the maximum age of this claim F5). Thus, an IdP can promise to update the affiliation within a month or even a day, which allows the SP to make a corresponding risk assessment. This indirectly reflects the IT process of the organization behind the IdP and its ability to apply changes in a person's status to their digital identity.

Conformance Criteria: In addition to the concrete assurance components, the framework defines some high level requirements for the general security of the IdP (F6). Thereby no specific criteria are given, instead the security of the IdP should be basically aligned to the security of the organization itself. It is therefore assumed that every organization in a federation is basically able to guarantee secure IT operation and it must only be ensured that this also applies to the IdP provided. Instead of strict security requirements, this procedure is based on mutual trust within the federations. While this would not be applicable in a commercial environment, it is satisfactory for a partnership scenario like this, which is ultimately based on a pure self-assessment.

4.2   Authentication Assurance

The aim of authentication assurance is to define a set of criteria which handles the authentication strength in the R&E scope. It originates from requirement F4 (password authentication) given that the use of a password credential is the most common use case within this web-based R&E scope. Nevertheless, we decided to abstract from password-based authentication and created a profile which covers authentication using a single factor independent of its type. Solely biometrics is excluded due to its lacking capability as a single factor.

The SFA Profile [11] defines a minimum security baseline for authentication using a single factor. "Minimal" on the one hand, that it tries not to dispense with key criteria of existing frameworks. On the other hand, that the defined criteria must be fulfilled as a minimum in order to qualify to this profile. Federations or organizations with existing stronger policies on passwords may then be compliant to the SFA Profile without additional effort. This is achieved by the definition of high-level requirements that allow some freedom of action. In general, the SFA profile distinguishes between two major criteria: the requirements for the authentication factor itself and the requirements for the replacement of a lost authentication factor. The first criteria is then further divided into four high-level requirements. List item 1 and 2 define quantitative thresholds which must at least be met.

Table 2. Authenticator secret length and basis [11]

Authenticator type	Secret basis	Min length
Memorized secret	≥52 characters (e.g. 52 letters)	12 characters
	≥72 characters (e.g. 52 letters + 10 digits + 10 special characters)	8 characters
Time based OTP-Device	10–51 characters (e.g. 10 digits)	6 characters
Out-of-band Device	≥52 characters (e.g. 52 letters)	4 characters
Look-up secret	10–51 characters (e.g. 10 digits)	10 characters
Sequence based OTP-Device	≥52 characters (e.g. 52 letters)	6 characters
Cryptographic	RSA/DSA	2048 bit
software/device	ECDSA	356 bit

(1) The authenticator secret length and the secret basis used for secret generation as shown in Table 2
(2) The maximum secret lifetime according to the way of secret delivery
(3) Threat protection: prevention of online guessing attacks
(4) Threat protection: cryptographic protection of authentication secrets (at rest/in transit)

The other criteria deals with the replacement of a lost authentication factor. It is composed of a set of requirements specifying (in)valid replacement procedures (e.g. knowledge based, human based), but also for restoring a lost factor using OTPs (e.g. recovery links) and the handling of backup authenticators.

Compliance to this profile is communicated in SAML via the AuthnContextClassRef and the acr claim (id token) in OIDC respectively.

4.3 RAF Profiles

To simplify the use of the identity assurance framework and the orthogonal components described therein, two predefined *RAF profiles* (Cappuccino, Espresso) were defined. These provide a meaningful selection of identity related values from the different components to support different security needs of the community (Fig. 2).

The **Cappuccino profile** aims at covering the requirements of the low-risk use cases. The required identity proofing is more demanding then basic procedures (i.e. self asserted) and a combination with the SFA profile is recommended.

The **Espresso profile** aims at high-risk use cases. It requires a strong identity proofing process and recommends a combination with the MFA profile.

For reasons of flexibility, these RAF profiles have been decoupled from the authentication profiles, i.e. any combination of RAF profile and authentication profile is possible in principle. A recommendation for a certain security level remains, however. While the combination of Low-Identity (Cappuccino) and High-Authentication (MFA) makes sense, it is doubtful for High-Identity

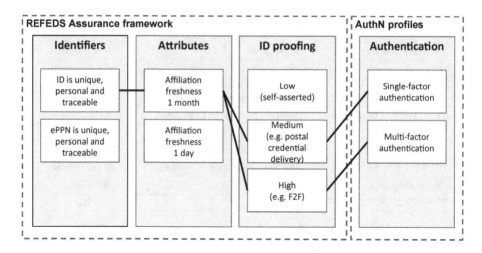

Fig. 2. REFEDS identity and authentication profiles

(Espresso) and Low-Authentication (SFA). It is recommended to choose a combination where the authentication security is higher or equal than the identity LoA.

4.4 Comparison with Existing Frameworks

This paper presented the REFEDS assurance suite, which is a lightweight assurance framework derived from existing frameworks to fulfill the special requirements of the R&E community. The suite defines assurance requirements for all functional requirements defined in Sect. 2.2 and imposes a consistent granularity across all requirements. While they were written in a level of detail that clearly states the boundaries of a requirement, for example secrets lengths, they are at the same time high level enough to allow different implementations.

Even though most functional requirements are met by existing frameworks as well (see Sect. 3), they lack the non-functional requirements which are crucial for its acceptance in the community.

Especially NF2 (Implementability) is a requirement that cannot be met by sophisticated frameworks like NIST or Kantara. In the context of the SFA profile, an attempt was made to identify the most important requirements and to reuse them as basic requirements. The minimum requirements it defines for authentication factors are derived from those in NIST, but reduces the number and demands of these requirements. The profile pursues a mixture of requirements-based and risk-based approaches. Strict requirements are used to define a baseline in order to guarantee a minimum quality, such as the length and composition of secrets. Soft requirements, on the other hand, are based on the mitigation of certain threats. Although the goal is specified, such as prevention of online guessing attacks or protection of secrets at rest, no exact measure or key figures are defined on how these are to be met. In comparison, NIST and KANTARA define exact values and consequences for a rate limit, as well as technologies with which secrets are to be protected. Although these are reasonable specifications, they make it difficult to apply them in existing infrastructures. Therefore, it makes more sense at this point to abstract these and comparable requirements and to give the organization the possibility to treat the associated risk in a way that is possible in its existing infrastructure and appropriate for its user group.

Similar difficulties apply to NF3 (Understandability), since existing frameworks demand security knowledge. It turned out in review discussions with the community that frameworks like NIST and KANTARA are comprehensive and therefore difficult to understand by many people without a security background.

The reason for this is probably that eduGAIN and NRENs are the only form of SAML-based R&E federations, at least on a global scale. The specific requirements of this heterogeneous community are therefore not fully covered by standard frameworks. For this reason, their requirements do not fully match the simple needs in the target scope. Many specifications are based on the availability of external resources to verify the identity verification process and the associated processes. Furthermore, there are also business aspects which needs to be considered. R&E organizations, like universities, aim at supporting their researchers' collaboration but also protecting their own assets with the same IAM systems. Commercial CSPs aim at minimising the costs while complying the specifications. Therefore Kantara and other standards are much more detailed.

To put it in a nutshell, the REFEDS Assurance Suite aims to extract the essential requirements from existing assurance frameworks and cast them to a high level representation to make them applicable in a heterogeneous environment.

5 Evaluation and Piloting

The developed assurance and authentication framework was publicly evaluated by the R&E community and other interested parties and tested in a pilot study by organizations from different NRENs and countries. In this way it was ensured that the framework meets the requirements initially set by the community, is internationally applicable and can be implemented by common IdP and SP products.

5.1 Public Consultation

During the preparation process, the SFA profile was reviewed in one, RAF in two public consultations [10]. In a time period of each 6 weeks the R&E community, interested parties and members of REFEDS were asked to provide their feedback on the assurance suite.

Results: Regarding the quantitative evaluation results of RAF public consultation round one, we received 26 queries from an international basis. RAF public consultation round two produced 10 queries on european level while SFA public consultation produced four. To track these queries a change log was created, the derived actions were specified in several discussion rounds. Due to the large number of queries received in the first RAF round, the revised RAF specification was resubmitted for a second public consultation. Given the number and complexity of the queries received for the SFA profile, no second consultation was considered necessary.

In terms of qualitative evaluation results in RAF round two, we received besides some general formatting and the resolution of minor issues in RAF, feedback to clarify the usage of identifiers in the identifier uniqueness component, especially in terms of the eduPersonPrincipleName attribute (ePPN). For ePPN, the eduPerson specification does per default not specify any ePPN reassignment practices so that needed to be specified more precisely with language that leaves less room for misinterpretation.

Furthermore, some examples for each identity proofing level (low, medium and high) were added given that the identity proofing component derives its levels from one or more existing LoA.

In addition to that, the definitions on attribute quality and freshness values (1 day, 1 month) were considered too ambiguous, leaving room for misunderstandings. The institutions have heterogeneous practices on when they decide a researcher or student departs and loses the grounds for their affiliation. Additional clarification was necessary to show that these values only refer to the latency of the organizational IAM system after the person has departed.

In terms of the SFA Profile, the community was largely satisfied. Merely a refinement of the boundaries to existing frameworks (i.e. NIST 800-63-3) and guidance for authenticator types, its secret basis and minimum length was provided by adding two informative appendices to the profile.

5.2   Piloting the REFEDS Assurance Suite

In parallel to the feedback gained from the consultation, a pilot [12] was deployed to identify any remaining vagueness or (technical) issues but also to gain practical experience on the specifications in the R&E environment. In total, four SAML identity providers (all Shibboleth-based) and four service providers (Shibboleth as well as SimpleSAMLphp software) participated in the pilot phase over a period of three to four month. The pilot participants first familiarized themselves with the specifications. The IdPs were then configured to populate and support RAF and authentication context values of SFA/MFA, while SPs were configured to request and interpret the values.

Results: Technically all participating entities (IdPs, SPs) were successfully configured. An IdP/SP test matrix [12] was produced to keep records of the successful exchange of RAF, SFA and MFA between the involved pilot participants. We did not explicitly pilot with Microsoft ADFS product but additional research has shown that RAF support is straightforward. Regarding the authentication profiles, ADFS only supports a predefined set of authentication contexts and so far cannot handle the custom ones defined in the SFA/MFA profiles.

As an overall conclusion, we received positive feedback from the R&E community. A bunch of federations/organizations is already checking compliance to the criteria defined in the REFEDS assurance suite and a few IDPs/SPs already start asserting/requiring these values. In terms of implementing the REFEDS assurance suite, the main challenge is the proper configuration of the RAF values and the SAML authentication context at the IdP. Therefore, supporting implementation guidance has already made publicly available.

6   Conclusion and Further Work

In this paper we presented the REFEDS assurance suite tailored to the needs of the research and education sector. Due to the special, federated environment and the lack of a hierarchical organizational structure, no mandatory regulations can be imposed on the participating federations or organizations. This complicates the usage of existing frameworks such as NIST 800-63-3 or Kantara and makes it even impossible to enforce them. Furthermore, numerous individual policies at federational or organizational level are in place, which additionally burden the adoption of an overall, common assurance framework. This is why in this paper we have presented a lightweight solution, which is to the best as possible in line with existing policies and takes into account relevant criteria from existing frameworks. Even though the assurance suite is tailored to the needs of the R&E community, the framework may also be used in other non-research related organizations, as it defines a set of fundamental identity & authentication related requirements. By using high-level criteria, the approach allows some room for action to keep the implementation effort for all participants as low as possible. Its practical approach enables implementation in any identity federation and is therefore applicable to other SAML/OIDC based scenarios, which are not specifically addressed by any other framework at the moment.

The REFEDS assurance suite presented in this paper is based on a requirement analysis (i.e. interview) with several research-/e-infrastructures. Subsequently, existing frameworks (e.g. NIST 800-63-3, Kantara, IGTF) were checked in terms of their suitability, but were considered too complex for the R&E environment. Based on the findings of the requirement analysis and some key criteria of existing frameworks a lightweight approach has been designed. The REFEDS assurance suite is modular and extensible and decouples the identity assurance from the authentication assurance. The identity assurance (REFEDS Assurance Framework) is built on the concept of three orthogonal components, which are independently assertable. A proposal to combine the values of these components is provided by means of two profiles (Cappuccino, Espresso). The authentication assurance relies on two authentication profiles to handle one or multiple authentication factors. Following, an evaluation within the R&E community was carried out with its findings fed into a revised assurance suite. Simultaneously, a pilot with SAML software, i.e. Shibboleth and SimpleSAMLphp, to test practical applicability was performed. Both public consultation and piloting showed positive feedback from the R&E community.

As an outlook on further work, the REFEDS assurance suite aims to be implemented on a large scale in a given R&E environment. For this purpose, the approach first needs to be advertised to all participating federations/organizations. As this approach is self-asserted due to the lack of mandatory regulations, it needs to be ensured that all criteria are correctly understood and that a correct self-assessment has taken place. For this reason a self-assessment tool provided to the community to test individual compliance could help encouraging adoption.

Acknowledgment. The research leading to these results has received funding from the Europeans Union's Horizon 2020 research and innovation programme under Grant Agreement No. 731122 (GN4-2) and 730941 (AARC2). The authors wish to thank the project members of GÉANT, AARC2 as well as the REFEDS community for helpful discussions and feedback to continuously improve the work presented in this paper.

References

1. eduGAIN Homepage (2018). https://edugain.org/. Accessed 10 Nov 2018
2. Cantor, S., et al.: Assertions and Protocols for the OASIS Security Assertion Markup Language (SAML). OASIS (2005)
3. Cantor, S.: SAML V2.0 Subject Identifier Attributes (2018)
4. Groep, D.: IGTF Levels of Authentication Assurance (2015)
5. International Standard Organization: ISO/IEC 29115: Entity Authentication Assurance Framework, first edn. (2013)
6. Internet2/MACE: eduperson object class specification (2016). http://software. internet2.edu/eduperson/internet2-mace-dir-eduperson-201602.html. Accessed 10 Nov 2018
7. ITU: X.1254: Entity authentication assurance framework (2012)
8. Linden, M., et al.: Recommendations on Minimal Assurance Level Relevant for Low-risk Research Use Cases (2015). https://aarc-project.eu/wp-content/uploads/2015/11/MNA31-Minimum-LoA-level.pdf. Accessed 10 Nov 2018
9. National Institute of Standards and Technology: Special Publication 800–63-3: Digital Identity Guidelines (2017)
10. REFEDS: REFEDS Public Consultation (2018). https://wiki.refeds.org/display/CON/Consultations+Home. Accessed 07 Dec 2018
11. REFEDS: REFEDS Specifications (2018). https://refeds.org/specifications. Accessed 02 Dec 2018
12. REFEDS: REFEDS wiki: RAF pilot final report (2018). https://wiki.refeds.org/display/GROUPS/RAF+pilot+final+report. Accessed 07 Dec 2018
13. Richer, J., Johansson, L.: RFC 8485: Vectors of Trust. IETF (2018)
14. Wilsher, R.G.: Identity Assurance Framework: Service Assessment Criteria. Kantara Initiative Inc, 5.0 edn. (2016)

Audit-Based Access Control with a Distributed Ledger: Applications to Healthcare Organizations

Umberto Morelli[1]⬤, Silvio Ranise[1]⬤, Damiano Sartori[2]⬤,
Giada Sciarretta[1]⬤, and Alessandro Tomasi[1(✉)]⬤

[1] Security & Trust, Fondazione Bruno Kessler,
Via Sommarive 18, 38123 Trento, Italy
{umorelli,ranise,giada.sciarretta,altomasi}@fbk.eu
[2] EIT Master School, Trento, Italy
damiano.sartori@studenti.unitn.it
https://st.fbk.eu

Abstract. We propose an audit-based architecture that leverages the Hyperledger Fabric distributed ledger as a means to increase accountability and decentralize the authorization decision process of Attribute-Based Access Control policies by using smart contracts. Our goal is to decrease the trust in administrators and users with privileged accounts, and make the a posteriori verification of access events more reliable. We implement our approach to the use case of Electronic Health Record access control. Preliminary experiments show the viability of the proposed approach.

Keywords: Access control · Hyperledger fabric · Distributed ledger · Trust

1 Introduction

Controlled information sharing among the users of a system or a platform operated by an organization is key to achieve business objectives, prevent unauthorized disclosure (confidentiality) and malicious or accidental unauthorized changes (integrity), while ensuring accessibility by authorized users whenever needed (availability). The main security mechanism to achieve this is access control: the process of mediating every request to resources maintained by the organization and determining whether the request should be granted or denied. Defining, deploying, and enforcing the access control policies in complex organizations is a difficult task because of the following three main problems.

First, an organization wishes to define a reference set of policy rules through a single point of administration for uniformity and enforce them in a distributed way for efficiency. In large and geographically dispersed organizations, this requires placing trust in several policy administrators to align the local copy

S. Mauw and M. Conti (Eds.): STM 2019, LNCS 11738, pp. 19–35, 2019.
https://doi.org/10.1007/978-3-030-31511-5_2

of evolving policy rules and maintain the integrity of the policy enforcement and decision points.

Second, *a priori* access control – i.e. granting or denying an action before it is performed – is not always possible or desirable. Predicting all possible circumstances under which access should be granted or denied is a daunting task, given the complexity of the workflows supported by modern organizations and the additional authorization conditions imposed for instance in compliance with privacy regulations, such as the General Data Protection Regulation (GDPR) [8]. Taking a permit-override approach may cause security issues, while a deny-override may cause unacceptable frictions in accessing data and ultimately safety issues; for example, frictionless accessibility to patient data is crucial to taking effective and timely clinical decisions.

Third, given the impossibility to adopt a purely *a priori* approach to access control, as observed in e.g. [5], the use of an audit log to record the evidence of each request and decision that has been made during access control enforcement is of paramount importance to enable the *a posteriori* verification of privilege abuses – e.g., doctors using patient data for clinical trials, even when consent had been granted for the purpose of treatment only. Integrity of the log is a mandatory requirement for auditing but is not trivial to guarantee; it requires technical measures – setting up an isolation boundary around the audit log so that it can only be accessed through a pre-defined set of functionalities – and requires additional trust to be placed on administrators that are assumed not to exploit their legitimate access rights to the audit log.

As a result of the difficulties of solving the three problems above, administrators and users with privileged accounts may abuse their rights, either inadvertently or maliciously, enabling insider attacks with severe impact. Recent reports show that insiders are involved in 23% of data breaches on average, and in 56% in healthcare organizations in particular [28,29].

To address these problems and mitigate the risks related to privilege abuses, the main contribution of this paper is an Audit-Based Access Control Enforcement (AuBACE, Sect. 3): we leverage Distributed Ledger Technology (DLT) to provide *(i)* strong integrity of the audit log, *(ii)* a single point of administration to define a uniform policy for the entire organization, and *(iii)* efficient and distributed enforcement with less trust in administrators. Although our discussion and findings hold for arbitrary organizations, we consider a healthcare scenario (Sect. 1.1) for concreteness and because the three problems identified above are particularly severe for these organizations.

In addition, we provide the following two contributions: a security assessment against insider attackers (Sect. 4) and an experimental evaluation (Sect. 5) of a prototype implementation based on Hyperledger Fabric (HF), a widely used private and permissioned DLT. HF is particularly suited to our application, as it uses Public Key Infrastructure (PKI) for the enrolment and authentication of users without the need to define ad-hoc identity management contracts, all communications can be protected by TLS, and transactions are immediately final, i.e. if an authorization decision appears in an honest peer's ledger, it will appear in every other honest peer's ledger in the same position. This is critical because an access control enforcement in which decisions were not guaranteed to be final would always be subject to argument. We contrast some significant examples of previous uses of DLT and HF in Sect. 6.

1.1 Use Case and AuBACE: Discussion

The main goal of an Electronic Health Record (EHR) system is that of sharing health information among healthcare professionals to provide patients with effective and timely treatments. Of the many possible deployment models, we consider a centralized EHR system as our use case scenario. In this model, patients or staff at local Health Service Providers (HSP) – e.g. hospitals, laboratories, or Local health authorities – interact with one or more HSPs using a custom application to store and retrieve EHR, and for each interaction with the HSPs, a centralized Health Authority (HA) is obliged to authenticate the involved parties and authorize the interaction based on their credentials.

In the presence of insider attackers – which are the main problem in the healthcare sector – the integrity of the audit log itself may also be at risk. To overcome this problem, our approach is to have a single point of administration for access control policies managed uniquely by the HA and use a distributed ledger for the evaluation of policies that shall be performed by the HA and the local HSPs.

The main benefits of this approach are to increase the confidence of patients as well as officials in the assurances given by the system: in particular, that data will be handled according to the reference policy dictated by the HA, and that the access log is tamper-proof for auditing. Earning the trust of patients is particularly important, given the sensitive nature of the data stored in the EHR and the contrasting needs of controlling unauthorized access while enabling timely access of crucial information by healthcare professionals, especially in case of an emergency.

We assume that users can authenticate to the system by using credentials provided in different ways; these may include electronic identity cards for patients, which are becoming more and more widespread in many European countries, as well as credentials provided by local organizations for healthcare professionals when they are hired. The HA is responsible for specifying the access control policies that should be used for the evaluation of authorization requests by the nodes of the distributed ledger associated with the organizations.

In some legislations there may be a higher degree of centralization than others. For instance, in France there is a national authority in charge of providing access to a common EHR system, while Italy is in the process of migrating from regional authorities overseeing local providers to a national authority.

We also note that the use case described above is subject in Europe to the EU General Data Protection Regulation (GDPR). For instance, patients are considered *Data Subjects* and the centralized nature of the policy administration is a consequence of the need to clearly establish a *Data Controller* who is legally responsible for the treatment of subject data. Data subjects also have to expressly consent to the treatment.

For concreteness, two examples of the policies we implemented are: *(P1)* nursing staff can read or update a patient record for the purpose of provision of care; *(P2)* emergency medical technicians can read or update patient records for the purpose of emergency services, even without consent.

2   Background

We briefly recall the traditional architecture for implementing an access control mechanism and present the main components of the Hyperledger Fabric technology that will be used in our experiments.

2.1   Access Control

We adopt the Attribute-Based Access Control (ABAC) framework for its flexibility not only to simulate and combine a wide range of classical access control models – e.g. Role-based, Discretionary, or Mandatory Access Control – but also refine them so as to supplement rather than supplant the classical models; see, e.g. [18] for a discussion on these and related issues. We do not choose a particular language for expressing ABAC policies – any one of the available choices, e.g. eXtensible Access Control Markup Language (XACML, [23]) would do – but rather focus on policy evaluation and logging.

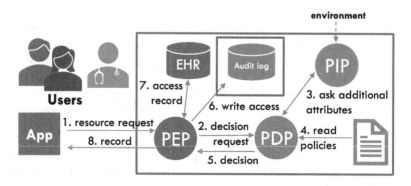

Fig. 1. ABAC framework with an audit log.

We recall the ABAC framework [9,10,14] in Fig. 1. The Policy Enforcement Point (PEP) intercepts every authorization request to access resources, such as Electronic Health Records, performed by users, e.g. patients or healthcare professionals, and then returns the requested resource based on the decision provided by the Policy Decision Point (PDP) after the evaluation of the rules specified in an access control policy. The expressive power of ABAC policies derives from the fact that rights are granted or denied depending on security-relevant features – called attributes – of users and resources, together with environment attributes, such as location, time, or the state of certain variables provided to PDP by the Policy Information Point (PIP).

Given this framework, an isolation boundary blocks all access to resources except over the channel that passes through the PEP. To determine the user's attributes, the sender of an authorization request is identified based on credentials, e.g. digital certificates.

In addition to the ABAC framework we require an audit log (Step 6 of Fig. 1), i.e. a complete and integral record of the authorization decisions taken by the PEP. As highlighted by Lampson in [20], the audit log is a crucial, and sometimes overlooked, component of an access control system, and to ensure its integrity, an isolation boundary must protect the audit log from tampering even by those principals entitled to operate within the isolation boundary of the access control system, e.g. system admins; in other words, the only way to write to the access log must be through a channel connecting it to the PEP.

We would emphasize the importance of the two isolation boundaries in Fig. 1 for the security of the enforcement of access control policies. There are several possible ways to implement these depending on the particular technological scenarios in which policies must be enforced. Since the precise evaluation of risks related to the implementation of the outer isolation boundary in Fig. 1 depends on many implementation details, in the following we assume that an appropriate choice has been made for it and we focus on the part inside the outer box. In particular, our proposal (Sect. 3) involves avoiding the use of an isolation boundary around the audit log by using distributed ledger technology.

2.2   Hyperledger Fabric

Hyperledger Fabric (HF) is a private and permissioned distributed ledger providing an execution environment for smart contracts. We refer to reports by ENISA [7] and NIST [30] on blockchain and distributed ledgers in general, and to the official Fabric documentation [12] for details of HF as a whole. Here we focus on the features of HF that are most important to our case.

The HF components of main interest for our purpose are *clients* – applications to make function calls to smart contracts – and *peers*, who collectively enforce the access control policies to those functions and commit authorized changes to the shared database. Each organization participating in the consortium setting-up an HF network may run one or more peer nodes. The read and write requests issued by clients are known as *transactions* and are collected in a blockchain structure; valid transactions are used by peers to update the database.

Another essential component is a *membership service provider* (MSP). Every peer has an MSP, which is responsible for determining which principal has administrative or participatory rights within the scope of that MSP. Each MSP manages lists of X.509 certificates, including: a root CA and TLS root CA; certificates for itself, administrators, and a certificate revocation list; and a keystore with its own private key. Certificates issued by external CAs may be relied upon to authenticate users, or a built-in Fabric CA may be used.

In HF, smart contracts are referred to as *chaincodes*. These programs represent a shared operational logic among a group of *organizations* agreeing on common rules and establishing a private *channel*. The Fabric network is designed to enforce these common rules and policies, and maintains a shared database, ensuring its consistency among all participants.

Smart contracts are digitally signed by their owners at creation, and only their owners may update them. They also specify a policy of peer nodes that are required to participate in their execution, called *endorsement policy*. They need not be installed on every peer, but must be installed on peer nodes sufficient to satisfy the endorsement policy.

Lastly, HF is designed to guarantee a total ordering of the blocks [2]. In particular, it is designed to guarantee that correct submitted transactions eventually appear in every correct peer's chain, and transactions always appear in the same order. These properties are particularly desirable for access control applications because one peer's blockchain does not run the risk implicit in bitcoin-like solutions that a longer, equally valid chain will replace it, so decisions based on a transaction in a correct peer's chain can always be audited with certainty.

3 AuBACE Proposal

We build Audit-Based Access Control Enforcement (AuBACE) on a private and permissioned DLT. We believe that it is the ideal choice to design and implement an access control enforcement mechanism capable of satisfying the following requirements: (R1) centralized policy definition and administration, (R2) distributed policy evaluation and enforcement, (R3) audit log integrity. Such requirements naturally stem from scenarios in which organizations are legally responsible for defining a reference set of security policies to protect the personal data of users, minimizing abuse by administrators, and identifying malicious behavior of privileged users. This is the case for instance under GDPR [8].

A private and permissioned DLT allows one to limit the capability of writing policies to a single peer of the network (satisfying R1) while smart contracts can be used, in combination with the consensus algorithm, to implement the distributed evaluation of access requests (satisfying R2). The strong integrity properties of the blockchain data structure underlying the DLT allows auditing of the access control history with a high level of assurance (satisfying R3).

A high-level representation of our proposal architecture can be seen in Fig. 2. Compared to the ABAC framework in Fig. 1, the main differences are the distributed evaluation of policies, and the use of a blockchain-based audit log not as information storage but as the basis for granting authorization to access resources. Only the information relevant to access control is recorded in the blockchain; resources are stored off-chain for efficiency and privacy.

We map the functional points defined by the ABAC standard to concrete entities in our specific solution in Sect. 3.1, summarize the proposed access request

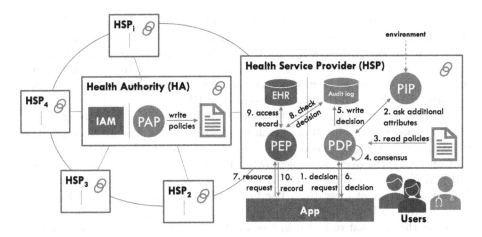

Fig. 2. High-level architecture.

flow in Sect. 3.2, and discuss more in detail how policies and attributes are set and updated in Sect. 3.3.

3.1 Functional Points

The HF network is created and administered by a central Health Authority (HA) with a data controller running a Policy Administration Point (PAP) managing the creation and update of the HF chaincode containing the policies themselves. The HA is also responsible for digital identity and access management (IAM).

The HA recognizes local Health Service Providers (HSPs) with their own HF peer nodes. The HSPs have been given permission to join the network and enroll new users with their MSP. Each principal has been assigned an X.509 certificate that is recognized by the network, with a corresponding private key. Users make requests to the network through their application (App), which acts as a client with respect to the HF peer node network. Keys are securely stored by each client and peer node in their local keystore. Each peer node, represented in Fig. 2 with the chain symbol, also has a local copy of the blockchain. Specifically, it is necessary for the Policy Enforcement Point (PEP) in each HSP to have a peer node in order to read the policy decision from the blockchain. Indeed, the PEP is the gateway to the medical records, stored off-chain to support user privacy: while the distributed ledger can decide whether to grant access and record that decision, the access itself must be granted by the service storing the record. In this proposal, we assume that the HSP has direct access to an HF peer node and grants access to resources based on HF transaction outcomes. More specifically, if a user making a request through an App has been granted access to a resource, then the decision will be written in the blockchain; the PEP can then authenticate the user based on the HF certificate in her App, check the network for the decision, and thus fulfil her request.

The Policy Decision Point (PDP) is distributed, in the sense that the decision is made by HF peers running their copy of the decision-making smart contract. The network consensus algorithm ensures that all peers run the same copy of chaincodes, prevents dishonest peers from influencing the final result that all peers commit, and ensures that the committed decisions are not subject to change in the future thanks to the design of HF.

The Policy Information Point (PIP) is distributed, in the sense that principal attributes are contained in their certificate, resource attributes are written in the HF database, and environment attributes are gathered from other sources.

Concretely, the decision request (Step 1 in Fig. 2) is made by the App using a HF SDK. The App has access to the user's HF certificate and private key, limited by the client's keystore. The final resource request (Step 7 in Fig. 2) is made to the PEP by the App on another channel and the access is granted based on the decision recorded in the audit-log (Step 8 in Fig. 2). In this way, the audit-log becomes the source of truth for authorization decisions (hence the name AuBACE) and differs from typical practice of putting the PEP in charge of translating access requests into a language the PDP will understand.

Finally, we note that environmental conditions are challenging to handle on a distributed ledger. In order to reach consensus on a transaction, participating nodes are usually required to execute completely deterministic code without external input, such as in Ethereum. While HF is capable of handling non-deterministic code, e.g. lists without a specific ordering (see [2]), it still requires a sufficient number of peers to return the same set of values. Alternatively, they must accept single points of trust, such as Corda oracles [4], which provide network participants with statements of external facts, such as timestamps. We discuss in Sect. 3.3 how specific attributes may be implemented in our proposal.

3.2 Processing Authorization Requests

As shown in Fig. 2, the following steps are taken by both patients (data subjects) and doctors (data processors) to request access to the EHRs handled by HSPs:

1. The user makes an access request through her App. Transparently to the user, the App first invokes a decision request chaincode on HF.
2. The PDP (chaincode installed on peer nodes) checks the PIP for attributes, e.g. resource attributes from the HF database, principal attributes from their certificate, or environment attributes from the local host.
3. The PDP evaluates the request against the policies.
4. The HF network reaches consensus.
5. The PDP's decision is committed to the immutable log of all peers.
6. The decision is available to be referenced by the user's App.
7. If the decision was to grant access, the App can establish an off-chain secure channel to request the EHR from the HSP. The App creates a signed token referencing the transaction id containing the decision, and signs this token with the same key used to request access in HF. Concretely, this can be achieved with a standard JSON web token (JWT) [16].

8. The PEP of the HSP validates the signed token, composes an HF network query for a valid transaction with the correct id, and checks that the public key validating the token signature corresponds with the public key of the identity that created the transaction.
9. If the token is validated, the keys correspond, and the decision was to grant access, the PEP accesses the requested EHR.
10. Finally, the PEP releases the requested EHR to App.

Step 1 is performed by the App to obtain an access decision through a HF channel; while Step 7 is performed for requesting access to a resource through an off-chain channel.

3.3 Attributes

User attributes are written in HF certificates. It is the responsibility of CA and MSP registrars – admins with the `registrar` attribute in their certificate – to ensure that attributes are correctly assigned to users when their certificates are issued, and to perform all associated duties such as maintain revocation lists and re-issue certificates as appropriate.

The PAP remains centralized in this proposal. Only users registered by the administrative organization (HA in Fig. 2) with an attribute of *policy administrator* are authorized to invoke the administration chaincode. Each policy is evaluated by a chaincode and assigned a unique identifier, so that it may be selected for update and deletion.

Resource attributes can be set by chaincode on resource creation, associated with a resource ID r. The EHR server (PEP) only knows r.

A resource attribute we consider is *consent*. Patients (data subjects) may invoke a consent chaincode to record their explicit consent to the treatment of their EHR for a given purpose, recorded on the ledger as a boolean value.

The *purpose* for data treatment is an environment attribute. Following [27], the notion of purpose is inherent to the whole sequence of actions needed to achieve a certain goal, and does not pertain to individual steps. Purpose should be declared at the outset; indeed, our access control requires the requesting principal to declare a purpose with each request. Only at the end of the whole sequence of actions is it possible to establish whether the purpose had been as declared in an a posteriori audit analysis step, which our proposal does not encompass.

The purpose attribute has a small set of possible values. Examples in our proof-of-concept are *provision of care* and *emergency* (see policy examples in Sect. 1.1). Access for the declared purpose is granted only if the policies are satisfied. In the special case of emergency access, the requesting principal must have the corresponding subject attribute in their certificate, and the consent resource attribute is ignored.

An environment attribute we may consider in future work is the time of access request - for instance, in case a policy were to specify a restriction on the time of the request to be within business hours. It would not be possible for all peers to agree on a synchronized time of arrival of a request, but we consider it feasible to ask each peer to return a boolean value in answer to whether their locally measured time falls within a sufficiently wide range.

4   Security Assessment Against Insider Attackers

We focus our security assessment on the properties that distinguish our proposal from other access control solutions, in particular how the distributed PDP and the strong guarantee on the integrity of audit logs prevent *log erasure* and mitigate *legitimate privilege abuse*.

Our analysis is based on the following trust and security assumptions: ($A1$) the HF distributed ledger is robust in the sense of [11], i.e. it guarantees the liveness and persistence of the committed transactions; and ($A2$) no means exist for admins of the PEP to disable the check against the log before granting an access request.

Following NIST [22], we define an insider as *"an entity inside the security perimeter that is authorized to access system resources but uses them in a way not approved by those who granted the authorization"*. Given the focus of our analysis, the threat model consists of two specific insiders:

- *Admin of PDP:* maintainers of IT services, who will for instance have access to the HF peer nodes; these are the accounts with the highest level of security-critical access.
- *User with privileged accounts:* medical staff at all levels; for instance, doctors and emergency staff may have a wider access to information if they declare that access is being requested for a specific purpose.

In the following, we argue how AuBACE mitigates threats from these insiders, based on assumptions $A1$ and $A2$.

Actively deleting a log entry from the network is made infeasible by the distributed ledger, even for admins of PDP. During the decision check performed by the PEP (Step 8 in Fig. 2), a network query is performed. Even if an admin of PDP locally modifies a log entry, given assumption $A1$, we are sure that the right log entry value is returned. This is an effective mitigation against collusion between admins of PDP and users with privileged accounts. The use of a Byzantine fault-tolerant consensus protocol for the DLT also mitigates against collusion between several admins of PDP.

In addition, compared to a classic ABAC system, in our proposal it is infeasible for admins of PDP to install a valid copy of the policies that differs from the one defined by the entitled peer (admin of PAP); policy tampering attempts are mitigated by digital signatures on the smart contract.

A user with privileged accounts in possession of a genuine certificate may abuse the trust that policies afford them. For instance, while emergency medical technicians are allowed to read any EHR without consent from the data subject (see policy P2 in Sect. 1.1), this policy is designed to support specific use cases in rare circumstances. Given assumption $A2$ and the strong integrity properties of the blockchain data structure underlying the DLT, our proposal allows auditing of the access control history with a high level of assurance. This, together with being forced to declare the specific purpose for which one is requesting that access, is an effective deterrent.

Finally, since AuBACE is based on classical ABAC and IAM solutions, we do need further trust and security assumptions to prevent common attacks, which we consider out-of-scope of this security assessment. For example, we assume admins of the PAP are trusted in writing the policies – i.e. no one is able to create a fake policy – and admins of the PEP are trusted in managing the resources – i.e. no one is able to access resources without the policy and decision validation. In addition, we assume the robustness of the PKI infrastructure underpinning the HF trust model itself. In particular, we assume registrars will not create fake identities. There are mitigation strategies to prevent malicious issuance of certificates – a robust standardized and automated procedure has recently been proposed in [17] – but they lie outside the scope of our current proposal. We do highlight this as an area of potential future work, particularly in regards to integration with existing identity providers, which we think is quite reasonable for the public healthcare sector use case.

5   Prototype and Experiments

Our sample implementation is concerned only with the distributed ledger part of the architecture, specifically a Fabric network with organizations, users, and policies defined to support the use case of EHR access control. We have not implemented any part beyond the DLT itself. What we have implemented is available in the github repository[1], and can be run as docker containers.

5.1   Policy and Data Structure

Principals i are identified by their HF X.509 certificate, which contains attributes associated with the principal – in particular their unique identifier, to which resources are associated.

The action requested can be one of the following: Add EHR, Get EHR, Update EHR, Update consent. The first three requests are for permission to interact with the PEP; in addition, Add EHR creates a new entry on the ledger, and Update Consent sets an associated variable on the ledger to true or false.

EHRs are created at patient enrolment. The data subject expresses their consent c to data treatment, and the policies specify for which purpose p consent may be granted. We take a *deny-by-default* approach and only specify the policies in which principals are explicitly granted access.

The HF database stores the following data for each EHR: (i_s) *data subject*, (r) a unique identifier linking the data subject to the data (EHR), (t) *last request* time, as declared by the client application in the transaction proposal, (i_q) *requesting principal*, and (c) *data subject consent* to the treatment of data.

---

[1] https://github.com/stfbk/AuBACE.

Policies are evaluated by using HF smart contracts. Each access request Req is an HF transaction. We refer the reader to the online documentation [12] for the detailed HF transaction protocol, but each Req contains at least the following fields: (Req.i_q) the certificate of the requesting principal, (Req.$action$) the action requested, (Req.r) the resource identifier, and (Req.$purpose$) the declared purpose for access. The certificate i_q is an integral part of the HF transaction protocol; transactions could not be built without one. The remaining fields are parameters to be evaluated by the access control smart contract.

It is not difficult to devise a procedure capable of generating pseudo-code for any given finite set of attributes. We leave as future work the design and implementation of a translator that takes an ABAC policy expressed in some formal language (e.g. XACML) and automatically generates a set of equivalent smart contracts that can be deployed in HF for evaluation.

5.2   Fabric Set-Up

In our implementation, we used the HF SDK for node.js, with a client app to call the SDK and make transaction proposals to HF. Each peer node is run in its own docker container. The control interface is designed for test purposes to switch between identities and retrieve different views of the ledger, provided the local keystore contains the appropriate keys and certificates; this allows to test the correct execution of policies.

In our proposal, only the single policy administration node is the owner of the access control policy smart contract.

We deployed the architecture detailed in Sect. 3.1 by using 3 organizations, each with 2 peers and 1 admin user; 1 Certificate Authority and, as end-users: 100 patients, 10 doctors, 3 nurses and 1 user with the emergency attribute.

Users are registered by the admin with the CA and then enrolled at the MSP.

5.3   Experimental Evaluation

We deployed our prototype on a Linux testbed[2] and evaluated user requests for all actions listed in Sect. 5.1. We distinguish cases when the action is *authorized* (A), when it is *denied* (D) after policy evaluation; or when the policy is not evaluated (NE). To support NE operations, we specifically modified the smart contract.

We do not attempt to assess the entire HF architecture, which has been the focus of a thorough and recent study [26]. Rather, we report our measurements of the overhead introduced by the policy evaluation functions and the handling of concurrent requests. Platform-independent metrics to evaluate the performance of blockchain technologies have been proposed in [15]. We adapt the ones most suitable to our use case, namely *Transaction Latency* and *Transaction Throughput*, to investigate the performance of AuBACE in an HF-based

---

[2] Tests were run using Apache JMeter [19] version 5 on a server equipped with Intel Xeon E3-1240 V2 3.40 GHz CPU and 16 GB RAM.

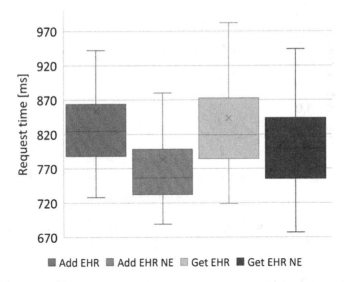

Fig. 3. *Transaction Latency* [ms] of the Add EHR and Get EHR operations with authorized and Not Evaluated (NE) access requests, as boxplot. The distribution of times is shown as a boxplot: the box is bounded by lower and upper quartiles; the line indicates the median, and the cross indicates the average. Upper and lower whiskers are computed as the default – 1.5× upper and lower interquartile range; outliers have been omitted.

prototype implementation. In particular, the speed in serving *Get EHR* requests is of interest to evaluate the use of AuBACE with a real-world EHR system: we believe requests for EHRs to be significantly more frequent than the remaining supported operations.

Transaction Latency is the amount of time taken for requests to produce visible results on the majority of nodes of the network. Figure 3 provides the distribution of latencies [ms] when performing 100 consecutive *Add EHR* and *Get EHR* requests.

The results indicate that the policy evaluation mechanism itself has a small effect on the request latency, with the difference between authorized and not evaluated request times being approx. 50 ms. An additional, intrinsic delay is due to the creation time of each block in the chain, for which a channel-specific delay parameter is defined – which in our experiments was set to 100 ms.

To measure *Throughput* – the capacity to handle parallel requests – we configured our testbed to continuously perform requests for different resources over 15 s, and repeated this experiment by increasing the number of concurrent requesting users on different JMeter threads from 1 up to 10. Requests in this proof-of-concept set-up were addressed to the same Peer. Each thread waited for a reply before sending a new request. The results shown in Fig. 4 indicate that the policy evaluation mechanism slightly affects the Throughput: compared to not evaluated requests, the authorized ones had a Throughput of −5,6% requests/s

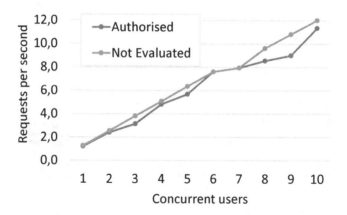

Fig. 4. *Throughput* of the authorized and NE *Get EHR* requests when simulating up to 10 concurrent users.

with one user, and up to 20% with 9 concurrent users (162 authorized requests instead of the 135 not evaluated ones).

Finally, we can report the *Access Latency* of the HF prototype, measured as the time interval between an *Add EHR* request being sent from JMeter to the App and the HA Peer receiving an HF transaction request from the App; 15 ms on average over 100 requests. Additionally, the *Propagation Latency*, measured as the difference between the first and the last Peer on the channel committing a transaction to their local database: 45 ms averaged over 100 *Add EHR* requests.

Although the performance of our tests might be optimized by means of hardware or software, e.g. by load-balancing requests or upgrading the HF infrastructure and the smart contracts to support the latest 1.4 release, we believe the results to be satisfactory for our use case. Indeed, a medium-sized healthcare organization in Trento (Italy) serving a population of approximately 500,000 reported to us that their peak access request throughput is approx. 200 per minute.

6   Comparison with Related Work

The use of smart contracts for policy evaluation, and the exploitation of the strong integrity properties of blockchain for auditing, have been previously explored in the design and implementation of middleware for controlled information sharing or access control enforcement – see [13] for a recent review. The prevalent paradigm has been to fully decentralize access control to the highest degree to put individual users in complete control of policies, while keeping the data off-chain, going back at least to [32]. [6] proposes a similar approach, with a more specific reference to XACML [23] for attribute-based policy specification. See also e.g. [3, 24, 31].

Our work argues that private and permissioned DLT solutions are better suited than public and permisionless blockchains – used in, e.g. [6, 31, 32] –

precisely characterizes the use case scenarios in which such an approach is useful, and conducts a security assessment showing that access right abuses by privileged users or administrators are effectively mitigated. As reported in [28,29], such threats affect specific sectors disproportionately and clearly demonstrate the relevance of AuBACE. Another advantage of using a private and permissioned DLT is the possibility to more easily comply with existing regulations (such as the GDPR) recognizing that the responsibility for the safekeeping and processing of personal data lies with a single entity, referred to as data controller in the GDPR, while supporting the distributed deployment of the system. This was already observed in [24].

A specific advantage in using HF to build our prototype implementation, to our knowledge not previously exploited, is the immediate finality of transactions, as noted in Sect. 1. This is a benefit for an access control mechanism over using public and permissionless blockchains adopted in previous work (e.g. [6,31]) in which availability and partition tolerance are usually preferred over consistency, as is the case e.g. for Bitcoin. Additionally, the reliance on a well-established PKI avoids the need to define ad-hoc identity management contracts as in e.g. [3].

One previous proposal of interest in particular [21] integrates mobile devices and a HF service. It is unclear whether their implementation uses the distributed ledger as more than a log since they provide no examples of their policy rules or an indication of where these are evaluated, and their only experimental evidence is a measure of the efficiency with which proofs of integrity of the medical data are generated. A major difference with respect to our work is that it also appears as though the only Fabric client they use to send transactions is present on a cloud server, while it is left unspecified how requesting principals are enrolled and authenticated.

7   Conclusion

We have presented AuBACE an access control architecture built in a private and permissioned DLT (HF) designed to increase accountability and decentralize the authorization decision process. This allows us to decrease the trust in administrators, mitigate insider attacks by privileged users, and make the a posteriori verification of access events more reliable while maintaining a reasonable overhead for access control enforcement. The main differences between AuBACE and a standard architecture (cf. Fig. 1) are the following:

- policy administration is performed through a single point while access control decisions are performed by smart contract on the DLT;
- an access request is made to be granted access as a matter of policy, and one is made to be granted access to the resource itself (a separate channel is required to communicate with the distributed PDP and the PEP);
- the audit log is not a black-box information storage, but rather it is the fundamental evidence of security assertions on which the PEP bases its enforcement: no resource access is granted without prior evidence of the decision in the log;

– security is based on the assumption that an attacker will not be able to compromise a sufficiently large number of nodes at once in the DLT.

The distributed evaluation of policies and the distributed storage of logs on a DLT increase an auditor's confidence that the log could not have been manipulated, either at the initial write stage or by subsequent tampering.

We recall that auditing is composed of two phases [25]: *(i)* the collection and storage of audit data, and *(ii)* their analysis to detect security violations. Our work offers a solution for step *(i)* and can be combined with available techniques for *(ii)*, such as [1,5]. An interesting line of future work is to investigate how to combine one of these techniques with AuBACE while complying with data protection regulations such as the GDPR.

Another line of future work is to improve consent management, in particular concerning its update, and the presentation to users of the policies they are asked to consent to.

References

1. Alizadeh, M., Lu, X., Fahland, D., Zannone, N., van der Aalst, W.M.: Linking data and process perspectives for conformance analysis. Comput. Secur. **73**, 172–193 (2018). https://doi.org/10.1016/j.cose.2017.10.010
2. Androulaki, E., et al.: Hyperledger fabric: a distributed operating system for permissioned blockchains. In: EuroSys 2018. ACM, New York (2018). https://doi.org/10.1145/3190508.3190538
3. Azaria, A., Ekblaw, A., Vieira, T., Lippman, A.: MedRec: using blockchain for medical data access and permission management. In: OBD 2016, pp. 25–30. IEEE (2016). https://doi.org/10.1109/OBD.2016.11
4. Introduction to oracles. Corda online documentation v3.3. https://docs.corda.net/oracles.html
5. Dekker, M.A., Etalle, S.: Audit-based access control for electronic health records. Electron. Notes Theor. Comput. Sci. **168**, 221–236 (2007). https://doi.org/10.1016/j.entcs.2006.08.028
6. Di Francesco Maesa, D., Mori, P., Ricci, L.: Blockchain based access control. In: Chen, L.Y., Reiser, H.P. (eds.) DAIS 2017. LNCS, vol. 10320, pp. 206–220. Springer, Cham (2017). https://doi.org/10.1007/978-3-319-59665-5_15
7. ENISA: Distributed Ledger Technology & Cybersecurity (2017). https://doi.org/10.2824/80997. https://www.enisa.europa.eu/publications/blockchain-security
8. EU: General Data Protection Regulation (GDPR) (2016). https://data.europa.eu/eli/reg/2016/679/2016-05-04
9. Ferraiolo, D., Chandramouli, R., Hu, V., Kuhn, R.: A Comparison of Attribute Based Access Control (ABAC) Standards for Data Service Applications: Extensible Access Control Markup Language (XACML) and Next Generation Access Control (NGAC). NIST (2016). https://doi.org/10.6028/NIST.SP.800-178
10. Fisher, B., et al.: Attribute-Based Access Control. NIST (2017). https://nccoe.nist.gov/projects/building-blocks/attribute-based-access-control
11. Garay, J., Kiayias, A., Leonardos, N.: The bitcoin backbone protocol: analysis and applications. In: Oswald, E., Fischlin, M. (eds.) EUROCRYPT 2015. LNCS, vol. 9057, pp. 281–310. Springer, Heidelberg (2015). https://doi.org/10.1007/978-3-662-46803-6_10

12. Hyperledger fabric documentation. https://hyperledger-fabric.readthedocs.io/
13. Hölbl, M., Kompara, M., Kamišalič A., Nemec Zlatolas, L.: A systematic review of the use of blockchain in healthcare. Symmetry **10**(10) (2018). https://doi.org/10.3390/sym10100470
14. Hu, V., et al.: Guide to Attribute Based Access Control (ABAC) Definition and Considerations. NIST (2014). https://doi.org/10.6028/NIST.SP.800-162
15. Hyperledger Performance and Scale Working Group (PSWG): Hyperledger Blockchain Performance Metrics. https://www.hyperledger.org/resources/publications/blockchain-performance-metrics
16. IETF RFC: JSON Web Token (JWT) (2015). https://tools.ietf.org/html/rfc7519
17. IETF RFC: Automatic Certificate Management Environment (ACME) (2019). https://tools.ietf.org/html/rfc8555
18. Jin, X., Krishnan, R., Sandhu, R.: A unified attribute-based access control model covering DAC, MAC and RBAC. In: Cuppens-Boulahia, N., Cuppens, F., Garcia-Alfaro, J. (eds.) DBSec 2012. LNCS, vol. 7371, pp. 41–55. Springer, Heidelberg (2012). https://doi.org/10.1007/978-3-642-31540-4_4
19. Jmeter. https://jmeter.apache.org/
20. Lampson, B.: Practical principles for computer security, NATO Security through Science Series - D: Information and Communication Security, vol. 9, pp. 151–195. IOS Press (2007)
21. Liang, X., Zhao, J., Shetty, S., Liu, J., Li, D.: Integrating blockchain for data sharing and collaboration in mobile healthcare applications. In: PIMRC, pp. 1–5. IEEE (2017). https://doi.org/10.1109/PIMRC.2017.8292361
22. Glossary of key information security terms. https://csrc.nist.gov/glossary
23. OASIS: The eXtensible Access Control Markup Language (XACML) (2013). https://docs.oasis-open.org/xacml/3.0/xacml-3.0-core-spec-os-en.pdf
24. Dias, J.P., Sereno Ferreira, H., Martins, Â.: A blockchain-based scheme for access control in e-health scenarios. In: Madureira, A.M., Abraham, A., Gandhi, N., Silva, C., Antunes, M. (eds.) SoCPaR 2018. AISC, vol. 942, pp. 238–247. Springer, Cham (2020). https://doi.org/10.1007/978-3-030-17065-3_24
25. Sandhu, R., Samarati, P.: Authentication, access control, and audit. ACM Comput. Surv. (CSUR) **28**(1), 241–243 (1996). https://doi.org/10.1145/234313.234412
26. Thakkar, P., Nathan, S., Viswanathan, B.: Performance benchmarking and optimizing hyperledger fabric blockchain platform. In: MASCOTS 2018, pp. 264–276. IEEE (2018). https://doi.org/10.1109/MASCOTS.2018.00034
27. Tschantz, M.C., Datta, A., Wing, J.M.: Formalizing and enforcing purpose restrictions in privacy policies. In: S&P 2012, pp. 176–190. IEEE (2012). https://doi.org/10.1109/SP.2012.21
28. Verizon: Data breach investigations report (2018). https://enterprise.verizon.com/resources/reports/2018/DBIR_2018_Report.pdf
29. Verizon: Protected health information data breach report (2018). https://enterprise.verizon.com/resources/reports/phi/
30. Yaga, D., Mell, P., Roby, N., Scarfone, K.: Blockchain Technology Overview. NIST (2018). https://doi.org/10.6028/NIST.IR.8202
31. Zhang, P., White, J., Schmidt, D.C., Lenz, G., Rosenbloom, S.T.: FHIRChain: applying blockchain to securely and scalably share clinical data. Comput. Struct. Biotechnol. J. **16**, 267–278 (2018). https://doi.org/10.1016/j.csbj.2018.07.004
32. Zyskind, G., Nathan, O., Pentland, A.S.: Decentralizing privacy: using blockchain to protect personal data. In: SPW, pp. 180–184. IEEE (2015). https://doi.org/10.1109/SPW.2015.27

Is a Smarter Grid Also Riskier?

Karin Bernsmed[1], Martin Gilje Jaatun[1(✉)], and Christian Frøystad[2]

[1] SINTEF Digital, Trondheim, Norway
{karin.bernsmed,gilje}@sintef.no
[2] Secure Practice, Trondheim, Norway

Abstract. The smart grid evolution digitalizes the traditional power distribution grid, by integrating information communication technology into its operation and control. A particularly interesting challenge is the integration of grid topology monitoring and decision support systems with the remote control of breakers in the grid and at the subscribers' premises. In this paper we outline and discuss the results from a recent information security risk assessment of such an integrated system.

Keywords: Smartgrid · Cyber security · Risk assessment

1 Introduction

Energy supply is vital for almost all parts of our daily lives. Failure in the delivery of power will have direct consequences for all sectors in our society and for the digital systems that these sectors rely on. Today, it is already common practice to use Information and Communication Technology (ICT) to support the operation and control of electric power transmission systems and the SCADA systems that supervise them. To meet the modern society's demand for efficient and reliable power supply, SCADA systems are increasingly being interconnected with other systems, such as Distribution Management Systems (DMS), Geographical Information Systems (GIS), Network Information Systems (NIS) and systems for Customer Relationship Management (CRM). In addition, the introduction of the Advanced Metering Infrastructure (AMI) with smart electricity meters, which will provide the power utility companies with information on the current status of the power distribution grid, will also increase the reliance on ICT in this sector.

Increased digitalization and integration of these systems into an envisioned smart grid will yield increased utility, but will potentially also bring increased risk [4]. In particular the increased complexity will make it difficult to understand how the different parts interact, and this will also increase the risk of technical failures, human errors and cyber security threats.

In this paper we outline results from a information security risk assessment of the integration of AMI, DMS and SCADA systems that we performed on behalf of the Norwegian Water Resources and Energy Directorate[1] during the fall of

---

[1] https://www.nve.no/english/.

© Springer Nature Switzerland AG 2019
S. Mauw and M. Conti (Eds.): STM 2019, LNCS 11738, pp. 36–52, 2019.
https://doi.org/10.1007/978-3-030-31511-5_3

2018. The focus of the risk assessment was not on the security of the individual systems per se (this has already been covered in numerous publications; cf. next section), but rather on new threats and risks that may materialize when these systems become more closely integrated. Further, our analysis focuses on risks that stem from breaches of information security, i.e. attacks; we have not included random failures and other types of unwanted events in our study.

The paper is organised as follows. Section 2 provides an introduction to the threat picture faced by the energy sector today, as well as an overview over existing studies of threats and risks related to smart grid security. Section 3 explains the methodology that have been used to perform the risk assessment. In Sect. 4 we outline the system that has been our target of evaluation. Sections 5 and 6 outline the assets and the evaluation criteria that we have used in the risk assessment. Section 7 contains the risk identification, analysis and evaluation and Sect. 8 provides a set of countermeasures that can be implemented to mitigate the most serious risks. Finally, in Sect. 9 we conclude our work.

2   Background

The Stuxnet attack against uranium enrichment centrifuges in the Iranian Bushehr nuclear power plant [3] was the first publicly known external cyber attack against industrial control systems. At the time, the power distribution industry professed confidence that a similar incident could not happen in their systems [11], but only a few years later saw the Dragonfly campaign targeting industrial control systems in the power sector [15]. Dragonfly was primarily an information gathering exercise, but in December 2015 the gloves came off when almost a quarter of a million Ukrainians suddenly found themselves without power for more than 6 hours due to a cyber attack on several Ukranian Distribution System Operators (DSOs). The trick was repeated one year later by the Industroyer malware [1], blacking out parts of Kiev for an hour.

Nowadays, cyber security is high on the agenda, both for the industry as well as in the academic community. Piètre-Cambacédès et al. [11] review 21 "myths" about cyber security that exist in the power industry. The very first one is the common perception that the different control systems are isolated. According to the authors, most systems are already (to a varying degree, of course) connected in one way or the other. In the paper, the authors also neutralize the common belief that cyber security incidents will not impact operations. An interview study of power distribution system operators (DSOs) from 2014 indicates that, even though the power industry is very well prepared for traditional threats, such as physical attacks, they are not yet ready to meet targeted cyber attacks.

Security threats and challenges to smart grids have been highlighted by, for example, Goel and Hong [5], Hawk and Kaushiva [6], Sanjab et al. [12] and Cleveland [2] (the last one already in 2008). An excellent overview and classification of threats to smart grid cyber security is provided by Otuoze et al. [10]. While the scope of these articles do not cover all parts of the system that we have assessed, the threats identified has been a valuable input in our study when identifying risks to the integrated system.

3 Methodology

The risk assessment presented in this paper has been performed in accordance to ISO/IEC 27005 Information Security Risk Management standard [7]. The standard prescribes five different steps; (1) Context establishment, which includes understanding the system that is to be assessed, defining the scope of the analysis, identifying assets and agreeing on scales and acceptance criteria for risk assessment and evaluation, (2) Risk identification, which includes identifying threats and understanding how these threats may lead to unwanted events, (3) Risk analysis, which includes assessing the consequence and likelihood of each of the identified risks, (4) Risk evaluation, which includes comparison of risk analysis results with risk criteria to determine which risks should be considered for treatment, and (5) Risk treatment, which includes identifying and selecting means for risk mitigation and reduction.

Since our assessment concerns an envisioned system rather than an existing one, lots of effort was put into the context establishment phase; more specifically to define what such a system would look like and agreeing on the scope of the analysis. To gather necessary information, we arranged a workshop with key stakeholders from the energy sector, which included participants from energy producers and suppliers, Distribution System Operators (DSOs), vendors of relevant equipment as well as representatives from the national regulatory body. In this workshop we used the world café methodology[2] to facilitate the discussion and to gather the stakeholders' perspectives on how the integration of AMI, DMS and SCADA will manifest. We also briefly discussed what are the critical assets that will need to be protected and what risks the stakeholders envision with this future system.

To identify risks, we then performed a thorough walk-through of all the identified assets, in which we analyzed their need for confidentiality, integrity and availability, where in the system they will be stored, how they will processed and used, and how they will be transmitted between the different parts of the system. Using Microsoft STRIDE [13] we were then able to identify a number of relevant threats. The vast body of existing literature on AMI and SCADA security (cf. Sect. 2) was also of great help in this process. Since ISO/IEC 27005 is a generic standard, applicable to any kind of domain, we also needed to adapt the risk evaluation step to the domain at hand. More specifically, we used a existing guidance document for risk assessment of AMI and its adjacent systems [9] to derive the scales for consequence and likelihood evaluation and the risk evaluation criteria that we later relied on in our assessment.

Finally, when all the steps in the risk assessment were completed, we sent a draft report to a selected number of stakeholders from the workshop, to gain their feedback on the identified risks, the risk acceptance criteria and the list of countermeasures that we had proposed for mitigating the unacceptable high risks.

---

[2] http://www.theworldcafe.com/key-concepts-resources/world-cafe-method/.

4 System Description

The scope of the analysis presented in this paper is the integration of AMI, DMS and SCADA systems in the context of power grid operation. Here we first present an overview over the individual subsystems (Sects. 4.1–4.3) before we outline the integrated system that has been assessed (Sect. 4.4). We will refer to this integrated system as *Integrated DMS, AMI and SCADA (IDAS)*.

4.1 DMS

The Distribution Management System (DMS) is a map application with an overlay network topology, which provides the grounds for predicting consequences of planned and unplanned breaker operations in the SCADA system, and for assessing the severity of failures and downtime of the different links and components in the power distribution grid. The main purpose of the DMS is hence to facilitate a better understanding of potential changes to the grid. At the DMS operation centre, the Shift Operation Manager is the sole person authorized to approve changes to the grid and he/she is also responsible for making sure that such changes are reflected in the DMS. The DMS receives incoming data in terms of state information from the automatic and/or remotely controlled breakers in the SCADA system, but at the time of writing, it is very rare that a DMS has implemented outbound communication, i.e. transmission of breaker operation commands from DMS to SCADA[3].

Data from the DMS is also replicated and transmitted as status information to 3rd party actors and other types of systems. DMS also receives information from other sources, such as the AMI Head End System (see Sect. 4.3), however, such data is not processed automatically; instead it is sent to the Shift Operation Manager who manually reviews it and decides whether the DMS should be updated or not.

4.2 SCADA

Supervisory Control And Data Acquisition (SCADA) resides between the physical and the digital world. A SCADA system consists of a collection of hardware (Programmable Logical Controllers (PLCs), servers and switches) and software that monitors and controls (parts of) the power distribution grid. Per today, it is straightforward to retrofit sensors in the SCADA system whenever needed, but the use of actuators is less common. All transformer substations in the SCADA network have already been automated, but so far is has not been considered worth the effort to automate the smaller components. Hence, today the majority of the power distribution grid is still operated manually, i.e. not controlled by the SCADA system, which means personnel need to be dispatched to execute changes in, for example, the switches in the grid.

---

[3] Systems that control SCADA operations are subject to dedicated legislation, which today in practice is considered a showstopper in most European countries.

4.3   AMI

The Advanced Metering Infrastructure (AMI) measures the power consumption of the individual households in the power distribution grid by collecting and analyzing data from smart meters installed at the subscribers' premises. The AMI can also log and report events, such as local earth faults, and send and receive control messages; the most controversial one being the envisioned breaker operation that will shut down the power supply to one or more subscribers. The smart meters are in most cases connected to a central Head End System (HES) through local master nodes. The master nodes are connected to the HES through the mobile network (GPRS, 4G, 3G or 2G), while the remaining smart meters (slave nodes) are connected to the master node through a mesh based network. Note that there are also other ways to connect the smart meters to the HES, for example by installing a dedicated transmitter that nearby smart meters can connect to, or by installing radio communication equipment in the smart meter themselves.

4.4   Integrated DMS, AMI and SCADA (IDAS)

Increased integration of the power distribution grid indicates that existing systems are tied more closely together. This becomes particularly interesting when systems that have been designed to avoid being classified as "operation control systems" (such as the DMS) are being connected with existing operation control system (such as SCADA). Closer integration between AMI, DMS and SCADA means that DMS is being more closely connected the power distribution grid operations, in addition to its current status as a segregated system whose main purpose is to provide increased situation awareness. In case the integration of these three subsystems are performed to such a degree that the new system-of-systems can do both the job of the DMS, as well as sending control signals to SCADA and AMI, such an integrated system would also fall into the category of "operation control systems". In this paper, we refer to this future integrated system as "IDAS" (Integrated DMS, AMI and SCADA).

Note that these systems have already, in some cases, been partly integrated; there exist installations where the HES in the AMI delivers data to the DMS (the HES is then often implemented as a cloud service), and where the SCADA system delivers sensor data and breaker status data to the DMS.

Figure 1 outlines the state-of-the-art in the energy sector where most actors already operate a DMS. The purple dashed line shows where IDAS will manifest, in terms of closer integration of systems and functionality. The purple arrows show communication to and from IDAS. As can be seen in the figure, integration of data from AMI is expected to be more direct and possibly also automatic. At the same time, IDAS will be allowed to control the SCADA system directly. These changes increase the attack surface for all the systems that used to be more separated. In the not-so-distant future, we may also envision the IDAS as a system-of-systems that automatically manages the existing tasks of the human operators at DMS, AMI HMI and SCADA HMI.

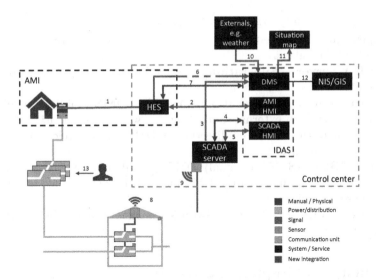

Fig. 1. System overview

The different communication interfaces are identified by numbers in Fig. 1, and are detailed as follows:

1. **Smart Meter – HES** (bidirectional): The smart meter periodically sends meter readings to HES, including eventual error messages. In the case of power cut, a "last gasp" diagnostic message is sent, and some meters can also send updated information after power cut. The HES sends control messages to the smart meter. The HES can request readings outside the planned interval, activate breaker function, and set limit on allowed consumption before breaker is automatically activated (throttling function).
2. **HES – AMI HMI** (bidirectional): HES offers an API for interaction. The DSOs can either use the interface offered by HES, or implement their own.
3. **SCADA server – DMS** (unidirectional): SCADA transfers status information on breakers and sensors in the grid to DMS.
4. **SCADA server – IDAS** (bidirectional): IDAS transfers control signals to SCADA to effectuate physical changes in the grid. This implies that breakers may alter state.
5. **SCADA server – SCADA HMI** (bidirectional): SCADA HMI is the user interface to the SCADA controller. All state information is sent from SCADA server to SCADA HMI, and commands are sent from SCADA HMI to SCADA-server.
6. **HES – DMS** (unidirectional): HES transfers alarms from the grid so that they may be put in an operational context in DMS.
7. **HES – IDAS** (bidirectional): Operation of breaker and throttling for each individual smart meter.

8. **Substation – SCADA Server** (unidirectional): Sensor data (humidity, temperature, door open/closed, etc.), measurement on transformer load, and state of breakers.
9. **SCADA Server – Substation** (unidirectional): Control signals for operation of breakers.
10. **External entity (e.g., weather service) – DMS** (unidirectional): Relevant updates from external sources such as weather information to DMS.
11. **DMS – Situation map** (unidirectional): DMS transfers relevant data (i.e., data to be published)
12. **DMS – NIS/GIS** (bidirectional): DMS is based on the NIS/GIS data base, hence will changes made in the DMS interface be reflected in the NIS/GIS data base, and vice versa.
13. **Service technician – manual breaker** (manual): Manually changing the state of breakers.

5   Primary and Supporting Assets

ISO/IEC 27005 stipulates that the risk assessment should focus on assets. The standard distinguishes between *primary assets*, which are the information and services that are crucial for the business operation, and *supporting assets*, which are related IT infrastructure and human resources that also will need to be protected in order to ensure the confidentiality, integrity and availability of the primary assets. The focus of our analysis is mainly information security. As described in the previous three subsections, closer integration of AMI, DMS and SCADA will entail that breaker operations (or "ops") will be pushed from DMS to SCADA, which is new compared to today's situation. In addition, the status of the breakers in the power distribution network will form the basis for (possible automated) decisions in the IDAS. We have therefore identified three primary assets, which we call "SCADA Breaker ops", "SCADA Breaker status" and "AMI Breaker ops". These are further described in Table 1. In addition, we have identified twelve supporting assets, which, if manipulated or misused, may affect the primary assets. These are:

- AMI Breaker status: reports breaker status for individual power consumers. Manipulation of AMI status reports may lead to a misconception of the status of the grid, leading to the execution of erroneous SCADA breaker operations that, in worst case, can have harmful consequences.
- Sensor data: reports the status (power output, temperature, wind, humidity, wear out, etc) of different parts of the power distribution grid. Sensor data is aggregated in the network and transmitted to the SCADA server, which in turn forwards the data to the SCADA HMI and the DMS. Sensor data can be correlated with breaker status to detect deviations in the network. Manipulation of sensors may be used to avoid the detection of malicious breaker operation commands or and breaker status reports.

- NIS/GIS data: imported to the DMS and used to model and visualize the topology of the power distribution network. Correct topology information is a necessity for the usage of breaker status in decision making and for performing remote execution of breaker operations.
- AMI measurements: reports power consumption and events to the HES. This information is used to support AMI breaker operations (P3).
- Authentication credentials: need to be protected to ensure that only authorized personnel have access to the AMI and SCADA HMIs.
- Encryption keys: used to ensure confidentiality protection of data in transit and stored data. Encryption is currently implemented in smart meters, the HES, the SCADA servers and the PLCs.
- System documentation: contains detailed information about the IDAS architecture, functionality and current configuration. Should be kept confidential.
- Head End System (HES): collects data from smart meters and receives and forwards control commands to the smart meters. Protecting the HES is necessary to secure the execution of AMI breaker commands.
- SCADA server: the heart of the SCADA system. Transmits commands to the remotely controlled breakers and collects sensor data from the grid.
- IDAS software: provides monitoring and control of the complete power distribution grid, including the ability to execute changes to the grid and to control smart meters.
- Software/firmware updates: all updates to any part of the system need to be protected and controlled.
- Network communication infrastructure: need to be available and have sufficient capacity to ensure that control commands can reach the breakers and that sensor data and breaker status can reach the SCADA server.

6   Risk Assessment Criteria

Risk assessment in accordance to ISO/IEC 27005 [7] includes the identification and assessment of unwanted events, which in the scope of our study include threats that cause a breach of confidentiality, integrity or availability of the three primary assets "SCADA Breaker ops", "SCADA Breaker status" and "AMI Breaker ops" that we have identified[4]. Further, risk is a combination of likelihood and consequence. The threats have therefore been assessed in terms of what *impact* they will have on the relevant stakeholders, which in our case is the DSOs, the power consumers (subscribers) and the society overall, and the *likelihood* that the threat will occur. In the energy sector, reliable power supply should always be included as a dimension of impact [9]. Here we have also included safety and economy as additional dimensions when assessing the impact of each identified threat. Likelihood is a notoriously difficult dimension to assess in a security risk assessment. Here we have made a qualitative assessment based on "expert opinion", which takes into account how easy/difficult it would be to perform the

---

[4] Note that some of the threats will also implicitly affect the supporting assets.

Table 1. Description of primary assets

Id	Primary asset & rationale	C	I	A	Storing	Processing	Communication
P1	**SCADA Breaker ops.** A remotely executed command that changes the state of a breaker in the power distribution grid. Unauthorized breaker operations may disconnect (parts of) the grid. Such events may require the operator to disable remote control altogether and revert to manual control of the grid	Yes	Yes	Yes	n/a	Processed by SCADA HMI and IDAS (receive decisions from the Shift Operation Manager), SCADA server (receives commands from SCADA HIM or DMS and forward them to the breakers) and remote breakers (receive commands and changes the state of the breakers)	Transmitted from IDAS or SCADA HMI to SCADA server and further to the PLC (using cable or wireless)
P2	**SCADA Breaker status.** A (real-time) status report of the breakers in the power distribution grid. User by the operation central. Breaker status is important because it (1) can be used by unauthorized persons to survey the grid, (2) erroneous breaker status may lead to the execution of erroneous actions from the control center that damages the grid, and (3) lack of updated breaker status may in worst case cause operators to execute unnecessary change sin the grid, or changes that may have adverse safety effects	Yes	Yes	Yes	DMS (stored until the next update) and SCADA (stored continuously)	Processed by sensors at the breakers (generates and transmits status of automatized breakers), SCADA server (receives signals from sensors at breakers and forwards these to the SCADA HMI) and SCADA HMI and IDAS (displays information to the operators)	Transmitted from the breaker sensors to the SCADA server over cable or 4G, and further to the SCADA HM and IDAS (over cable)
P3	**AMI Breaker ops.** Manipulation of AMI breaker operations could lead to loss of power for one or more subscribers. Unavailability of this function will require personnel to be dispatched to manually connect or disconnect the subscriber. In the longer term, unavailability may also prevent serious failures at subscribers to be isolated form the rest of the grid	No	Yes	Yes	n/a	Processed by HES, IDAS and the smart meters	Transmitted from HES to smart meters over through master nodes, mesh network or dedicated transmitters (cf Sect. 4.3). The communication link will be encrypted. NB: AMI breaker operations will allegedly never be broadcasted; only unicast will be implemented

attack, whether there exist any security mechanisms that could prevent, detect and/or react to such a threat, and whether such events have been observed in the past.

The scale that was used to assess likelihood is:

1. Unlikely
    - Expected to occur less than every 10th year.
    - Security mechanisms exist and are expected to work as intended.
    - Existing security mechanisms can only be circumvented by resourceful insiders with thorough knowledge of the system.
    - External attackers need to have advanced technical skills and help from insiders.
    - There are no known examples of this attack.
2. Less likely
    - Expected to occur once a year.
    - Security mechanisms exist and are expected to work as intended.
    - Existing security mechanisms can be circumvented by insiders with some knowledge of the system.
    - External attackers must be resourceful and have detailed knowledge of the system.
    - Similar attacks have occurred in other sectors and may, in theory, also be applied in the energy sector.
3. Possible
    - Expected to occur several times a year.
    - Security mechanisms are not fully implemented or do not work as intended.
    - Existing security mechanisms can easily be circumvented by insiders.
    - External attackers need some knowledge of the system. There may be existing exploit tools that can be used to perform the attack.
    - Such attacks have been observed in the energy sector before.
4. Likely
    - Expected to occur several times a month.
    - Security mechanisms do not exist, or can be easily circumvented by either insiders or external attackers.
    - The attack can be performed without any specific knowledge of the system.
    - The incident may be caused by negligence, either by own personnel or attackers.
    - Such incidents are common in the energy sector.

The scale that was used to asses impact is:

1. Minor
    - Minor or insignificant impact on the subscribers.
    - No interruption of power supply.
    - No damage to equipment.
    - Insignificant economic loss.

2. Moderate
    – Local impact affecting a small number of subscribers.
    – A limited number of subscribers lose power for a limited amount of time.
    – Minor damage to equipment.
    – Small (recoverable) economic loss
3. Major
    – Serious consequences in a local community.
    – Loss of power for a long period of time for a limited number of subscribers.
    – Damages to the grid and/or on personnel
    – Major economic loss
4. Critical
    – Essential services, such as health care or other critical infrastructure, are affected.
    – Loss of power for large parts of the grid during a long period of time
    – Severe damages to equipment and/or loss of human life
    – Irreparable economic loss.

The risk of each identified incident have then been calculated as likelihood × impact and evaluated as

– High (red) for values between 12–16,
– Medium high (orange) for values between 8–9,
– Medium low (yellow) for values between 4–6,
– Low (green) for values between 1–3.

7   Risk Identification, Analysis and Evaluation

We have identified 11 threats that may have direct consequences for primary assets; these are detailed in Table 2. For each identified threat, we indicate whether it affects Confidentiality (C), Integrity (I) or Availability (A) of the affected primary asset(s). We also calculate the risk using the scales outlined in the previous section.

Figure 2 shows an overview over the risks. As can be seen, two risks are unacceptably high:

– R2: Unauthorized entities send fake commands with breaker operations to remotely controlled breakers in the distribution grid.
– R7: Unauthorized entities perform changes in the DMS part of IDAS that lead to undesirable SCADA breaker operations are effectuated.

The severity of these threats are comparable with the incidents that occurred in Ukraine in 2015 and 2016 [8] and may cause a loss of power for large parts of the grid during a long period of time, possibly also affecting essential services, such as health care and other critical infrastructure.

Two risks have also been assessed as medium high:

– R6: Reporting of false breaker status to the SCADA server.

Table 2. Threats with direct consequences for the primary assets

ID	Threat	Pri. asset(s)	C	I	A	Consequence	Impact	Likelihood	Risk
R1	Eavesdropping of commands that modify state of breakers, or status messages from remotely controlled breakers in the distribution grid	SCADA Brk. ops (P1) SCADA Brk. status (P2)	X			Mapping of network topology, communication pattern analysis	1	3	3
R2	Unauthorized entities send fake commands with breaker operations to remotely controlled breakers in the distribution grid	SCADA Breaker ops (P1)		X		Can disconnect (parts of) distribution grid, as well as inflict damage on equipment and grid that leads to greater and more long-lasting power cuts. In the worst case, this can lead to disconnection of large areas, including hospitals and other critical infrastructures	4	3[a]	12
R3	Denial of service attack against the communication link to a single or a few remotely operated breakers in a limited area of the distribution grid	SCADA Brk. ops (P1) SCADA Brk. status (P2)			X	Reduced overview of status, delay in ability to make changes in the distribution network (due to need for sending out personnel)	1	2[b]	2
R4	Targeted attack against SCADA servers so that breakers in the distribution grid cannot be remotely controlled	SCADA Breaker ops (P1) SCADA Breaker status (P2)			X	Significantly reduced overview of status in own grid, delay in ability to make changes in the distribution grid (due to need for sending out personnel to observe and make changes)	2	2	4
R5	Attack against central communication infrastructure that prevents communication with remotely operated breakers	SCADA Breaker ops (P1) SCADA Breaker status (P2)			X	Significantly reduced overview of status in own network, delay in ability to make changes in the distribution network (due to need for sending out personnel to observe and make changes)	2	3	6
R6	Reporting of false breaker status to the SCADA server	SCADA Brk. status (P2)		X		Can spur grid changes that may cause damage to the grid or people	3	3[c]	9

(continued)

Table 2. (*continued*)

ID	Threat	Pri. asset(s)	C	I	A	Consequence	Impact	Likelihood	Risk
R7	Unauthorized entities perform changes in the DMS part of IDAS that lead to undesirable SCADA breaker operations are effectuated	SCADA Breaker ops (P1) SCADA Breaker status (P2)		X		Can disconnect (parts of) grid, cause damage to equipment and grid that leads to major and long-term power loss. In worst case blackouts in larger areas, including hospitals and other critical infrastructure	4	3[d]	12
R8	Denial of service attack that affects communication link to one or more subscribers in the grid	AMI Breaker ops (P3)			X	Breaker functionality and throttling is expected to be rarely used per subscriber, but loss of communication link may cause reduced overview of own grid. Delays in restoration due to use of manual labor to make changes	1	4[e]	4
R9	An unauthorised entity gains control over the AMI breaker functionality for a single subscriber	AMI Breaker ops (P3)	X			A single subscriber disconnected	1	2	2
R10	An unauthorised entity gains control over the AMI breaker functionality for a group of subscribers	AMI Breaker ops (P3)	X			Arbitrary number of subscribers disconnected	4	2[f]	8
R11	An unauthorised entity immobilises an arbitrary number of smart meters ("bricking")	AMI Breaker ops (P3)	X	X		Loss of overview in the grid, loss of ability to disconnect subscribers with serious errors. Loss of DSO revenue, and extra maintenance cost	2	2	4

[a] Observed in Ukraine in the case of fully integrated DMS and SCADA.

[b] The major DSOs in Norway are required to have redundant communication in their SCADA system, which implies that fault in a single communication link will not cause a failure.

[c] Observed, e.g., in Stuxnet.

[d] If today's DMS is integrated unchanged with IDAS, the likelihood will be higher due to DMS having more contact points to the outside world, and lower security requirements.

[e] With use of combined communication technology (radio, cellular, copper, etc.) communication failures must be expected.

[f] Lower likelihood of finding many keys for group disconnection, than to find a single key to disconnect one subscriber. There is no function for group disconnection in AMI, but seems easy to script if keys are available.

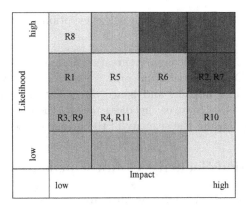

Fig. 2. An overview of the risks identified for the IDAS. (Color figure online)

– R10: An unauthorised entity gains control over the AMI breaker functionality for a group of subscribers.

These threats will only have consequences for local communities. The effect will hence be less severe than if the attacker have had direct access to the execution of SCADA breaker operations (as in R2 and R7).

The rest of the identified risks were considered to be either medium low (yellow) or low (green). It is therefore not necessary to treat these, but as will be discussed below, some of the countermeasures that we propose to mitigate the four higher risks will also reduce the likelihood or impact for some of these lower risks.

We have also identified the following threats to the supporting assets:

T12 Unauthorised entities can read meter values from the smart meter (AMI meter data – S4)

T13 Manipulation of meter values (AMI meter data – S4)

T14 Eavesdropping on messages that contain breaker status (Status AMI breaker – S1)

T15 Reporting fake breaker status to HES (Status AMI breaker – S1)

T16 Field Area Network (FAN) access used to break into central systems (HES and beyond) and subsequent unauthorised modification of HES Software (HES – S10)

T17 Unauthorised eavesdropping on sensor data (Sensor data – S2)

T18 Unauthorised manipulation of sensor data (Sensor data – S2)

T19 Unauthorised access to NIS/GIS (NIS/GIS data – S3)

T20 Unauthorised manipulation of NIS/GIS (NIS/GIS data – S3)

T21 Unauthorised access due to data breach involving authentication information (Authentication information – S7)

T22 Unauthorised access due to weak authentication (Authentication information – S7)

T23 Data breach involving encryption keys (Encryption keys – S8)

T24 Broken encryption due to use of weak encryption algorithms (Encryption keys – S8)

The assessment of these secondary threats will depend on the actual implementation in each DSO's distribution grid, so we have not ventured to make guesses at likelihood or impact, and hence do not attempt to rank the risks to the secondary assets. However, needless to say, these will also need to be protected in order to ensure the security of the primary assets.

8   Recommended Security Countermeasures

The recommended security countermeasures are

- Implement authenticity, integrity and confidentiality protection of all SCADA breaker operations and SCADA status reports. This can be achieved by, for example, setting up secure sessions between the communicating entities. For connectionless communications, each single message needs to be protected. This will reduce R1, R2 and R6.
- Ensure that only authorized actors have access to the AMI breaker functionality. This can be achieved by following the instructions in the guidance report [14]. This will reduce R9 and R10.
- Define and enforce procedures and criteria for user access control to all systems and equipment that will be part of IDAS (DMS, AMS-HMI and SCADA HMI). This will reduce R7.
- Use independent and redundant communication links, preferably over different media (wireless/fiber/etc) and delivered by different service providers. This will reduce R3, R5 and R8.
- Perform hardening of the SCADA server, i.e., remove unnecessary services and configure the remaining ones to the highest possible security level. This will reduce R4 and R5.
- Implement segmentation of the SCADA network, by splitting the logical network into two or more different security zones. This will reduce R3, R4 and R5.
- Install a firewall between IDAS and the outside network. This will reduce R3 and R4.
- Set up an Intrusion Detection System that monitors the SCADA server and its inbound and outbound connections. This will reduce R4.
- Introduce a regime for signing and verifying all software updates and patches of the SCADA server. This will reduce R11.
- Perform regular vulnerability scanning of the different parts of the IDAS, including any external services. This will reduce all the identified risks.
- Perform a penetration test of the different subsystem in IDAS, including any external services. This will reduce all the identified risks.
- Use whitelists to control all incoming connections from external systems. This will reduce all the identified risks.

– Use digital certificates for secure communication and ensure that all root certificates are securely stored. This will reduce R1, R2, R6, R9, R10 and R11.

The above list is not meant to be a silver bullet; the proposed countermeasures will mitigate the most pressing risks, but in the end it is up to the stakeholders in the energy sector to decide what risks are unacceptable and what countermeasures that are worth investing in.

9 Conclusion

Increased integration of AMI, DMS and SCADA means that systems that originally were designed as separate entities now are being connected and will be dependent on each other. This is particularly challenging when systems that are have been designed with the intention of avoiding falling into the category of "operation control systems" suddenly are connected with such systems. In this paper we have assessed risks that stem from threats to SCADA breaker operations, SCADA breaker status reports and AMI breaker operations. Our assessment shows that the highest risks with an integrated system are related to the execution of unauthorized SCADA breaker operations, which in worst case can have severe consequences on our whole society. The proposed list of security countermeasures is meant to serve as a starting point for stakeholders who want to implement a more integrated system, but we emphasize that the details of each new architecture needs to be thoroughly scrutinized in order to ensure that it is sufficiently secure. It would also be useful to pay more attention to the risk of cyber security threats causing *black swans*, i.e. unexpected events that are hard to predict but that may have severe safety consequences. Such events are typically not picked up by an information security risk assessment like the one that we have presented in this paper.

Acknowledgments. This paper is based on a risk assessment assignment performed for NVE, and further developed as part of the RCN FME Cineldi research centre, project no. 257626 (www.sintef.no/projectweb/cineldi).

References

1. Cherepanov, A., Lipovsky, R.: Industroyer: Biggest threat to industrial control systems since stuxnet. WeLiveSecurity by eset (2017). https://www.welivesecurity.com/2017/06/12/industroyer-biggest-threat-industrial-control-systems-since-stuxnet/
2. Cleveland, F.: Cyber security issues for advanced metering infrastructure (AMI), pp. 1–5 (2008)
3. Falliere, N., Murchu, L.O., Chien, E.: W32.Stuxnet Dossier (2011). http://www.symantec.com/content/en/us/enterprise/media/security_response/whitepapers/w32_stuxnet_dossier.pdf

4. Frøystad, C., Jaatun, M.G., Bernsmed, K., Moe, M.: ROS-analyse AMS-DMS-SCADA - risikoanalyse av økt integrasjon mellom AMS, DMS og SCADA. Technical report, 2018:01083, SINTEF Digital (2018). http://publikasjoner.nve.no/eksternrapport/2018/eksternrapport2018_15.pdf
5. Goel, S., Hong, Y.: Security challenges in smart grid implementation. Smart Grid Security. SC, pp. 1–39. Springer, London (2015). https://doi.org/10.1007/978-1-4471-6663-4_1
6. Hawk, C., Kaushiva, A.: Cybersecurity and the smarter grid. Electricity J. **27**(8), 84–95 (2014). http://www.sciencedirect.com/science/article/pii/S1040619014001791
7. ISO: Information technology - security techniques - information security risk management. ISO/IEC Standard 27005:2018 (2018). https://www.iso.org/standard/75281.html
8. Lee, R.M., Assante, M.J., Conway, T.: Analysis of the cyber attack on the Ukrainian power grid, defense use case. SANS ICS and E-ISAC white paper (2016). https://ics.sans.org/media/E-ISAC_SANS_Ukraine_DUC_5.pdf
9. Norges vassdrags- og energidirektorat: Veiledning i risiko- og sårbarhetsanalyser for kraftforsyningen. Technical report, Norges vassdrags- og energidirektorat (2010). http://publikasjoner.nve.no/veileder/2010/veileder2010_02.pdf
10. Otuoze, A.O., Mustafa, M.W., Larik, R.M.: Smart grids security challenges: classification by sources of threats. J. Electrical Syst. Inf. Technol. **5**(3), 468–483 (2018). http://www.sciencedirect.com/science/article/pii/S2314717218300163
11. Pietre-Cambacedes, L., Tritschler, M., Ericsson, G.N.: Cybersecurity myths on power control systems: 21 misconceptions and false beliefs. IEEE Trans. Power Deliv. **26**(1), 161–172 (2011)
12. Sanjab, A., Saad, W., Güvenç, I., Sarwat, A.I., Biswas, S.: Smart grid security: threats, challenges, and solutions. CoRR abs/1606.06992 (2016). http://arxiv.org/abs/1606.06992
13. Shostack, A.: Experiences threat modeling at Microsoft. In: Proceedings of the Workshop on Modeling Security (MODSEC08). CEUR Workshop Proceedings (2008). http://ceur-ws.org/Vol-413/paper12.pdf
14. Skapalen, F., Jonassen, B.: Veileder til sikkerhet i avanserte måle- og styringssystem. Technical report, Norges vassdrags- og energidirektorat (2012). https://www.nve.no/Media/5525/veiledertil-sikkerhet-i-ams.pdf
15. Symantec Security Response: Dragonfly: Cyberespionage attacks against energy suppliers (2014). https://www.symantec.com/content/en/us/enterprise/media/security_response/whitepapers/Dragonfly_Threat_Against_Western_Energy_Suppliers.pdf

BioID: A Privacy-Friendly Identity Document

Fatih Balli[1]($\boxtimes$), F. Betül Durak[1,2], and Serge Vaudenay[1]

[1] Ecole Polytechnique Fédérale de Lausanne (EPFL), Lausanne, Switzerland
{fatih.balli,serge.vaudenay}@epfl.ch
[2] Robert Bosch LLC – Research and Technology Center, Pittsburgh, USA
betul.durak@us.bosch.com

Abstract. We design a suite of protocols so that a small tamper-resistant device can be used as a biometric identity document which can be scanned by authorized terminals. We target both strongly secure identification and strong privacy. Unlike biometric passports, our protocols leak no digital evidence and are essentially deniable. Besides, getting the identity information from the device requires going through access control. Access control can follow either a strong PKI-based path or a weak password-based path which offer different functionalities. We implemented our protocols on JavaCard using finger-vein recognition as a proof of concept.

Keywords: Privacy · Deniability · ID document · Smart card

1 Security vs Privacy in Identification

Informally, *secure identification* means that (1) acceptance of invalid identities do not happen, (2) making multiple copies of the same identity document is hard, and (3) the identity of the holder matches the identity indicated by the document. Public-key cryptography, tamper-resistance, and biometry solve these problems. However, the same cannot be said for privacy, which used to come as a secondary goal in the design process. Fortunately, EU has recently passed GDPR to enforce companies and institutions to put forth "appropriate technical and organizational measures" to protect users' privacy. In identification context, privacy means that (1) identity documents leak no tracking information to unauthorized terminals, (2) the information transferred to authorized terminals is always deniable, and (3) biometric templates leave the card only if the terminal is strongly authenticated, i.e. the certificate of the interacting terminal is still valid.

The full version of this paper includes security models and proofs and it is accessible at eprint [1]. This work was supported by Innosuisse project 19339.1 PFES-ES and done in collaboration with Global ID SA, Switzerland.

F. B. Durak—This work was done when the author was at EPFL.

S. Mauw and M. Conti (Eds.): STM 2019, LNCS 11738, pp. 53–70, 2019.
https://doi.org/10.1007/978-3-030-31511-5_4

PREVIOUS WORK. International Civil Aviation Organization standardized globally recognized passports as Machine Readable Travel Documents (MRTD) [2]. The MRTD standard realizes the goals of secure identification and some minimalistic level of privacy. In a more detail, false or invalid recognition of identities are prevented with classical digital signatures and Public-Key Infrastructures (PKI) in the MRTD standard. This is referred to as the Passive Authentication Protocol. Although this solution is simple and effective in terms of secure identification, it leaks a transferable evidence to the communicating terminal. An adversarial terminal can collect these identities with signatures and sell them on the black market (because their validity is provable), or use them in a global surveillance system. Therefore, it ignores the privacy of the bearer.

Even worse, the MRTD standard allows the chip to communicate with the terminal only through a password-authenticated channel (formerly BAC, currently PACE protocol). Although this prevents arbitrary devices from communicating with the chip and skim the contained data, a state-level adversary collecting password page copies can easily thwart this protection. In practice, passwords are printed in the photo pages of passports and they are frequently shared via instant messaging, emails or even uploaded to the cloud. These passwords can also be guessed as they are sampled from a small domain.

The MRTD standard also proposes an Active Authentication Protocol (version 1). In order to prove its genuineness, the chip signs a challenge message chosen by the terminal. Although it allows the terminal to ensure that it is talking to the genuine chip but not a copy, it leaks a signature to the terminal and harms the privacy of the owner.

To address some of the problems above, German Federal Office for Information Security (BSI) has proposed eIDAS tokens with TR-03110 standard which is an improvement over the MRTD [3]. The first main contribution is the introduction of the Extended Access Control (EAC). One of the motivations behind the EAC proposal was to provide a better alternative for the terminal authentication based on a PKI instead of a shared password. The EAC consists of the Terminal Authentication and the Chip Authentication protocols. The Terminal Authentication (version 2) is a simple challenge-response protocol based on digital signatures. The Chip Authentication (version 2) is an authenticated key-exchange protocol based on a PKI and a fixed public-key of the chip. The security of both protocols is proven with respect to the Bellare-Rogaway model [4], which is weaker than eCK [5]. However, the privacy of the Chip Authentication is not addressed and neither formalized as a security game. It actually leaks undeniable and transferable information from the chip. Finally, the hash values of privacy-sensitive data groups are stored in a publicly readable security object called $EF.SO_D$. Hence, if these data groups leak, $EF.SO_D$ can be used as evidence of their validity [6].

Bichsel et al. [7] proposes an identification scheme based on smart cards. Their idea (henceforth referred to as eID) is implementation of an RSA-based anonymous credential scheme on smart cards. Each eID contains a credential and it can be used to sign arbitrary messages, e.g. a proof of having a certain age. In that sense, eID is treated as a trusted platform module (TPM), where tamper-resistance of smart cards acts as a core security assumption. Hence, if tamper-resistance of a (single) smart card is circumvented, then the security of the whole identification scheme is threatened, i.e. the terminals will accept inaccurate statements or even fake identity information[1]. Even though eID scheme supports revocation of leaked credentials, it is unclear how to detect leakages in a timely manner and prevent malicious identification sessions during the transient periods, i.e. the interval from leakage of a credential to its revocation. Moreover, signatures released by an eID can be linked later if its credential is released (happens when an eID is revoked), and thus anonymous credential scheme destroys deniability in order to support a revocation scheme.

Overall, ICAO's design solves secure identification, but fails with respect to the aforementioned privacy goals of identification systems. On the other hand, eID of Bichsel et al. [7] provides a more generic solution through anonymous credentials, yet treating smart cards as TPM provides weaker security in identification, and at the same time prevents deniability.

OUR DESIGN PARADIGM. Our design from scratch allows us to keep the privacy goals in mind at every step, in order to place *appropriate measures* encouraged by the GDPR. We refer to the identity document as *chip*, and any device which supports the same contactless communication technology as *terminal*. We adhere to the following list of rules:

1. Privacy-sensitive biometric data should be stored on chips but not on a central database. The data inside the chip must also be clearly separated with clear boundaries based on the sensitivity level.
2. The communication with the chip should be allowed only if the terminal can prove its authorization, (interchangeably if the chip can authenticate the terminal). The interactions from two different chips in the same domain[2] should look indistinguishable to unauthorized terminals.
3. The self-authenticating data, e.g. signatures verifiable with a public key, of the identity should never leave the chip. This authentication should be done via deniable zero-knowledge interactive protocols. On the contrary, both MRTD and EAC disclose signatures on all data groups with the document security object $EF.SO_D$[3] as discussed by Monnerat et al. [6].
4. If a transferable proof is leaked from the chip, then it should not be publicly-verifiable and undeniable, e.g. a trusted third-party is required for verification. On the contrary, both MRTD and EAC releases publicly-verifiable undeniable proofs with $EF.SO_D$.

---

[1] In comparison, in our scheme if tamper-resistance of a single device is violated, only the data contained in the card is affected. It does not lead to a system-wide collapse of identification.

[2] We cannot guarantee that two chips with different hardware or software configuration remain indistinguishable.

[3] In practice, this means that anyone who can get hold of passport can extract undeniable, transferable, universally-verifiable proofs of its identity with the help of a NFC reader e.g. an Android phone.

5. Any biometric comparison must be done on the chip if computational resources of the chip permits. Otherwise it must be strictly restricted to authorized terminals. The EAC strengthens the MRTD with the Terminal Authentication Protocol.
6. Interactions should be deniable from the chip's perspective. No terminal should be able to store information which can be later used to prove a previous interaction of the chip, e.g. the owner was at given location at some specific time[4]. On the contrary, interactions with the MRTD (even when enhanced by the EAC) cannot be denied because of EF.SO$_D$.

Deniability remains vulnerable to adversaries in the trusted agent model [8]: if a tamper-proof device implements the terminal and outputs a signed result and if it can be proven that the signing key never left this device, then any protocol leaks undeniable evidence. This is an inherent limitation to deniability. We exclude this attack model in our contribution.

Our suite does not necessarily address the scenarios involving passports and border controls, but instead provides a more generic treatment to the identification problem. Namely, our design can be used by governments to identify their citizens, hospitals to identify patients, and companies to issue cards to its employees. For this reason, our main goal is to improve privacy, ensure that the identification session is deniable and no evidence leaks. The use cases where a user wants to obtain an evidence for a successful session, e.g. a tourist proving a valid entry/exit to/from a country, falls outside the scope of our work.

Section 2 defines our notation and common cryptographic primitives. In Sect. 3, we give the high level picture of our design. The detailed descriptions of our protocols are in Sects. 4 (strong path) and 5 (weak path). The results of a prototype implementation can be found in Sect. 6. Security models and the proofs of our protocols are presented in the full version [1].

2   Preliminaries

2.1   Notation

We use $\mathcal{G} = (p, a, b, G, G_2, G_3, q, h)$ to represent elliptic curve (EC) defined over $\mathbb{F}_p$ with $y^2 = x^3 + ax + b$ such that G generates a group with a prime order q, and the cofactor is h. We use additive notation for groups. $\mathcal{O}$ denotes the neutral element and $\langle G \rangle$ denotes the subgroup generated by G. G_2, G_3 are additional generators uniformly sampled from $\langle G \rangle \setminus \mathcal{O}$. We further assume that membership to this subgroup is easily verifiable, i.e. given a point R on the elliptic curve, we can decide whether $R \in \langle G \rangle \setminus \mathcal{O}$ by checking $q \cdot R = \mathcal{O}$ and $R \neq \mathcal{O}$.

We denote bitstring concatenation operator with '|'. For encoding a field element x, we use fixed-length encoding, i.e. each $x \in \mathbb{F}_p$ is mapped to $\lceil \log_2 p \rceil$

---

[4] More formally, any information obtained by the terminal after interacting with the chip should remain indistinguishable from some simulated information obtained without interaction.

bits exactly by left-padding with zeros. In our notation, we omit this conversion and leave it implicit, e.g. $H(x)$ means binary-encoding of the field element x is fed to hash function H. Similarly, conversions from bitstrings to integers are implicit. We assume that a point R on the elliptic curve is represented by (x, y). We consider the binary encoding of R as the concatenation of x and y as bitstrings. We denote with $(R)_X$ the x-coordinate of the point R on the elliptic curve. With $x \leftarrow_{\$} \mathcal{D}$, we mean that x is uniformly sampled from the domain $\mathcal{D}$. With $x \leftarrow_{\$} A(y)$, we mean that the algorithm A takes y as input along with some implicit random coins and returns x.

2.2   PKIs and Entities

We rely on Public-Key Infrastructures (PKI) to bootstrap trust among entities. The public/private keys of an entity A are denoted by A_{pub}/A_{prv}. When a higher level authority A issues a certificate for a lower level entity B, we denote this certificate by $\langle A, B \rangle$. We extend the same notation to chains of certificates, e.g. $\langle A, C \rangle$ is a shorthand for the combination of $\langle A, B \rangle$ and $\langle B, C \rangle$.

   We assume the following three operations below can be performed on a given certificate $\langle A, B \rangle$: (1) verify the certificate using A_{pub}, by "verify $\langle A, B \rangle$", (2) extract the public key, by "extract $B_{pub} \leftarrow \langle A, B \rangle$", (3) extract the expiration date, by "extract $t_e \leftarrow \langle A, B \rangle$"[5]. They can also be applied to chains of certificates.

   Our design consists of the following PKIs:

- *Identity Signer PKI* is managed by an autonomous authority whose task is to produce signatures for identity cards, e.g. the government. CA-ID is the root certificate authority, identity signers IS_i are sub-authorities, and identity documents are leaf-level entities.
- *Terminal PKI* issues/authorizes devices (called terminals) who support the same communication technology with chips. Authorized terminals can communicate with chips and eventually decide whether the presented identity is valid or not. CA-T is the root certificate authority, Term-S is a sub-level authority, and terminals T are leaf-level entities.

Furthermore we employ the following entities:

- *Time server* TS is the entity whose task is to provide secure time information to chips, so that chips can check whether the valid certificate presented by the terminal has not expired.
- *Confirmer* Cnf is a third-party authority whose task is to check whether given message authentication code (MAC) is valid or not. It is trusted from the privacy perspective.
- *Chips* are tamper-resistant devices with small secure memory (henceforth denoted with C).
- *Terminals* are devices which communicate with chips (denoted with T).

---

[5] We consider the earliest expiration date from all certificates in the chain.

2.3 Primitives

HASH FUNCTION. We use SHA256 [9]. In our security proofs, each hash function is treated as an independent random oracle. Hence, we need to separate each of them with a fixed padding: $H_i(x) := \mathsf{SHA256}(\mathsf{encode}(i)|x)$ where encode maps integer i to a single byte value.

PSEUDORANDOM FUNCTION, MESSAGE AUTHENTICATION CODE. For MAC and PRF, we use HMAC [10], where the underlying hash function is SHA256 [9].

AUTHENTICATED ENCRYPTION [11]. A (variable-length) authenticated encryption is a symmetric encryption scheme comprising two algorithms $(\mathsf{Enc}, \mathsf{Dec})$. Enc takes (K, IV, H, pt) as input, that is a symmetric key K, initialization vector IV, authenticated header H and message pt respectively, and returns a ciphertext ct. Dec takes (K, IV, H, ct) as input and returns either a special failure symbol $\perp$ or a message pt. The security of the AE primitive is formally defined by Rogaway [11]. Our practical choice for AE is AES-GCM [12].

SCHNORR SIGNATURES [13]. The Schnorr signature scheme over $\mathcal{G}$ is a tuple of algorithms $(\mathsf{Kg}, \mathsf{Sign}, \mathsf{Ver})$ with arbitrary-length bitstrings as the message domain. Below, sk, vk denotes signing, verifying key pair respectively; σ denotes the signature. All algorithms have access to $\mathcal{G}$ which includes G and q.

$\mathsf{Kg}(\mathcal{G})$:	$\mathsf{Sign}(\mathsf{sk}, m)$:	$\mathsf{Ver}(\mathsf{vk}, m, \sigma)$:
$\mathsf{sk} \leftarrow_\$ \mathbb{Z}_q^*; \mathsf{vk} \leftarrow \mathsf{sk} \cdot G$	$k \leftarrow_\$ \mathbb{Z}_q; R \leftarrow k \cdot G$	$\sigma \rightarrow (s, R)$
return $(\mathsf{sk}, \mathsf{vk})$	$h \leftarrow H_1(m|R)$	$h \leftarrow H_1(m|R)$
	$s \leftarrow (k - \mathsf{sk} \cdot h) \bmod q$	$R' = s \cdot G + h \cdot \mathsf{vk}$
	$\sigma \leftarrow (s, R)$	**return** $[R' = R]$ //true or false
	return σ	

A Schnorr tuple (vk, m, σ) is valid if $\mathsf{Ver}(\mathsf{vk}, m, \sigma) = \mathsf{true}$. Assuming that the discrete logarithm problem is hard, this signature scheme is existentially unforgeable with chosen message attack in the random oracle model, as proven by Pointcheval and Stern [14].

For our Data & Chip Authentication Protocol (Sect. 4.2), we require that the signature to be of Schnorr type. However, it is possible to use other elliptic-curve-based signature schemes for implementing PKIs. Our efficiency calculations are based on the assumption that signing takes one scalar multiplication on $\mathcal{G}$, where verification takes two. Hence, verifying a certificate chain takes $2d$ scalar multiplications, where d is the depth of the PKI.

3 Suite Overview

In this section, we explain the high-level organization of the protocols. The data contained in the chip is stored at enrollment and is never updated. We categorize the information inside the chip into few data groups depending on their privacy sensitivity:

– DG_1: It contains all necessary public parameters for our protocols. It contains no privacy-sensitive data that can be exploited for tracking.

- DG_2: The data contained in this group is related to the basic identity information of the holder. It is revealed only after the successful completion of either the Strong Access Control Protocol (SAC) (Sect. 4.1) or the Weak Access Control Protocol (WAC) (Sect. 5.1).
- DG_3: The data contained in this group is privacy-sensitive, e.g. biometric templates. It can only be given to the terminal if the session is established through the SAC (Sect. 4.1).
- DG_4: The data contained in this group is highly privacy-sensitive such as signatures of the identity, and never leaves the chip.

In Table 1, we give the actual contents of the data groups. $DG_{2\text{-}3}$ is a shorthand for the combination of DG_2 and DG_3, and it is authenticated by the identity signer IS such that $\sigma_{DG_{2\text{-}3}}$ is a Schnorr signature over $DG_{2\text{-}3}$.

Table 1. Content of data groups. The password pwd lays printed on the front page.

Printed	Public	pwd (password for WAC)
DG_1	Public	$\mathcal{G}$ (curve domain parameters), $CA\text{-}T_{pub}$ (public key for the terminal authority), TS_{pub} (public key for the time server), ℓ (nonce length)
DG_2	Personal	ID (identity info e.g. full name), u_{chip} (identifier value tied to K_{chip} for DCA)
DG_3	Sensitive	BIO_{ID} (biometric reference template), $\langle CA\text{-}ID, IS \rangle$ (certificate chain of IS)
DG_4	Chip-only	$\sigma_{DG_{2\text{-}3}}$ (signature over $DG_{2\text{-}3}$), K_{chip} (MAC key for CDA), G_{pwd2} (precomputed pwd$\cdot G_2$), G_{pwd3} (precomputed pwd$\cdot G_3$)

The protocol works in two different paths as shown in Fig. 1: strong and weak paths. The control flow can follow either one based on the choice of the terminal. The holder has no control on this choice but he can accept or refuse to have his biometry scanned, which is necessary in the strong path[6]. If either T or C encounters an error, then the session is aborted immediately.

The strong path continues in the following order:

SAC: C proceeds to verify the authorization of T. On success, both C and T end up deriving a shared secret key K.
TCH: C requests a reliable time information from TS and the communication between the two is relayed through T.
SSE: C and T use the shared key K to establish secure communication. After this protocol, any following interaction between the two is encrypted.
$DG_{2\text{-}3}$: C transfers DG_2 and DG_3 to T.
DCA: C proves the authenticity of $DG_{2\text{-}3}$ and that the chip is genuine.

---

[6] We cannot guarantee that the biometric scanner is not malicious and will not store or share the real-time template obtained from the user during the session. Each time a user accepts (or coerced) to give a biometric sample, she inherently faces the risk that the scanner will store the real-time sample.

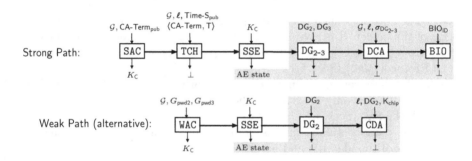

Fig. 1. The high-level picture of the suite. The protocols with gray background are encapsulated by the secure session. Input/output of the chip for protocols are shown.

BIO: T checks if the real-time biometric template matches the reference template BIO_{ID} included in DG_3 by running the biometric matching algorithm. On success, T successfully accepts the presented identity and terminates.

In the strong path, C ensures that T is authorized for access by the authority. This allows C to trust T and release its biometric template for biometric matching. On the other side, T ensures that (1) the identity information on C is valid, (2) C is genuine (not a skimmed copy) and (3) the holder's biometric identity matches the one carried by C. The strong path requires the online connectivity between T and TS. All security and privacy goals of identification are fulfilled in the strong path.

The weak path continues in the following order:

WAC: C proceeds to verify that T knows the password. On success, both C and T end up deriving a shared secret key K.

SSE: Same as in the strong path.

DG_2: C transfers only DG_2 to T (but not DG_3).

CDA: C proves the authenticity of DG_2 with a confirmer-based proof. T terminates after receiving the proof. Later, T needs to interact with the remote confirmer Cnf to verify the authenticity of the proof. On success, T concludes that the presented identity is valid and that C is genuine. T never receives access to DG_3 in this path and no biometric matching is made.

The weak path provides a more lightweight solution and does not require T to have online connection to TS (or the revocation server) during the interaction. C ensures that T has a visual access to the front page of the identity document and thereby knows the password. This does not necessarily mean that T is authorized by the identification system. It could be a rogue device who had access to the front copy of the identity document. Therefore, C shares its basic identity information with T along with the confirmer-verifiable proof of the identity. Also, C does not release its biometric template. On the other side, T cannot decide on the validity of the identity information by itself. T keeps the offline proof and later requests from the trusted confirmer to verify the proof. Only when the confirmer validates the proof, T is fully convinced that the presented identity is valid, and the interacting chip is genuine. There is no guarantee that the holder's biometric identity matches the one carried by C. Therefore, the weak path cannot be used to securely identify the holder. It can only be used to authenticate the document. This sort of verification could be useful for mobile terminals that does not have a reliable connection to TS (or the revocation server), e.g. in a refugee camp.

4   Strong Path

4.1   Strong Access Control (SAC)

Given the current wide-spread use of NFC-enabled smart phones, attackers have a large number of devices that can be exploited to act as terminals. To prevent arbitrary devices from communicating with chips, we rely on a PKI. When T prompts C to establish a communication session, T is asked to provide a chain of *valid* certificates as an attestation. The chip comes embedded with $CA\text{-}T_{pub}$. On success, both C and T end up with a shared secret, that is the key material for the following symmetric session. Hence, the access control protocol serves two purposes: (1) C is convinced that it is talking to an authorized terminal, (2) C and T derive the key material.

The full description of our *strong access control* (SAC) is given in Fig. 2. The security model and proofs are given in the full version [1]. Briefly, the security argument states that (1) the passive adversary cannot distinguish the derived session key from random, and (2) the active adversary cannot make C accept by modifying the exchanged messages. The final derived key material remains secure even if T_{prv} is given to the adversary after the protocol is completed, i.e. forward-secrecy.

Efficiency: The chip has to perform 1 scalar multiplication for checking the subgroup membership of R^7; 4 multiplications for computing X_1, X_2, K_C; and $2d_T$ multiplications for verifying the certificate chain. d_T is the depth of the Terminal PKI ($d_T = 2$ is a reasonable choice). The chip does $5 + 2d_T$ multiplications in total[8]. The terminal does 5 multiplications.

Deniability: Because the protocol does not require a private input from C side, any execution transcript can be later denied by C. I.e. C can claim that T produced the transcript by simulation. For terminals, we do not need to consider deniability; as they do not carry any personal information.

Forward-Secrecy: Gathered executions will not be useful, even if the key of the terminal is compromised. This assumes that the values x_2 and r are destroyed

---

[7] Note that asserting $R \in (\langle G \rangle \setminus \mathcal{O})$ is done by $(R \neq \mathcal{O}) \wedge (q \cdot R = \mathcal{O})$; so each group membership check takes 1 multiplication.

[8] As a speed up technique, the chip can store the hash of the previously seen certificate chains in its non-volatile memory. If the chip interacts with a small set of terminals, simple hash-then-compare saves $2d_T$ multiplications in each interaction.

SAC: Strong Access Control Protocol

Chip C		Terminal T
IN: $\mathcal{G}$, CA-T$_{\text{pub}}$		IN: $\mathcal{G}$, T$_{\text{prv}}$, $\langle$CA-T, T$\rangle$
verify $\langle$CA-T, T$\rangle$	$\xleftarrow{\langle\text{CA-T, T}\rangle}$	
extract T$_{\text{pub}}$ $\leftarrow$ $\langle$CA-T, T$\rangle$		
assert $R \in \langle G\rangle \setminus \mathcal{O}$	$\xleftarrow{\quad R \quad}$	$r \leftarrow_\$ \mathbb{Z}_q^*$; $R \leftarrow r{\cdot}G$
$x_1 \leftarrow_\$ \mathbb{Z}_q^*$; $X_1 \leftarrow x_1{\cdot}G$		
$x_2 \leftarrow_\$ \mathbb{Z}_q^*$; $X_2 \leftarrow x_2{\cdot}G$	$\xrightarrow{\quad X_1, X_2 \quad}$	assert $X_1, X_2 \in \langle G\rangle \setminus \mathcal{O}$
$K_{\text{C}} \leftarrow (x_1{\cdot}\text{T}_{\text{pub}} + x_2{\cdot}R)_{\mathbb{X}}$		$K_{\text{T}} \leftarrow (\text{T}_{\text{prv}}{\cdot}X_1 + r{\cdot}X_2)_{\mathbb{X}}$
erase x_2		erase r
$K_v' \leftarrow \mathsf{H}_2(K_{\text{C}}\vert\text{trans}_{\text{C}})$	$\xleftarrow{\quad K_v \quad}$	$K_v \leftarrow \mathsf{H}_2(K_{\text{T}}\vert\text{trans}_{\text{T}})$
assert $K_v' = K_v$		
OUT: K_{C}		OUT: K_{T}

Fig. 2. T's key pair is such that $(\text{T}_{\text{prv}}, \text{T}_{\text{pub}}) \in \mathbb{Z}_q^* \times (\langle G\rangle \setminus \mathcal{O})$. On "assert" and "verify", parties abort with failure if given statement is false or given certificate/signature is invalid. "erase" means given parameters must be destroyed. trans$_{\text{T}}$, trans$_{\text{C}}$ are the local transcripts, i.e. the concatenation of R, X_1, X_2 seen by each party.

by the chip and the terminal following the "erase" instruction in SAC. If the Gap Diffie-Hellman Problem remains intractable in $\mathcal{G}$, then all past sessions will be protected against key leakages of the future. More lightweight solution without forward-secrecy can be obtained by letting the chip pick $x_2 = 0$ and removing assert $X_2 \in \langle G\rangle \setminus \mathcal{O}$ on the terminal side.

4.2 Data & Chip Authentication (DCA)

DATA AUTHENTICATION. C is obliged to prove to T that $\text{DG}_{2\text{-}3} = \text{DG}_2\vert\text{DG}_3$ is valid, i.e. has a signature verifiable w.r.t. the identity server PKI. We propose an interactive zero-knowledge (ZK) protocol for proving the authenticity of the presented identity that is similar to offline non-transferable authentication protocol [15]. Briefly, C carries a Schnorr tuple $(\text{IS}_{\text{pub}}, \text{DG}_{2\text{-}3}, \sigma_{\text{DG}_{2\text{-}3}})$ along with the certificate chain $\langle$CA-ID, IS$\rangle$. T knows CA-ID$_{\text{pub}}$ in advance, and also receives $\text{DG}_{2\text{-}3}$ as described in Fig. 1. Then, C and T follow the interaction described in Fig. 3; in which C proves the knowledge of a valid signature, that is $\sigma_{\text{DG}_{2\text{-}3}}$. During this interaction, R point of the signature $\sigma_{\text{DG}_{2\text{-}3}} = (s, R)$ is revealed to the verifier in clear. This allows us to develop a very efficient Σ-protocol, which yields a zero-knowledge proof of knowledge interactive protocol with a commitment scheme under the random oracle assumption. The security of this generic commitment based transformation is proven by Monnerat et al. [15], and our proofs for Σ-protocol can be found in the full version [1]. Preferring interactive proofs over

DCA: Data & Chip Authentication Protocol

Chip C		**Terminal T**
IN: $\mathcal{G}, \ell, \sigma_{\mathsf{DG}_{2\text{-}3}}$		**IN:** $\mathcal{G}, \ell, \mathsf{DG}_{2\text{-}3}, \mathsf{CA\text{-}ID}_{\mathsf{pub}}$
$(s, R) \leftarrow \sigma_{\mathsf{DG}_{2\text{-}3}}$		**extract** $\langle \mathsf{CA\text{-}ID}, \mathsf{IS} \rangle \leftarrow \mathsf{DG}_{2\text{-}3}$
		extract $\mathsf{IS}_{\mathsf{pub}} \leftarrow \langle \mathsf{CA\text{-}ID}, \mathsf{IS} \rangle$
		verify $\langle \mathsf{CA\text{-}ID}, \mathsf{IS} \rangle$
		$r \leftarrow_\$ \{0,1\}^\ell \; ; \; v \leftarrow_\$ \mathbb{Z}_q^*$
	$\xleftarrow{\quad h \quad}$	$h = \mathsf{H}_5(r\|v)$
$u \leftarrow_\$ \mathbb{Z}_q; \; U \leftarrow u{\cdot}G$	$\xrightarrow{\quad U, R \quad}$	**assert** $R \in (\langle G \rangle \setminus \mathcal{O})$
assert $(v \in \mathbb{Z}_q^*) \wedge (r \in \{0,1\}^\ell)$	$\xleftarrow{\quad r, v \quad}$	**assert** $U \in \langle G \rangle$
assert $h = \mathsf{H}_1(r\|v)$		
$s' \leftarrow (s + v{\cdot}u) \bmod q$	$\xrightarrow{\quad s' \quad}$	**assert** $s' \in \mathbb{Z}_q$
		$e \leftarrow \mathsf{H}_1(\mathsf{DG}_{2\text{-}3}\|R)$
		assert $(s'{\cdot}G + e{\cdot}\mathsf{IS}_{\mathsf{pub}} = R + v{\cdot}U)$

Fig. 3. The identity signature $\sigma_{\mathsf{DG}_{2\text{-}3}}$ over $\mathsf{DG}_{2\text{-}3}$ is actually a tuple $(s, R) \in \mathbb{Z}_q^* \times \langle G \rangle$.

signature schemes has two benefits in our scenario. First, the transcript remains deniable from the chip's perspective, hence he can later deny the interaction, even if the transcript is released by the terminal[9]. Secondly, the actual signature is never released to the terminal, which prevents the terminal from obtaining publicly-provable and transferable proof over the identity.

Efficiency: The chip only performs one scalar multiplication. The terminal performs $4 + 2d_{\mathsf{IS}}$ multiplications, where d_{IS} is the depth of the Identity Signer PKI ($d_{\mathsf{IS}} = 2$ is a reasonable choice).

CHIP AUTHENTICATION. With the assumption that the memory of C is secure and the ZK property of DCA, $\sigma_{\mathsf{DG}_{2\text{-}3}}$ does not leak. Hence, the proof of knowledge of $\sigma_{\mathsf{DG}_{2\text{-}3}}$ is also a proof that C is genuine.

4.3   Time Check Protocol (TCH) & Revocation Check Protocol (REV)

To protect against compromise of long-term secret keys, we need a secure revocation verification in the Terminal PKI.

First remedy is the revocation-through-time. Briefly, we enforce that the terminal server issues certificates only for a limited amount of time. The compromised certificates remain useful only for a short period of time. All required by the chip is a trusted clock to gradually expire certificates. As C usually has

---

[9] We exclude attacks from the trusted agent model [8].

TCH: Time Check Protocol

Chip C		**Time Server** TS
IN: $\mathcal{G}, \ell, \mathsf{TS_{pub}}, \langle\mathsf{CA\text{-}T}, \mathsf{T}\rangle$		**IN:** $\mathcal{G}, \ell, \mathsf{TS_{prv}}$
extract $t_e \leftarrow \langle\mathsf{CA\text{-}T}, \mathsf{T}\rangle$		
$n \leftarrow\!\!\$ \{0,1\}^\ell$	$\xrightarrow{\quad n \quad}$	**assert** $n \in \{0,1\}^\ell$
		$t \leftarrow$ current time
		$h \leftarrow \mathsf{H_3}(t\|n)$
$h' \leftarrow \mathsf{H_3}(t\|n)$	$\xleftarrow{\quad t, \sigma \quad}$	$\sigma \leftarrow\!\!\$ \mathsf{Sign}(\mathsf{TS_{prv}}, h)$
verify $(\mathsf{TS_{pub}}, h', \sigma)$		
assert $t_e > t$		

REV: Revocation Check Protocol

Chip C		**Rev. Server** Rev
IN: $\mathcal{G}, \ell, \mathsf{Rev_{pub}}, \langle\mathsf{CA\text{-}T}, \mathsf{T}\rangle$		**IN:** $\mathcal{G}, \ell, \mathsf{Rev_{prv}}, \mathsf{CA\text{-}T_{pub}}$
$n \leftarrow\!\!\$ \{0,1\}^\ell$	$\xrightarrow{\quad n, \langle\mathsf{CA\text{-}T}, \mathsf{T}\rangle \quad}$	**assert** $n \in \{0,1\}^\ell$
		verify $\langle\mathsf{CA\text{-}T}, \mathsf{T}\rangle$
		revoked? $\langle\mathsf{CA\text{-}T}, \mathsf{T}\rangle$
		$h \leftarrow \mathsf{H_3}(n\|\langle\mathsf{CA\text{-}T}, \mathsf{T}\rangle)$
$h' \leftarrow \mathsf{H_3}(n\|\langle\mathsf{CA\text{-}T}, \mathsf{T}\rangle)$	$\xleftarrow{\quad \sigma \quad}$	$\sigma \leftarrow\!\!\$ \mathsf{Sign}(\mathsf{Rev_{prv}}, h)$
verify $(\mathsf{Rev_{pub}}, h', \sigma)$		

Fig. 4. The instruction "revoked?" asserts that the input certificate is not revoked. $t_e > t$ means the certificate has not expired yet.

no such clock, it must query a time server. Concretely, C prompts T with a challenge value n to produce a signed timestamp value t (see Fig. 4). T acts as a proxy, relaying the communication between C and TS. Then, TS provides a signature over the timestamp t and nonce n to prevent replay attacks.

Alternatively, we can use OCSP-based approach to check the revocation status of certificates with the REV described in Fig. 4. In this case, the public key of the revocation server Rev is stored in C at enrollment time. Using REV instead of TCH could also allow us to outsource the verification of the certificate chain $\langle\mathsf{CA\text{-}T}, \mathsf{T}\rangle$ in SAC and save $2d_\mathsf{T}$ multiplications by trusting the revocation server.

Efficiency: The chip has to verify the validity of one signature, which takes 2 scalar multiplications over $\mathcal{G}$. The time server does $1 + 2d_\mathsf{T}$ multiplications.

4.4 Secure Communication (SSE)

We denote by $K = K_\mathsf{C} = K_\mathsf{T}$ the common secret which is derived by either SAC or WAC. We create an authenticated and confidential symmetric channel based on

K. For this, we use a variable-length authenticated encryption scheme AE which consists of two algorithm (Enc, Dec) as explained in Sect. 2.3. Each peer keeps an active state $st = (K_{AE}, i_0, i_1)$ for the live session where K_{AE} is the authenticated encryption/decryption key, and i_0, i_1 are nonce counters for each sent and received messages respectively. A peer has access to the pair of algorithms Send and Recv. Send takes (st, pt) as input and returns (st, ct), i.e. each send/receive updates the corresponding internal counter of the state. Similarly, Recv takes (st, ct) and returns (st, pt). Authenticated header in not used (so we put $\perp$ as input below). In case of $pt = \perp$, the receiver halts. The full description is given below:

Send(st, pt):	Recv(st, ct):	$\text{Init}_b(K)$:
$st \rightarrow (K_{AE}, i_0, i_1)$	$st \rightarrow (K_{AE}, i_0, i_1)$	$K_{AE} \leftarrow H_4(K\|\text{encode}(1))$
$ct \leftarrow \text{Enc}(K_{AE}, i_0, \perp, pt)$	$pt \leftarrow \text{Dec}(K_{AE}, i_1, \perp, ct)$	$IV_0 \leftarrow H_4(K\|\text{encode}(2))$
$st \leftarrow (K_{AE}, i_0 + 1, i_1)$	**if** $pt = \perp$ **then abort**	$IV_1 \leftarrow H_4(K\|\text{encode}(3))$
return (st, ct)	$st \leftarrow (K_{AE}, i_0, i_1 + 1)$	$st \leftarrow (K_{AE}, IV_b, IV_{\bar{b}})$
	return (st, pt)	**return** st

The initial state st is bootstrapped with algorithm Init_b (above) which takes the key material K as input. We swap the order of counters to synchronize the initial states. Hence, C runs Init_0 and T runs Init_1. encode is a byte-encoding function explained in Sect. 2.3 and $\bar{b}$ is the complement of b such that $\{b, \bar{b}\} = \{0, 1\}$.

5 Weak Path

5.1 Weak Access Control (WAC)

WAC is an alternative way of ensuring that a connection attempt is from an authorized terminal is based on a knowledge of a password instead of a PKI. This is done with PACE in the MRTD standard [2]. The password usually lays printed on the document and can be either typed manually by the inspector or directly read with visual scanning of the document.

Password-based authentication is already a well-established topic in the academic literature, as surveyed by Boyd and Mathuri [16]. The rigorous formalization of security can be found by Bellare et al. [17]. Nevertheless, password-based authenticated key exchange protocols did not receive its merit in practice, especially troubled by patents and legal ambiguities. Our own version in Fig. 5 is a reduced version of SPAKE which is available for royalty-free use, and has been drafted for a standardization [18].

In password-based access control protocols, passwords are chosen from a small domain, and it is feasible for an adversary to enumerate each possible password in this set. Therefore, the adversary always has an inevitable not negligible chance of guessing the password. In terms of security, the usual expectations from such protocols are that an adversary who obtains multiple execution transcripts of the protocol should not be able to eliminate any candidate password from the set and an adversary who is performing an active attack should only eliminate a single candidate password from the domain, and strictly no more.

WAC: Weak Access Control Protocol

Chip C		Terminal T
IN: $\mathcal{G}, G_{\mathsf{pwd2}}, G_{\mathsf{pwd3}}$		**IN:** $\mathcal{G}, \mathsf{pwd}$
$a \leftarrow\!\!\$\, \mathbb{Z}_q^*; \ A \leftarrow a \cdot G$		

$$M \leftarrow (A + G_{\mathsf{pwd2}}) \qquad \xrightarrow{\quad M \quad} \qquad b \leftarrow\!\!\$\, \mathbb{Z}_q^*; \ B \leftarrow b \cdot G$$

$$L \leftarrow B + \mathsf{pwd} \cdot G_3$$

$$K_\mathsf{T} \leftarrow (b \cdot M - b \cdot \mathsf{pwd} \cdot G_2)_\mathbb{X}$$

$$K_\mathsf{C} \leftarrow (a \cdot (L - G_{\mathsf{pwd3}}))_\mathbb{X} \quad \xleftarrow{\quad L, K_v \quad} \quad K_v \leftarrow \mathsf{H}_6 (K_\mathsf{T} | \mathsf{trans_T})$$

assert $K_v = \mathsf{H}_6 (K_\mathsf{C} | \mathsf{trans_C})$

OUT: K_C **OUT:** K_T

Fig. 5. T obtains pwd from the front page of the identity document. $\mathsf{trans_T}, \mathsf{trans_C}$ are the local transcripts, i.e. the concatenation of M, L seen by each party.

We specify the dictionary $\mathcal{D}$ as the password domain such that $\log_2 |\mathcal{D}|$ is far smaller than the security parameter λ. Each chip receives a randomly sampled password $\mathsf{pwd} \in \mathcal{D}$ at enrollment.

Efficiency: C and T do 2 and 4 scalar multiplications respectively. C also does 2 group additions.

5.2   Confirmer Data & Chip Authentication (CDA)

After a weakly secure session is established, C releases DG_2 as seen in Fig. 1. In order to convince T, without any publicly-verifiable proof of valid identity, C produces a MAC that can only be verified by Cnf. Therefore, without the help of Cnf, T can only learn the basic identity information without any proof.

We require that Cnf is in possession of a master secret $\mathsf{K_{Cnf}}$ that is sampled uniformly from the key domain of the pseudorandom function PRF. During enrollment, each chip receives a unique identity and key pair $(\mathsf{u_{chip}}, \mathsf{K_{chip}})$ from Cnf such that $\mathsf{K_{chip}} = \mathsf{PRF}(\mathsf{K_{Cnf}}, \mathsf{u_{chip}})$. When C and T interact, both of them add nonces to the protocol to guarantee freshness. By using timestamps, T commits to a specific time interval, i.e. $[t, t + \Delta_t]$, in which the authentication code will be useful. On the other side of the MAC verification, the confirmer decides on the value of Δ_t and applies this time interval policy (see Fig. 6).

This protocol allows weakly transferable proofs from the terminal side, but they are not publicly verifiable. Moreover, the confirmation protocol makes sure that a certain terminal can be kept accountable for verification requests. The proof σ_t is not deniable to the confirmer Cnf. If Cnf is honest, it provides verification access for a limited time Δ_t, thus σ_t is deniable to anyone else after this time. If Cnf is malicious, σ_t is deniable in the sense that it could have been forged by Cnf itself. We exclude attacks in the trusted agent model [8] which are inherent to deniability.

CDA1: Confirmer Data & Chip Auth. Protocol 1

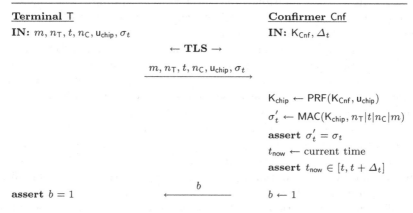

Chip C		**Terminal T**
IN: ℓ, DG_2, K_{chip}		**IN:** ℓ, DG_2
$m' \leftarrow H_7(DG_2)$		**extract** $u_{chip} \leftarrow DG_2$
		$t \leftarrow$ current time
		$m \leftarrow H_7(DG_2)$
assert $n_T \in \{0,1\}^{\ell}$	$\xleftarrow{\quad t, n_T \quad}$	$n_T \leftarrow\!\!\$\ \{0,1\}^{\ell}$
$n_C \leftarrow\!\!\$\ \{0,1\}^{\ell}$		
$\sigma_t \leftarrow MAC(K_{chip}, n_T\|t\|n_C\|m')$	$\xrightarrow{\quad n_C, \sigma_t \quad}$	**assert** $n_C \in \{0,1\}^{\ell}$
		OUT: $m, n_T, t, n_C, u_{chip}, \sigma_t$

CDA2: Confirmer Data & Chip Auth. Protocol 2

Terminal T		**Confirmer Cnf**
IN: $m, n_T, t, n_C, u_{chip}, \sigma_t$		**IN:** K_{Cnf}, Δ_t
	$\leftarrow$ **TLS** $\rightarrow$	
	$\xrightarrow{m, n_T, t, n_C, u_{chip}, \sigma_t}$	
		$K_{chip} \leftarrow PRF(K_{Cnf}, u_{chip})$
		$\sigma'_t \leftarrow MAC(K_{chip}, n_T\|t\|n_C\|m)$
		assert $\sigma'_t = \sigma_t$
		$t_{now} \leftarrow$ current time
		assert $t_{now} \in [t, t + \Delta_t]$
assert $b = 1$	$\xleftarrow{\quad b \quad}$	$b \leftarrow 1$

Fig. 6. We assume that T and Cnf can communicate through a mutually authenticated and confidential channel established through TLS.

Similar to DCA presented in Sect. 4.2, we place K_{chip} into the secure memory to obtain chip authentication at the same time. Since K_{chip} never leaves the chip, a terminal who verifies the validity of this offline proof can also be convinced that it was interacting with the genuine chip.

6   Implementation

We implemented our protocols on smart cards. We used a biometric finger-vein reader with infrared camera attached to Raspberry Pi that communicates through the WebSocket protocol. We developed the card applets with the technology of java cards (JCs) provided by Oracle. The JC we used is NXP JCOP version 2.4.2 with 144KB of EEPROM and 7.5KB of RAM [19].

Table 2. The running time and the number of operations (in $\mathcal{G}$) for each protocol. d_T is the depth of the terminal PKI. SAC is implemented without forward-secrecy (requiring no group addition).

	SAC	TCH	SSE	DG$_{2\text{-}3}$	DCA	WAC	SSE	DG$_2$	CDA
		Strong path				Weak path			
# of multiplications in $\mathcal{G}$	$5 + 2d_T$	2	0	0	1	2	0	0	0
# of additions in $\mathcal{G}$	1	0	0	0	0	2	0	0	0
Running time (in milliseconds)	1819			2815	2734	8765			

The general restrictions related to JCs are also summarized by Bichsel et al. [7], especially the fact that APIs related to group operations are quite limited and there are no big integer utilities. Since our design relies on elliptic curves (compared to their RSA-based group that requires modulus to be larger in terms of bit size), single scalar multiplication in the group takes much less time in our case (respectively 0.6 s versus 4.3 s). As a conclusion, our seemingly more detailed and fine-grained protocols take less time to complete than that of eID in total [7].

For scalar multiplications we use elliptic curve Diffie-Hellman key exchange (ECDH) API. However, group additions become more tricky (no closely related API). Therefore, we used an external library called JCMathlib [20]. It performs memory management and contains useful elliptic curve and big integer utilities. Despite the fact that we found some bugs in the library, it is a handy tool to implement elliptic curve cryptography on smart cards.

In JC API, ECDH algorithm returns the x-coordinate of a general purpose scalar multiplication. For scalar multiplications in the protocols, we use the ECDH hardware implementation through API which takes around 600 milliseconds per operation. However, the point addition is done in software through JCMathlib, and each addition operation takes more than 3 s (much slower than a scalar multiplication). This results in a considerable delay in WAC-CDA compared to SAC-TCH-SSE (where SAC is without forward-secrecy and contains no addition operation). It should be noted that this is solely due to over-restricted API imposed by smart cards. In general, point additions can be done much faster than multiplication. We used the secp256r1 curve. Our results are given in Table 2.

For the feature extraction algorithm, we used the maximum curvature method and for the matching algorithm, we used the Mirua Matching [21]. We integrated the biometric feature extraction and matching algorithm developed by IDIAP [22]. The algorithms are coded in python with reliable performance. They are easy to integrate with simple calls from the java code.

This implementation was a proof of concept. It was used as a demonstration during a science fair. We enrolled and matched about 300 people during the event. For this implementation, we simplified the protocols, mostly due to time constraints before the event. We used no forward secrecy in SAC (hence $x_2 = 0$). We did not implement TCH. Our PKI was flat (with depth 0). This way, only

WAC required a point addition to be made by the chip. Finally, the biometric extraction and matching were done by the terminal.

7   Conclusion

All of our protocols are designed to be efficient and they only require elliptic curve based operations. On the chip side, the strong path takes $8 + 2d_T$ scalar multiplications, and the weak path takes only 3 multiplications in total. On the terminal side, they take $10 + 2d_{IS}$ and 4 multiplications respectively. In practice, $d_{IS} = d_T = 2$ could be a realistic choice.

Our main improvement over the existing MRTD and EAC standards are in the privacy direction. Essentially, any interaction from the identity document can later be denied, and no transferable information is leaked. We achieved this with the help of interactive zero knowledge proofs instead of passively authenticating the data with digital signatures.

We thank Lambert Sonna for his support and valuable insights during the design and implementation of our protocols. We thank Innosuisse for providing financial support and Global ID for providing the necessary equipment for the implementation part.

References

1. Balli, F., Betül Durak, F., Vaudenay, S.: BioID: a Privacy-Friendly Identity Document. Cryptology ePrint Archive, Report 2019/894 (2019). https://eprint.iacr.org/2019/894
2. ICAO. Machine Readable Travel Documents Part 11 (Doc. 9303). International Civil Aviation Organization (2015)
3. BSI. Advanced Security Mechanisms for Machine Readable Travel Documents. TR-03110 Technical Guideline. in der Informationstechnik (2016)
4. Dagdelen, Ö., Fischlin, M.: Security analysis of the extended access control protocol for machine readable travel documents. In: Burmester, M., Tsudik, G., Magliveras, S., Ilić, I. (eds.) ISC 2010. LNCS, vol. 6531, pp. 54–68. Springer, Heidelberg (2011). https://doi.org/10.1007/978-3-642-18178-8_6
5. LaMacchia, B., Lauter, K., Mityagin, A.: Stronger security of authenticated key exchange. In: Susilo, W., Liu, J.K., Mu, Y. (eds.) ProvSec 2007. LNCS, vol. 4784, pp. 1–16. Springer, Heidelberg (2007). https://doi.org/10.1007/978-3-540-75670-5_1
6. Monnerat, J., Vaudenay, S., Vuagnoux, M.: About machine-readable travel documents. RFID Security 2007 (2007)
7. Bichsel, P., Camenisch, J., Groß, T., Shoup, V.: Anonymous credentials on a standard Java card. In: Proceedings of the 2009 ACM Conference on Computer and Communications Security, CCS 2009, Chicago, Illinois, USA, 9–13 November 2009, pp. 600–610 (2009)
8. Mateus, P., Vaudenay, S.: On tamper-resistance from a theoretical viewpoint. In: Clavier, C., Gaj, K. (eds.) CHES 2009. LNCS, vol. 5747, pp. 411–428. Springer, Heidelberg (2009). https://doi.org/10.1007/978-3-642-04138-9_29

9. National Institute of Standards and Technology. FIPS PUB 180–2: Secure Hash Standard (2004)
10. Krawczyk, H., Bellare, M., Canetti, R.: HMAC: Keyed-hashing for message authentication. RFC 2104, February 1997
11. Rogaway, P.: Authenticated-encryption with associated-data. In: Proceedings of the 9th ACM Conference on Computer and Communications Security, CCS 2002, pp. 98–107. ACM (2002)
12. Dworkin, M.J.: SP 800–38D. Recommendation for Block Cipher Modes of Operation: Galois/Counter Mode (GCM) and GMAC. Technical report, Gaithersburg, MD, United States (2007)
13. Schnorr, C.P.: Efficient identification and signatures for smart cards. In: Brassard, G. (ed.) CRYPTO 1989. LNCS, vol. 435, pp. 239–252. Springer, New York (1990). https://doi.org/10.1007/0-387-34805-0_22
14. Pointcheval, D., Stern, J.: Security proofs for signature schemes. In: Maurer, U. (ed.) EUROCRYPT 1996. LNCS, vol. 1070, pp. 387–398. Springer, Heidelberg (1996). https://doi.org/10.1007/3-540-68339-9_33
15. Monnerat, J., Pasini, S., Vaudenay, S.: Efficient deniable authentication for signatures. In: Abdalla, M., Pointcheval, D., Fouque, P.-A., Vergnaud, D. (eds.) ACNS 2009. LNCS, vol. 5536, pp. 272–291. Springer, Heidelberg (2009). https://doi.org/10.1007/978-3-642-01957-9_17
16. Boyd, C., Mathuria, A.: Protocols for Authentication and Key Establishment, 1st edn. Springer, Heidelberg (2010)
17. Bellare, M., Pointcheval, D., Rogaway, P.: Authenticated key exchange secure against dictionary attacks. In: Preneel, B. (ed.) EUROCRYPT 2000. LNCS, vol. 1807, pp. 139–155. Springer, Heidelberg (2000). https://doi.org/10.1007/3-540-45539-6_11
18. SPAKE2, a PAKE, draft-irtf-cfrg-spake2-04 (2017). https://tools.ietf.org/html/draft-irtf-cfrg-spake2-04. Accessed 18 Jan 2018
19. NXP JCOP J2E145 v2.4.2 R3 Java Card 144K (2018). https://www.cardlogix.com/product/nxp-j2e145-2-4-2-rel-3-java-card-145k-jcop-3-0-1. Accessed 01 Oct 2018
20. JCMathLib (2017). https://github.com/OpenCryptoProject/JCMathLib. Accessed 01 Oct 2018
21. Miura, N., Nagasaka, A., Miyatake, T.: Feature extraction of finger-vein patterns based on repeated line tracking and its application to personal identification. Mach. Vis. Appl. **15**(4), 194–203 (2004)
22. IDIAP finger-vein matching (2016). Accessed 01 Oct 2018

On the Statistical Detection
of Adversarial Instances
over Encrypted Data

Mina Sheikhalishahi[1]([✉]), Majid Nateghizad[2], Fabio Martinelli[1],
Zekeriya Erkin[2], and Marco Loog[2]

[1] Istituto di Informatica e Telematica, Consiglio Nazionale delle Ricerche (CNR),
Pisa, Italy
{mina.sheikhalishahi,fabio.martinelli}@iit.cnr.it
[2] Department of Intelligent Systems, Delft University of Technology,
Delft, The Netherlands
{m.nateghizad,z.erkin,m.loog}@tudelf.nl

Abstract. Adversarial instances are malicious inputs designed to fool machine learning models. In particular, motivated and sophisticated attackers intentionally design adversarial instances to evade classifiers which have been trained to detect security violation, such as malware detection. While the existing approaches provide effective solutions in detecting and defending adversarial samples, they fail to detect them when they are encrypted. In this study, a novel framework is proposed which employs statistical test to detect adversarial instances, when data under analysis are encrypted. An experimental evaluation of our approach shows its practical feasibility in terms of computation cost.

Keywords: Privacy · Adversarial machine learning ·
Homomorphic encryption

1 Introduction

Machine learning algorithms are generally constructed under the assumption that models are trained on instances drawn from a distribution expected to be the representative of test instances exploited for making the prediction. In an ideal scenario, the training and test distributions are identical. However, this hypothesis does not hold in the presence of adversaries. In a real scenario, every learning-based system which is trained and employed over economic, political, military, and security-critical data, is in the certain risk of attracting adversaries who gain advantages by manipulating the system to influence its decisions [1]. Such activities include, but are not limited to, Spam detection [2], terrorist Tweet analysis, adversarial advertisements, malware PDF file detection [3], and sign detection in autonomous vehicles [4].

The problem of adversarial machine learning has attracted considerable attention since 2014, when Szegedy et al. [5] showed that deep convolutional

© Springer Nature Switzerland AG 2019
S. Mauw and M. Conti (Eds.): STM 2019, LNCS 11738, pp. 71–88, 2019.
https://doi.org/10.1007/978-3-030-31511-5_5

neural network, utilized for object recognition, can be fooled by perturbed input image which is visually indistinguishable. From then on a lot of work has been devoted to this field, spanning from physical consequences of adversarial instances presented in autonomous vehicles [6], the analysis of classifiers' robustness against adversarial perturbation [7], to defenses designed to mitigate issues caused by adversarial instances [8]. Still, the majority of proposed defenses, e.g. defensive distillation [9], are not effective in adapting to changes in attack strategies.

To provide an arm race that is independent of the kind of attacks, Grosse et al. [10] proposed an approach based on the intuition that adversarial instances must inherently show some *statistical* differences with the correct data. More precisely, an attacker generally designs adversarial instances in such a way that it is similar to the training records labeled as he expects. These new fake elements – independently from how they have been created – must have different distributions compared to the training data. Grosse et al. [10] showed that *statistical tests* work efficiently in detecting adversarial instances, even when these instances have been generated through different adversarial instance crafting techniques.

However, their proposed approach fails to detect adversarial instances when they are crafted in an *encrypted* format. Generally, the primary organizations who determine and mandate laws about the way sensitive data may be utilized, such as European General Data Protection Regulation (GDPR)[1], Payment Card Industry Data Security Standard (PCI DSS)[2], and the Health Insurance Portability and Accountability Act (HIPAA)[3], permit the analysis of data only when they are encrypted. Encryption mechanisms, which are defined based on rigorous mathematical rules, provide the possibility of confirming security at every step they are employed [11].

In this study, as a very first work in addressing issues caused by adversarial samples in private setting, we propose encryption-based protocols, which enable the system to detect adversarial instances when they are encrypted. The proposed mechanism *securely* performs a statistical test on encrypted data to measure the distribution difference between two datasets. In the case that the difference is high, the crafted instances are suspicious of being designed by an adversary.

The contribution of the current study can be summarized as follows:

- We propose a novel framework that can be deployed as a tool to *securely* detect adversarial instances in private settings.
- We propose a mechanism for transforming a non-integer-based statistical test into an integer-based one.
- We propose a new protocol for computing the exponential function. The security proof for this protocol is provided.

---

[1] https://www.eugdpr.org/.

[2] https://www.pcisecuritystandards.org/.

[3] https://www.hhs.gov/hipaa.

- We report the computation cost of our protocol for different values of adversarial instances, number of features, and size of training data.
- Finally, we prove the security of our architecture.

The remainder of this paper is structured as follows. The next section presents the preliminary notations utilized in the current study. In Sect. 3, the motivating example and the architecture of our approach are proposed. In Sect. 4 the integer-based representation of statistical test is reported. The security proof of our architecture is presented in Sect. 5. We analyze the performance of our protocols in Sect. 6, and in Sect. 7 we discuss the achievements and shortcomings of the proposed framework. In Sect. 8 the related work is presented. Finally, Sect. 9 concludes by briefly proposing future research directions.

2 Preliminaries

This section provide the background knowledge used in this work, including statistical detection of adversarial instances and Homomorphic encryption.

2.1 Statistical Detection of Adversarial Instances

To learn a classifier from training data, the real distribution of features $D_{real}^{C_i}$ for each subset C_i corresponding to a class i must be extracted. These subsets define a partition of the training data. Due to the limited number of training instances, each machine learning algorithm only learns an approximation of this real distribution, say learned feature distribution $D_{train}^{C_i}$. The existence of adversarial instances is a manifestation of the difference between $D_{real}^{C_i}$ and $D_{train}^{C_i}$. In this way, an adversary finds a sample from $D_{real}^{C_i}$ that does not adhere to $D_{train}^{C_i}$. Generally, an adversary has no knowledge about $D_{real}^{C_i}$, thus, the existing algorithms for generating adversarial instances perturb the legitimate instances drawn from $D_{train}^{C_i}$.

Independently of how adversarial instances have been generated, all adversarial instances for a class C_i will constitute a new distribution $D_{adv}^{C_i}$ of this class. This means that $D_{adv}^{C_i}$ is consistent with $D_{real}^{C_i}$, because each adversarial instance for a class C_i is still a data point that belongs to this class. However, for adversarial instances we have $D_{adv}^{C_i} \neq D_{train}^{C_i}$.

Following this argument, *statistical tests* are a natural candidate for adversarial instance detection [10]. The intuition is that adversarial instances have to be inherently distributed differently from legitimate instances during training.

Maximum Mean Discrepancy (MMD) Test: The *Maximum Mean Discrepancy (MMD)*, as a well-known two-sample statistical test, is defined in terms of particular function spaces that witnesses the difference between distributions through kernel function [12]. Formally, for two distributions $\mathcal{X} = \{X_1, \ldots, X_m\}$ and $\mathcal{Y} = \{Y_1, \ldots, Y_n\}$, the amount of MMD is computed as the following:

$$MMD(X, Y) = (\frac{1}{m^2} \sum_{i,j=1}^{m} \kappa(X_i, X_j) - \frac{2}{mn} \sum_{i,j=1}^{m,n} \kappa(X_i, Y_j) + \frac{1}{n^2} \sum_{i,j=1}^{n} \kappa(Y_i, Y_j))^{\frac{1}{2}}$$

$$(1)$$

where $\kappa(X, Y) = \exp(-\frac{\|X-Y\|^2}{2\sigma^2})$ represents the *Gaussian Kernel* function, in which σ is generally (as in this study) considered to be 1 [12]. Trivially, if two distributions are exactly equal in an ideal scenario, then $MMD(X, Y) = 0$. However, a threshold, say α, can be specified by an expert such that if $MMD(X, Y) \leq \alpha$, it is then said that the two distributions are close *enough*. It should be noted that fixing this threshold is out of the scope of the current study.

2.2   Homomorphic Encryption

We define our secure computation protocols based on a semantically secure homomorphic cryptosystem, named *Paillier* cryptosystem [13]. This scheme preserves a certain structure that can be employed to process ciphertexts without decryption. Given $\mathscr{E}_{pk}(m_1)$ and $\mathscr{E}_{pk}(m_2)$, a new ciphertext whose decryption yields the sum of the plaintext messages m_1 and m_2 can be obtained by performing a multiplication operation over ciphertexts under the additively homomorphic encryption scheme:

$$\mathcal{D}_{sk}(\mathscr{E}_{pk}(m_1) \otimes \mathscr{E}_{pk}(m_2)) = m_1 + m_2.$$

Moreover, exponentiation of any ciphertext with a public key yields the encrypted product of the original plaintext and the exponent as: $\mathcal{D}_{sk}(\mathscr{E}_{pk}(m)^e) = e \cdot m$.

In the rest of this study, we denote the ciphertext of a message m by $[m]$. In what follows, we present two additive homomorphic-based protocols, named secure *comparison* [14] and *multiplication* [15] protocols, which serve as building blocks in our framework.

Secure Comparison Protocol: We use a secure comparison protocol (e.g., [14]) to compare two encrypted values. Given two ciphertexts $[a]$ and $[b]$, the secure comparison between $[a]$ and $[b]$ is defined as follows:

$$SecureComp([a], [b]) = \begin{cases} [1] & \text{if } a \leq b, \\ [0] & \text{otherwise.} \end{cases}$$

Secure Multiplication Protocol: We use a secure multiplication protocol (e.g., [15]) to compute the multiplication between two encrypted values. Given two ciphertexts $[a]$ and $[b]$, the secure multiplication of $[a]$ and $[b]$ is defined as $Mult([a], [b]) = [a \cdot b]$.

3   Framework

This section presents the challenges in detecting adversarial instances over encrypted data through a running example within spam detection, and then an overview of our framework and security assumption is presented to address the associated challenges.

3.1   Motivating Example

Spam messages cause several problems, spanning from direct financial losses to misuses of Internet traffic, storage space and computational power. Spam emails are also becoming a tool to perpetrate different cyber-crimes, such as phishing, malware distribution, social engineering fraud, or propaganda distribution (e.g. by terrorist group). To reach his goal, the spammer generally hides himself behind infected devices (botnets) which send millions of spam messages with similar text and template (spam campaign), against their users' will (or even awareness) at the spammer command. Identifying the devices which are part of a botnet and consequent removal of malicious code from the device, helps in strongly limiting the amount of generated spam traffic [16]. Along with, in some dangerous scenarios, e.g. distributing terrorist messages, cyber-criminal police is able to catch the spammer through a thorough analysis of spam campaign. However, such an analysis brings several privacy implications resulting from this fact that data analyzer (cyber crime police) should have access to all outgoing users' emails. To mitigate this issue, it is essential that the email server be able to protect the confidential content of users' emails, while at the same time the data analyzer remains still capable in detecting dangerous spammers.

Our Solution: Homomorphic encryption serves as a privacy preserving technique which enables data analyzer to perform some desired operations over protected data, without needing them to be decrypted. Thus, email server homomorphically can encrypt a set of emails, belonging to a suspicious user, and send them to (semi-trusted) data server. Cyber crime police also provides two separate collections of records representing benign and spam messages. It also sends them encrypted to the data analyzer. Without decrypting any email, the data server– as an expert component in analyzing encrypted data– is capable to detect if data belonging to a suspicious user shows *considerable* difference compared to benign records sent by police.

3.2   Architecture and Workflow

To detect adversarial instances over encrypted data, we employ an interactive privacy model in which two additional components (plus the data analyzer and data provider) are needed to securely perform analysis. More precisely, this privacy model comprises four main components:

- *Data-analyzer* who is interested in detecting adversarial instances.

- *Data provider* who provides a dataset suspicious to be designed by a potential adversary
- *Semi Trusted Party (STP)* is a semi-honest component that generates public (p_k) and private (s_k) keys. This component is assumed to have limited storage and computation capabilities.
- *Data Server (DS)* is a remote component, generally in the cloud with high storage capability that stores encrypted data. DS is controlled by an expert who performs the analysis on encrypted data through secure communication with *STP*.

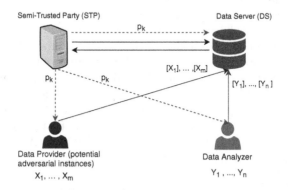

Fig. 1. Reference architecture

Figure 1 shows the architecture underlying the interactive privacy model along with the main components and their interactions. First, *STP* generates public (p_k) and private (s_k) keys; it sends the public key p_k to data analyzer, data provider, and to *DS*. After receiving the public-key, data analyzer and data provider encrypt their data and send the associated set of encrypted vectors, denoted respectively as $[X_1], \ldots, [X_n]$ and $[Y_1], \ldots, [Y_m]$, to *DS*. From now on, the secure computation protocols are performed between *STP* and *DS*.

We assume a semi-honest security model, where all participants are honest-but-curious. This means that all components follow the protocols properly, but they are interested in learning the input of other parties. In our motivating example, email server and cyber-criminal police can be considered as data provider and data analyzer, respectively. Data server and Semi-trusted Party are two external components expert in performing analysis over encrypted data. It is noticeable that in this specific scenario, the data provider and STP can be one unique component (the same for data server and data analyzer).

4   Private Detection of Adversarial Instances

This section transforms non-integer-based MMD statistical test to the integer-based formula; it then presents secure computation protocols to compute it over encrypted input.

4.1 Integer-Based MMD Evaluation

Considering that homomorphic encryption techniques are only applicable on integer numbers, and Maximum Mean Distance (Relation 1) is not defined based on integer numbers, in what follows we propose a methodology to evaluate MMD condition through an integer-based formula.

To this end, let's suppose that two datasets D_1 and D_2, and their associated encrypted versions as D_1' and D_2', respectively, are given. Let us denote the MMD distance of D_1 and D_2 as $MMD(D_1, D_2)$, and the (decrypted) MMD distance of encrypted formats as $MMD'(D_1', D_2')$. It is expected that if the MMD distance of two dataset as plaintexts is higher than α, then the MMD distance of equivalent ciphertexts also be higher than α, or equivalently, if $MMD'(D_1', D_2') \leq \alpha$ then $MMD(D_1, D_2) \leq \alpha$.

We first consider that x_i's are integer values. At the end of this section we will explain if this condition does not hold, how the problem can be addressed as well.

Given this assumption, the reason that Relation 1 may return a non-integer outcome is resulted from *Gaussian Kernel* function defined as $\kappa(X, Y) = e^{\frac{-1}{2}\|X-Y\|^2}$. In what follows, we transform it to integer-based relation.

By approximating the irrational value $e^{-\frac{1}{2}}$ with a rational value d (by rounding it to its t'th decimal number), we obtain $d \leq e^{-\frac{1}{2}} \leq (d+\delta)$, where $\delta = 10^{-t}$. Therefore, by denoting the squared Euclidean distance of two vectors X and Y as $n_{XY} = \|X - Y\|^2$, we have: $d^{n_{XY}} \leq \kappa(X, Y) \leq (d+\delta)^{n_{XY}}$.

Now, we are looking for α' such that the satisfaction of the following relation, results in the satisfaction of Relation 1.

$$n^2 \sum_{i,j=1}^{m} \frac{(d \cdot 10^t)^{n_{X_i X_j}}}{(10^t)^{n_{X_i X_j}}} - 2mn \sum_{i,j=1}^{m,n} \frac{(d \cdot 10^t)^{n_{X_i Y_j}}}{(10^t)^{n_{X_i Y_j}}} + m^2 \sum_{i,j=1}^{n} \frac{(d \cdot 10^t)^{n_{Y_i Y_j}}}{(10^t)^{n_{Y_i Y_j}}} \leq \alpha'$$

Theorem 1. *By setting* $\alpha' = \sqrt{\alpha^2 - 2d\delta}$ *(for negligible δ), the satisfaction of* $MMD'(D_1', D_2') \leq \alpha' \leq \alpha$ *results in* $MMD(D_1, D_2) \leq \alpha$.

Proof. Proof in Appendix. □

However, considering that additive homomorphic encryption does not provide secure division protocol, we multiply both sides by the common denominator of all fractions, i.e. $\tau = (10^t)^{\sum_{i,j=1}^{m} n_{X_i X_j} + \sum_{i,j=1}^{m,n} n_{X_i Y_j} + \sum_{i,j=1}^{n} n_{Y_i Y_j}}$:

$$n^2 \sum_{i,j=1}^{m} (d \cdot 10^t)^{n_{X_i X_j}} \tau_{X_i X_j} - 2mn \sum_{i,j=1}^{m,n} (d \cdot 10^t)^{n_{X_i Y_j}} \tau_{X_i Y_j} + m^2 \sum_{i,j=1}^{n} (d \cdot 10^t)^{n_{Y_i Y_j}} \tau_{Y_i Y_j} \leq \tau\alpha' = \alpha''$$

where for all $X, Y \in \mathcal{X}, \mathcal{Y}$, we have $\tau_{XY} = \frac{\tau}{(10^t)^{\|X-Y\|^2}}$, and since the phrase appeared in the denominators of the fractions, exists also inside the numerator as well, the outputs of this phrase is integer.

It is noticeable that although α is generally a decimal number (approximately 0.05), but since τ is a very big number, $\alpha'' = \tau\alpha'$ will be an integer at the end.

Thus, in the last relation all variables are integers. It also needs to be mentioned that we supposed x_is are integer numbers. If this hypothesis does not hold, it is just enough to round them to t''th decimal number and then multiply them by $10^{t'}$. The value of t' should be set beforehand from the context.

4.2 Preliminary Protocols

This section presents HE-based protocols, named *secure scalar, Euclidean distance*, and *exponential protocol*, which serve as preliminary protocols for evaluating the satisfaction of integer-based MMD distance.

Secure Scalar Product: Bob owns two vectors of encrypted values as $[X] = ([x_1], \ldots, [x_k])$, $[Y] = ([y_1], \ldots, [y_k])$, and he is interested in obtaining the scalar product of $[X]$ and $[Y]$ which equals to $\left[\sum_{i=1}^{k} x_i \cdot y_i\right]$. We propose the following formula to compute scalar product securely through the application of secure multiplication protocol:

$$Scalar([X], [Y]) = \left[\sum_{i=1}^{k} x_i \cdot y_i\right] = \prod_{i=1}^{k} Mult([x_i], [y_i])$$

Secure Euclidean Distance: Bob owns two vectors of encrypted values as $[X] = ([x_1], \ldots, [x_k])$, $[Y] = ([y_1], \ldots, [y_k])$, and he is interested in finding the (squared) Euclidean distance of these vectors in encrypted format. We remind that the (squared of) Euclidean distance of two vectors X and Y is equivalent to $X \cdot X - 2X \cdot Y + Y \cdot Y$, where "$\cdot$" refers to the scalar product of two vectors. The (squared) Euclidean distance of two encrypted vectors can be computed as the following:

$$Dist([X], [Y]) = Scalar([X], [X]) \cdot (Scalar([X], [Y]))^{-2} \cdot Scalar([Y], [Y])$$

Secure Exponential Protocol: Suppose Bob owns encrypted number $[b]$, and a is a public integer number. Bob is interested in finding $[a^b]$. We propose in Algorithm 1 a new protocol for secure computation of $[a^b]$. Our proposed procedure is based on masking b with $(\kappa + \ell)$-bit random integer value r, and afterwards secure multiplication protocol is applied to remove the noise.

4.3 Secure MMD Distance Computation

To detect adversarial instances over encrypted values, we design MMD protocol according to the integer-based relation presented in Sect. 4.1 applying HE-based building blocks. It is supposed that DS owns two sets of encrypted vectors, coming from potential adversary and data analyzer as $\mathcal{X} = \{[X_1], \ldots, [X_m]\}$ and $\mathcal{Y} = \{[Y_1], \ldots, [Y_n]\}$, respectively. The values m, n, t and α are known by DS. The following steps are executed between DS and STP:

Algorithm 1. *Exp(a, [b]):* Secure Exponential Function.

Data: *Alice* generates encryption keys. a is a public integer number. *Bob* owns
    encrypted integer numbers $[b]$.
Result: *Bob* obtains $[a^b]$.
1 *Bob* additively masks $[b]$ with r and sends $[b'] = [b + r] = [b] \cdot [r]$ to *Alice*.
2 *Alice* decrypts $[b']$ and sends $[a^{b'}]$ to *Bob*.
3 *Bob* obtains $[a^b] = Mult([a^{b'}], [a^{-r}])$.

- For $1 \leq i, r \leq m$ and $1 \leq j, t \leq n$, DS first obtains the encrypted
  values $Dist([X_i], [X_r])$, $Dist([X_i], [Y_j])$, and $Dist([Y_j], [Y_t])$ through secure
  Euclidean distance protocol. It then locally computes:

$$[Z] = \prod_{i,r,j,t} Dist([X_i], [X_r]) \cdot Dist([X_i], [Y_j]) \cdot Dist([Y_j], [Y_t])$$

- After obtaining $[Z]$, for $1 \leq i, r \leq m$ and $1 \leq j, t \leq n$, DS computes the
  following encrypted values through secure communication with STP:

$$[\tau_{X_i X_r}] = Exp(10^t, ([Z] \cdot (Dist([X_i], [X_r])^{-1})))$$
$$[\tau_{X_i Y_j}] = Exp(10^t, ([Z] \cdot (Dist([X_i], [Y_j])^{-1})))$$
$$[\tau_{Y_j Y_t}] = Exp(10^t, ([Z] \cdot (Dist([Y_j], [Y_t]))^{-1}))$$

At this step, by setting $a = d \cdot 10^t$, DS computes the encrypted value of MMD
distance through secure communication with STP, as the following:

$$[MMD] = \prod_{i,r,j,t} (Mult(Exp(a, Dist([X_i], [X_r])), [\tau_{X_i X_r}]))^{n^2}$$
$$\cdot (Mult(Exp(a, Dist([X_i], [Y_j])), [\tau_{X_i Y_j}]))^{m \cdot n}$$
$$\cdot (Mult(Exp(a, Dist([Y_j], [Y_t])), [\tau_{Y_j Y_t}]))^{m^2}$$

- Finally, secure comparison protocol is applied as *SecureComp* $([MMD], [\alpha''])$,
  where the outcome $[0]$ means that the data provider is suspicious to be an
  adversary.

5   Security Analysis

In this section, we present a security sketch of the proposed privacy preserving
protocols in the semi-honest model, where parties are assumed to be honest
in following the protocol description, while they are curious to obtain more
information than they are entitled to.

Based on this assumption, we provide proofs to show that our secure Maximum Mean Discrepancy (MMD) protocol is simulation secure in the semi-honest
security model. By providing the simulation security, the probability that an

adversary can learn private information from truly generated data by the parties in our protocols is at most negligibly more than the probability that an adversary can learn from given randomly generated data. We use the simulatability paradigm [17] in our proofs, where the adversary takes the control of the network and try to obtain the final result of the protocol by itself as the only party in the protocol. In this paradigm, security is defined as a comparison of computation work-flow in "real world" and "ideal world". In real world, a protocol can be broken into sub-protocols or computations that are carried out by each party throughout the protocol. Let us denote π as the MMD protocols; we can split π into two parts: $\pi = \pi_{DS}$ and π_{STP}, which are performed in parties DS and STP, respectively. π_{DS} takes X, $\mathcal{Y}$, γ', and α', which are the inputs, and outputs 1/0 (let's call this ϑ), $[\vartheta] \leftarrow \pi_{DS}(X, \mathcal{Y}, \gamma', \alpha')$. π_{STP} decrypts the given encryptions from DS, processes them, and sends their encrypted versions back to DS. Thus, to perform MMD the encrypted messages flow from one party to another party and together they generate the $[\vartheta]$ as the result of MMD. Assuming DS is corrupted by an adversary $\mathcal{A}$, then $\mathcal{A}$ has access to his inputs, and $[\vartheta]$. Similarly, when STP is corrupted, the adversary has access to the intermediate computation results.

In an ideal world, it is assumed that one of the parties is corrupted by an adversary. Then, he uses a simulator to generate the outputs of the other party. This would be similar to performing MMD with just one corrupted party. In the ideal world, an adversary $\acute{\mathcal{A}}$, who has control over DS, has only access to his inputs and the garbage inputs given from simulated STP instead of the correct result of π_{STP}. The goal is to show that $\mathcal{A}$ can learn equal or negligibly more than $\acute{\mathcal{A}}$, meaning that they are computationally indistinguishable, then we can claim that MMD is a simulation secure protocol.

Definition 1. *Let $a \in \{0,1\}^*$ represents the parties' inputs, $n \in \mathbb{N}$ to be a security parameter, and $X = \{X(a,n)\}_{a \in \{0,1\}^*; n \in \mathbb{N}}$ and $Y = \{Y(a,n)\}_{a \in \{0,1\}^*; n \in \mathbb{N}}$, two infinite sequences of random variables, are probability ensembles. Then, X and Y are computationally indistinguishable, denoted as $X \overset{c}{\equiv} Y$, if there is a polynomial $p(.)$ for every non-uniform polynomial-time probabilistic algorithm (nuPPT) D such that:*

$$|Pr[D(X(a,n)) = 1] - Pr[D(Y(a,n)) = 1]| < 1/p(n) \qquad (2)$$

The *Mult*, *SecureComp*, and *Equality* sub-protocols are proved to be secure in the same security setting [14,15], and [18], respectively. Moreover, since the *Scalar* and *Dist* sub-protocols are both built by only using *Mult*, we can claim that they are also simulation secure.

5.1 Security of SecureExp

Let denote the computation of b' as DS_{f_1}, $[a^{b'}]$ as STP_{f_1}, and $[a^b]$ as DS_{f_2}. Then, we have $DS_f = (A_{f_1}, A_{f_2})$, $STP_f = (B_{f_1})$, and $f = (DS_f, STP_f)$.

Theorem 2. *The protocol SecureExp is simulation secure and securely computes the functionality f, when the DS is corrupted by adversary $\mathcal{A}$ in the presence of semi-honest adversaries.*

Proof. We need to show that DS cannot computationally distinguish between generated messages and outputs from S_2 that is the simulation of STP, and randomly generated data. DS receives two outputs from S_2, $[a^{b'}]$ and result of $Mult$ sub-protocol. Given a, $[b]$, and 1^n (security parameter), DS works as follow:

1. DS chooses uniformly distributed random number r;
2. DS executes DS_{f_1} to obtain $[b']$, and sends it to S_2;
3. S_2 chooses a random number R, encrypts it and sends $[R]$ to DS.

The output of simulation can be written as: $Sim_{DS}(1^n, a, [b], DS_f, f) = (a, [b], r; [c]; [\hat{c}]; \phi))$. The real view of DS can be presented as $view^f_{DS}(a, [b]) = (a, [b], r; [a^{b'}])$. And the output of the real view is $output^f(a, [b]) = ([a^b], \phi)$. It can be observed that DS cannot computationally distinguish between $[a^{b'}]$ and $[c]$, since the underlying encryption scheme is semantically secure. Note that the $Mult$ sub-protocol is already proven secure in [15]. Therefore, we can claim that:

$$Sim_{DS}(1^n, a, [b], A_f, f) \overset{c}{\equiv} \{view^f_{DS}(a, [b]; \phi), output^f(a, [b]; \phi)\}$$

□

Theorem 3. *The protocol SecureExp is simulation secure and securely computes the functionality f, when the STP is corrupted by adversary $\mathcal{A}$ in the presence of semi-honest adversaries.*

Proof. STP works as follow:

1. S_1 chooses a $\kappa + \ell + 1$-bit random number r, encrypts it, and sends $[r]$ to STP.
2. STP executes STP_{f_1} and sends the result back to S_1.

Although STP has the decryption key, it cannot distinguish between r and b, since b is masked with a $(\kappa + \ell)$-bit integer. Therefore, we can claim that:

$$Sim_S TP(1^n, \phi, STP_{f_1}, f) = \{view^f_S TP(a, [b], \phi, n), output^f(a, [b]; \phi)\}$$

□

Since the *SecureExp* sub-protocol is proven to be secure, showing that simulation security of MMD protocol is straightforward. MMD protocol uses $Dist$, Exp, and $Mult$ sub-protocols, which all have been proven to be simulation secure; therefor, we can claim that MMD protocol is also simulation secure.

6   Performance Analysis

To compute the computational complexity of MMD protocol, let us assume that potential adversary and data analyzer uploaded m and n records on DS's server. Moreover, each record is a vector of size k, and each component of a vector is expressed maximum in ℓ-bit length. Based on MMD distance protocol, the number of times that building block protocols are employed equals to:

$$\mathcal{N}(m, n) = (m^2 + m \cdot n + n^2)(Scalar + Dist + Add + SExp. + SExp. + Mult) \tag{3}$$

Our building block protocols require primitive operations addition, encryption, decryption, and exponential, as the following:

- *Multiplication protocol (Mult)* requires 5, 4, 1, and $2_{\kappa+\ell}$ addition, encryption, decryption, and exponential, respectively.
- *Scalar product (Scalar)* needs 6k, 4k, k, and $2k_{\kappa+\ell}$ addition, encryption, decryption, and exponential, respectively.
- *Exponential protocol (SExp.)* employs 6, 7, 2, and $2_{\kappa+\ell}$ addition, encryption, decryption, and exponential, respectively.
- *Distance protocol (Dist.)* requires 2 and $1_{\kappa+\ell}$ addition and exponential, respectively.

Given the above argument, the number of times that Relation 3 employs addition, encryption, decryption, and exponential operations can be approximated as follows:

$$\mathcal{N}(m, n, k, \ell) = (m^2 + m \cdot n + n^2)$$
$$((6k + 21)Add. + (4k + 20)Enc. + (k + 6)Dec. + (2k + 6)Exp.) + \ell(Add. + Enc. + Dec.) \tag{4}$$

We implemented addition, encryption, decryption, and exponential protocols using $C++$ on a single machine running Ubuntu 14.04 LTS with 64-bit microprocessor and 8 GB of RAM. The cryptographic key length of Paillier is selected as NIST standard as 4096 bits. In our implementation, addition, encryption, and decryption for 10^6 records required 8.3, 5.6, and 9 s, respectively. Moreover, by considering $\kappa = 112$, each exponential operation needs 200 additions for element with ℓ-bit length equal to 20.

To assess the practical feasibility of our mechanism, we performed a number of experiments. Grosse et al. [10] showed that 50 adversarial instances are enough to infer a considerable MMD statistical distance between two datasets. Moreover, according to standard dimensioning technique, proposed in [19], the minimum size for a dataset to produce a reliable result is to dimension it as six times to the number of features. Therefore, to get a better insight on computation cost of the proposed approach, we consider the number of features to get their values as $k \in \{20, 50, 100, 200\}$, while the number of data in training set (m) is set to six times of k. The number of adversarial instances (n) varies from 50 and gets its value as $n \in \{50, 60, 70, 80, 90\}$.

Figures 2 and 3 show the computation costs (in log-scale) for different values of n and k, respectively. As explained previously, m is considered as a dependent variable to the number of features ($m = 6k$). From Fig. 2, it can be inferred that for fixed values of k and m, the required runtime increases linearly (with a slight slop) when n increases. On the other hand, for fixed value of n, when k varies from 20 to 200, the runtime increases from 0.5 h to 288 h. Figure 3 confirms that k has considerable impact on the computation cost. This result put the light on the fact that application of appropriate feature selection technique, prior to the adversarial instance detection over encrypted data, can noticeably reduce the computation cost.

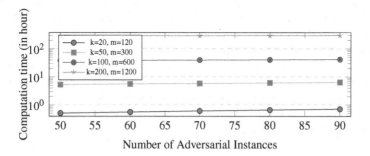

Fig. 2. Computation time (in hour) for different values of adversarial instances (n).

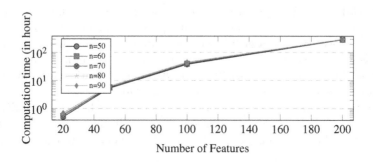

Fig. 3. Computation time (in hour) for different number of features (k).

7   Discussion

This section discusses some noticeable notions about the current study.

– We adapted the results of work done by Grosse et al. [10], which through mathematical explanation and experimental analysis proved the effectiveness of MMD statistical test in detecting adversarial samples. Therefore, we designed our experimental analysis not on detecting adversarial instances over encrypted data, but on evaluating the feasibility and efficiency of the proposed mechanism.

– Gaussian kernel is a de facto kernel which is employed in several data analysis approaches, e.g. image/signal processing, computational chemistry, SVM classifier, etc. Accordingly, the result of current study can be deployed in the aforementioned studies when analysis is desired to be performed over distributed encrypted data.

– The performance analysis of our approach shows that the proposed mechanism is effectively feasible when the number of features reduces. This result suggests that the application of an appropriate feature reduction technique considerably reduces the computation cost of our mechanism.

– Due to the fact that the current approach requires at least 50 adversarial samples from the attacker to be able to detect the adversarial instances, as one future work we plan to construct a robust classifier with one outlier class over encrypted data. The robust classifier is able to detect an adversarial instance upon being received [10].

8   Related Work

In this section we present works in the literature related to Adversarial Machine Learning and Encryption-based Mechanisms.

Adversarial Machine Learning: A growing body of work has been devoted to the field of adversarial machine learning, trying to solve the problem from different perspectives. A large number of work has been done (i) to develop attacks against machine learning, both at training time (poisoning attacks) [20], and at test time (evasion attack) [1], (ii) to design systematic methodologies for evaluation of the robustness of machine learning algorithms against such kinds of attacks [21], and (iii) to propose appropriate defense mechanisms for mitigating these threats [22]. However, there is no work in the literature which studies adversarial machine learning issues when the data under analysis are encrypted.

Encryption-Based Mechanisms: The main idea in encryption-based approaches is to obfuscate the privacy-sensitive data prior to processing. Cryptography-based techniques have been deployed in several domains of data analysis. In [23] the possible scenarios of applying homomorphic encryption on medical data is discussed. A working implementation of a prediction service in the cloud which takes private encrypted health data and returns the probability for suffering cardiovascular disease is returned in encrypted format. Erkin et al. in [15] propose a privacy-enhanced face recognition system, which allows to efficiently hide both biometrics and the result from the server for matching operation. Cryptography-based approaches have also been widely utilized in constructing data mining algorithms collaboratively, e.g. constructing on whole encrypted data a clustering algorithm [24], or a classifier [25], and collaborative private feature selection [26]. These techniques also have been used in other scenarios, *e.g.* private text analysis [27], the general framework for privacy preserving distributed data analysis [28], etc. However, to the best of our knowledge the problem of adversarial machine learning has not been addressed in private setting.

9   Conclusion

This paper presents a framework for detecting adversarial instances which are crafted through encrypted format. To this end, we employed statistical test which measures the distance of two encrypted datasets' distribution. Due to the fact that the proposed approach is based on homomorphic encryption, we proposed a mechanism to transform non-integer statistical test to an integer-based one. We showed the practical feasibility of the proposed approach in terms of computation cost.

In future research, we plan to address other challenges in adversarial machine learning, e.g. constructing robust classifier, over encrypted distributed data. We also plan to perform other statistical tests, e.g. *energy distance*, on encrypted datasets, and compare their effectiveness and efficiency. Moreover, we are interested in applying efficient secure multi-party computation, e.g. *data packing*, to speed up the process when size of data increases. We also plan to evaluate the effect of feature selection techniques on accuracy and efficiency of our methodology.

Acknowledgment. This work was partially supported by the H2020 EU funded project SECREDAS [GA #783119] and by the H2020 EU funded project C3ISP [GA #700294].

Appendix

In what follows we prove Theorem 1, claiming that if we set $\alpha' = \sqrt{\alpha^2 - 2d\delta}$ (for negligible δ), then from $MMD'(D_1', D_2') \leq \alpha'$ we can conclude that $MMD(D_1, D_2) \leq \alpha$.

Basically, we are looking for α' such that if the following relation holds:

$$n^2 \sum_{i,j=1}^{m} d^{n_{X_i X_j}} - 2mn \sum_{i,j=1}^{m,n} d^{n_{X_i Y_j}} + m^2 \sum_{i,j=1}^{n} d^{n_{Y_i Y_j}} \leq m^2 n^2 \alpha'^2$$

We can conclude that:

$$n^2 \sum_{i,j=1}^{m} \kappa(X_i, X_j) - 2mn \sum_{i,j=1}^{m,n} \kappa(X_i, Y_j) + m^2 \sum_{i,j=1}^{n} \kappa(Y_i, Y_j) \leq m^2 n^2 \alpha^2$$

To this end, we first find a relation between two above relations:

$$n^2 \sum_{i,j=1}^{m} \kappa(X_i, X_j) - 2mn \sum_{i,j=1}^{m,n} \kappa(X_i, Y_j) + m^2 \sum_{i,j=1}^{n} \kappa(Y_i, Y_j)$$

$$\leq n^2 \sum_{i,j=1}^{m} (d+\delta)^{n_{X_i X_j}} - 2mn \sum_{i,j=1}^{m,n} d^{n_{X_i Y_j}} + m^2 \sum_{i,j=1}^{n} (d+\delta)^{n_{Y_i Y_j}}$$

$$= n^2 \Big(\sum_{i,j=1}^{m} d^{n_{X_i X_j}} + \sum_{i,j=1}^{m} \big[\frac{n_{X_i X_j}(n_{X_i X_j} - 1)}{2} d^{n_{X_i X_j}-1}\delta + \ldots \big] \Big) - 2mn \sum_{i,j=1}^{m,n} d^{n_{X_i Y_j}}$$

$$+ m^2 \Big(\sum_{i,j=1}^{n} d^{n_{Y_i Y_j}} + \sum_{i,j=1}^{n} \big[\frac{n_{Y_i Y_j}(n_{Y_i Y_j} - 1)}{2} d^{n_{Y_i Y_j}-1}\delta + \ldots \big] \Big)$$

From the application of *binomial* theorem, we obtain:

$$(n^2 \sum_{i,j=1}^{m} d^{n_{X_i X_j}} - 2mn \sum_{i,j=1}^{m,n} d^{n_{X_i Y_j}} + m^2 \sum_{i,j=1}^{n} d^{n_{Y_i Y_j}}) + (n^2 \sum_{i,j=1}^{m} \big[\frac{n_{X_i X_j}(n_{X_i X_j} - 1)}{2} d^{n_{X_i X_j}-1}\delta + \ldots \big]$$

$$+ m^2 \sum_{i,j=1}^{n} \big[\frac{n_{Y_i Y_j}(n_{Y_i Y_j} - 1)}{2} d^{n_{Y_i Y_j}-1}\delta + \ldots \big]) \leq m^2 n^2 \alpha^2$$

This means that it is enough to set $\alpha'^2 = \alpha^2 - 2\delta d$, because:

$$\Rightarrow \alpha' = m^2 n^2 \alpha^2 - (n^2 \sum_{i,j=1}^{m} \big[\frac{n_{X_i X_j}(n_{X_i X_j} - 1)}{2} d^{n_{X_i X_j}-1}\delta + \ldots \big]$$

$$+ m^2 \sum_{i,j=1}^{n} \big[\frac{n_{Y_i Y_j}(n_{Y_i Y_j} - 1)}{2} d^{n_{Y_i Y_j}-1}\delta + \ldots \big])$$

$$\leq m^2 n^2 \alpha^2 - (n^2\delta \sum_{i,j=1}^{m} d + m^2\delta \sum_{i,j=1}^{n} d)$$

$$= m^2 n^2 \alpha^2 - 2m^2 n^2 \delta d$$

References

1. Srndic, N., Laskov, P.: Practical evasion of a learning-based classifier: a case study. In: Proceedings of the 2014 IEEE Symposium on Security and Privacy, SP 2014, pp. 197–211, IEEE Computer Society, Washington, DC (2014)
2. Lowd, D.: Good word attacks on statistical spam filters. In: Proceedings of the Second Conference on Email and Anti-Spam (CEAS) (2005)
3. Maiorca, D., Corona, I., Giacinto, G.: Looking at the bag is not enough to find the bomb: an evasion of structural methods for malicious PDF files detection. In: Proceedings of the 8th ACM SIGSAC Symposium on Information, Computer and Communications Security, ASIA CCS 2013, pp. 119–130. ACM, New York (2013)
4. Elsayed, G.F., et al.: Adversarial examples that fool both human and computer vision, CoRR abs/1802.08195 (2018)

5. Szegedy, C., et al.: Intriguing properties of neural networks, CoRR abs1312.6199 (2013)
6. Lu, J., Sibai, H., Fabry, E., Forsyth, D.A.: No need to worry about adversarial examples in object detection in autonomous vehicles, CoRR abs/1707.03501 (2017)
7. Fawzi, A., Fawzi, O., Frossard, P.: Analysis of classifiers' robustness to adversarial perturbations. Mach. Learn. **107**(3), 481–508 (2018)
8. Biggio, B., et al.: Evasion attacks against machine learning at test time. In: Blockeel, H., Kersting, K., Nijssen, S., Železný, F. (eds.) ECML PKDD 2013, Part III. LNCS (LNAI), vol. 8190, pp. 387–402. Springer, Heidelberg (2013). https://doi.org/10.1007/978-3-642-40994-3_25
9. Papernot, N., McDaniel, P.D., Wu, X., Jha, S., Swami, A.: Distillation as a defense to adversarial perturbations against deep neural networks, CoRR abs1511.04508 (2016)
10. Grosse, K., Manoharan, P., Papernot, N., Backes, M., McDaniel, P.D.: On the (statistical) detection of adversarial examples, CoRR abs1702.06280 (2017)
11. Potey, M.M., Dhote, C., Sharma, D.H.: Homomorphic encryption for security of cloud data. Procedia Comput. Sci. **79**, 175–181 (2016). Proceedings of International Conference on Communication, Computing and Virtualization (ICCCV) 2016
12. Gretton, A., Borgwardt, K.M., Rasch, M.J., Scholkopf, B., Smola, A.: A kernel two-sample test. J. Mach. Learn. Res. **13**, 723–773 (2012)
13. Paillier, P.: Public-key cryptosystems based on composite degree residuosity classes. In: Stern, J. (ed.) EUROCRYPT 1999. LNCS, vol. 1592, pp. 223–238. Springer, Heidelberg (1999). https://doi.org/10.1007/3-540-48910-X_16
14. Nateghizad, M., Erkin, Z., Lagendijk, R.L.: An efficient privacy-preserving comparison protocol in smart metering systems. EURASIP J. Inf. Secur. (1), 11 (2016)
15. Erkin, Z., Franz, M., Guajardo, J., Katzenbeisser, S., Lagendijk, I., Toft, T.: Privacy-preserving face recognition. In: Goldberg, I., Atallah, M.J. (eds.) PETS 2009. LNCS, vol. 5672, pp. 235–253. Springer, Heidelberg (2009). https://doi.org/10.1007/978-3-642-03168-7_14
16. Sheikhalishahi, M., Saracino, A., Mejri, M., Tawbi, N., Martinelli, F.: Fast and effective clustering of spam emails based on structural similarity. In: Garcia-Alfaro, J., Kranakis, E., Bonfante, G. (eds.) FPS 2015. LNCS, vol. 9482, pp. 195–211. Springer, Cham (2016). https://doi.org/10.1007/978-3-319-30303-1_12
17. Lindell, Y.: How to simulate it – a tutorial on the simulation proof technique. Tutorials on the Foundations of Cryptography. ISC, pp. 277–346. Springer, Cham (2017). https://doi.org/10.1007/978-3-319-57048-8_6
18. Nateghizad, M., Erkin, Z., Lagendijk, R.L.: Efficient and secure equality tests. In: 2016 IEEE International Workshop on Information Forensics and Security (WIFS), pp. 1–6 (2016)
19. Viola, P., Jones, M.: Rapid object detection using a boosted cascade of simple features. In: Proceedings of the 2001 IEEE Computer Society Conference on Computer Vision and Pattern Recognition, CVPR 2001, vol. 1 (2001)
20. Munoz-Gonzalez, L., et al.: Towards poisoning of deep learning algorithms with back-gradient optimization. In: Proceedings of the 10th ACM Workshop on Artificial Intelligence and Security, AISec 2017, New York, NY, USA, pp. 27–38 (2017)
21. Biggio, B., Fumera, G., Roli, F.: Security evaluation of pattern classifiers under attack, CoRR abs/1709.00609 (2017)
22. Jordaney, R., et al.: Transcend: detecting concept drift in malware classification models. In: 26th USENIX Security Symposium, Vancouver, BC, pp. 625–642. USENIX Association (2017)

23. Bos, J.W., Lauter, K., Naehrig, M.: Private predictive analysis on encrypted medical data. J. Biomed. Inform. **50**, 234–243 (2014)
24. Sheikhalishahi, M., Martinelli, F.: Privacy preserving clustering over horizontal and vertical partitioned data. In: 2017 IEEE Symposium on Computers and Communications, ISCC 2017, Heraklion, Greece, 3–6 July 2017, pp. 1237–1244 (2017)
25. Bost, R. Popa, R.A., Tu, S., Goldwasser, S.: Machine learning classification over encrypted data. In: 22nd Annual Network and Distributed System Security Symposium, NDSS 2015, San Diego, California, USA, 8–11 February 2015 (2015)
26. Sheikhalishahi, M., Martinelli, F.: Privacy-utility feature selection as a tool in private data classification. Distributed Computing and Artificial Intelligence, 14th International Conference. AISC, vol. 620, pp. 254–261. Springer, Cham (2018). https://doi.org/10.1007/978-3-319-62410-5_31
27. Costantino, G., Marra, A.L., Martinelli, F., Saracino, A., Sheikhalishahi, M.: Privacy-preserving text mining as a service. In: 2017 IEEE Symposium on Computers and Communications, ISCC 2017, Heraklion, Greece, 3–6 July 2017, pp. 890–897 (2017)
28. Martinelli, F., Saracino, A., Sheikhalishahi, M.: Modeling privacy aware information sharing systems: a formal and general approach. In: 2016 IEEE Trustcom/BigDataSE/ISPA, Tianjin, China, 23–26 August 2016, pp. 767–774 (2016)

Understanding Attestation: Analyzing Protocols that Use Quotes

Joshua D. Guttman$^{(\boxtimes)}$ and John D. Ramsdell

The MITRE Corporation, Bedford, MA, USA
{guttman,ramsdell}@mitre.org

Abstract. *Attestation* protocols use digital signatures and other crypto-graphic values to convey evidence of hardware state, program code, and associated keys. They require hardware support such as Trusted Execu-tion Environments. Conclusions about attestations thus depend jointly on protocols, hardware services, and program behavior.

We present a mechanized approach to modeling these properties, combining protocol analysis with axioms, that formalize hardware and software properties. Here, we model aspects of Intel's SGX mechanism. Above the underlying manufacturer-provided protocols, we build a mod-ular user-level that uses its attestations to make trust decisions.

1 Introduction

Cryptographic protocols are often designed for use with particular software and hardware. How can we craft the mechanisms so that they jointly achieve over-all security goals? In achieving their goals, the protocols may rely on specific assumptions about the remaining components' behaviors. These assumptions define security-relevant specifications for the remaining components, focusing the design and validation processes for these components.

This codesign process for protocols and other mechanisms requires protocol analysis to explore the executions that satisfy the axioms for the other com-ponents' expected behaviors. In this paper, we use the CPSA protocol analysis tool [33], which we have enriched with the ability to apply axioms or, as they are also called, *rules* [32]. CPSA with axioms checks if a protocol is using its con-text correctly. The analysis codifies what matters about this context, focusing attention—for further formal or empirical investigation—on whether the compo-nents satisfy the axioms. The axioms CPSA allows are implications, specifically universally quantified implications belonging to the *geometric fragment* of first order logic [14]. They formalize behavioral assumptions on the software and hardware context.

CPSA implements *enrich-by-need* protocol analysis. The analyst selects a sce-nario of interest—perhaps, that one participant has had a successful local run, a couple of keys are uncompromised, and a nonce has been successfully chosen to be fresh—after which CPSA displays all of the minimal, essentially different

© Springer Nature Switzerland AG 2019
S. Mauw and M. Conti (Eds.): STM 2019, LNCS 11738, pp. 89–106, 2019.
https://doi.org/10.1007/978-3-030-31511-5_6

executions compatible with it [18]. CPSA can also "read off" a strongest security goal (e.g. authentication or confidentiality) that holds for that scenario [35].

Other protocol analysis tools (e.g. Tamarin [29] and ProVerif [4]) can support variants of our method, which seems to increase its value. For instance, Tamarin's *restrictions* specify axioms, leading Tamarin to explore the set of traces that are compatible with the restrictions. This is used successfully on a substantial scale in Sapic to model protocols that manipulate state [25].

Attesting to Trusted Execution Environments. We illustrate our method by examining *attestation* for *trusted execution environments* or TEEs. A trusted execution environment is a software entity—either a thread with some memory or a virtual machine—that the processor promises to protect. Specifically, the processor will encrypt the TEE's memory before evicting it, and decrypt it only to return it to the same TEE.

An *attestation* for a TEE is a digital signature or Message Authentication Code that asserts that a TEE E is under the control of particular code C, and associated with other data D. Attestations, also called *quotes*, require support from the processor that must guarantee the TEE.

As we use TEEs, the data D always includes a public key K. The TEE generates the key pair K, K^{-1} on startup, and protects the private part K^{-1}, inserting K into D. Thus, any remote entity that obtains an attestation for $E, C, K, \ldots$ can use K to create secure channels to E. Messages over these channels are entrusted to the code C. If the code C faithfully implements a protocol Π, then E uses the private key K^{-1} only in accordance with that protocol Π.

TEEs—as threads with protected memory within user-level processes—are available on recent Intel processors. These so-called *enclaves* use the instruction set extension Software Guard Extensions (SGX) [22]. TEEs, as virtual machines, are available on AMD processors (Secure Encrypted Virtualization [24]). Other manufacturers may offer TEEs; academic work such as Sancus [31], for embedded systems, and Sanctum [10] also provide TEEs. Our methods are applicable well beyond SGX, which currently has weaknesses [7].

Case Study. Our case study justifies layering substantial mechanisms, using protocol analysis and assumptions about hardware and software.

At the lower level, we represent the original mechanisms for SGX attestation, which involve complications, such as online interaction with an Intel attestation server. We identify three axioms that jointly characterize what the hardware is intended to ensure, and how the provisioning of a signature key to the processor provides a supply-chain guarantee. On top of the lower layer, we illustrate how to use its attestations to draw conclusions about a user-layer protocol.

Contributions. We show how to combine rules and protocol analysis to design protocols targeted to hardware and software contexts. Our method provides simple descriptions of what the protocol requires from these contexts.

The rules in our case study fit three patterns that appear to be reusable for many attestation mechanisms.

Hardware rules codify the relevant behavioral consequences of the manufacturer's claims about the processor.

Trust rules formalize the decisions and practices of an organization about creating keys and certificates, and using the certified keys.

Attestation rules apply only when a TEE is executing known code C; they express a behavioral specification for that code C, such as how it will handle its private keys. Static analysis and empirical testing, such as for side channels, can justify these rules, or refute them [30]. Attestation rules furnish precise goals to prove or refute in these ways.

While other sorts of axioms also fit our formalism, these three types were central in applying the formalism to attestation and TEEs. They mechanize some of the reasoning in previous work on attestation for secure systems design, e.g. [9].

CPSA is an excellent interactive tool for determining the relevant rules. We derived the ones in this paper by observing what CPSA could *not* establish. We then introduced successive rules that would provide it with information it needs, respecting the intentions of the hardware and system designers.

Our work is a descendent of *authentication logics* [26], i.e. special-purpose logics for system designers to determine trust relations. Subsequent work showed how to use standard logics (Datalog as in [27]), and how to connect them with protocols [16,20]. We add a clear axiomatic structure for the combined analysis.

A *non-contribution* of this paper is any evidence that the rules are true. Instead, we identify simple, relevant rules that—*if* true—suffice to ensure that the application will meet its goals. To determine *whether* they are true in a particular instantiation calls for other—largely independent—methods, tuned to the claims of the hardware, trust, and attestation rules. Subramanyan et al. propose one basis for reasoning about enclaves in this complementary area [40].

Structure of this Paper. Section 2 presents our model of the SGX protocols for local (MAC-based) quotes, remote quotes using the EPID signature scheme, and online validation. A summary of CPSA appears in Sect. 2.3. Section 3 shows how an application level protocol can use SGX reliably. Sections 2.4 and 3 present the analysis at the successive layers, determining what the protocols can do subject to the rules. Overall patterns in these rules are discussed in Sect. 4, with related work and conclusions in Sect. 5.

The new CPSA is available [32], as are input and output files for this case study [21]. Our main notation is in Table 1.

Non-compromised Keys. We *do not* build into our notation that $K = \mathsf{sk}(A)$ or $\mathsf{dk}(A)$ is really uncompromised, which we instead express by writing $\mathsf{Non}(K)$.

The assertion $\mathsf{Non}(K)$ has two parts. The first is that no entity other than the intended one(s) possesses and can use the key K. Hardware and software must cooperate so a malicious adversary does not obtain its value.

The second part is that the intended entity uses it only in the ways that the protocol dictates. It is not used to sign/MAC/decrypt messages in any other situation. Thus, when the intended entity is an enclave E under the control of code C, then $\mathsf{Non}(K)$ induces a software requirement, namely to ensure that the

Table 1. Notation

$\#(m)$ is the result of a hash function applied to m;

$\mathsf{mac}(m, K)$ is a keyed hash or Message Authentication Code in which
K is the key and m is the value being authenticated;

mdk is the MAC key on a processor, regarding mdk as naming the processor.

$\{\!|m|\!\}_K$ is an encryption of m with K, either a symmetric or
an asymmetric encryption, depending on the type of K.

$[\![m]\!]_K$ is a digital signature prepared using K;

$[\![m]\!]_K^e$ is a digital signature using Intel's EPID algorithm.

$\mathsf{tag}\ m_0$ is the contents m tagged with the distinctive bitstring tag.

(K, K^{-1}) is a keypair for an asymmetric algorithm, with $(K^{-1})^{-1} = K$.

$\mathsf{sk}(A)$ is the principal A's private signing key, and

$\mathsf{vk}(A)$ is the public verification key other principals use to check them.

$\mathsf{pk}(A)$ is a public encryption key to prepare messages for A, and

$\mathsf{dk}(A)$ is the corresponding private decryption key.

Thus, $\mathsf{sk}(A)^{-1} = \mathsf{vk}(A)$ and $\mathsf{dk}(A)^{-1} = \mathsf{pk}(A)$.

---

code C uses the key only to prepare messages that the protocol dictates should be sent, and only subject to the control flow the protocol dictates.

The term of art "non-compromised" will cover these two parts.

The second aspect of Non justifies protocol analysis in taking cases based on the protocol definition when a key is known or assumed to be non-compromised.

The Adversary. CPSA works within a Dolev-Yao model [12], so we always assume that the adversary controls how messages are routed among participants. The adversary can also generate values, concatenate them and separate their parts, and can encrypt and decrypt using keys it possesses or can obtain. The adversary can obtain all long term secrets we do not assume non-compromised. The adversary can guess random values unless we assume them fresh and unguessable ("uniquely originating" in CPSA's terminology).

Software and hardware can misbehave at the convenience of the adversary, except when we make explicit behavioral assumptions expressed in rules.

Thus, limitations on the adversary are under the control of the modeler.

A Brief Introduction to Strands. A *strand* is a finite sequence of message transmission and reception events, which we call *nodes*. Some strands, called *regular* strands, represent the compliant behavior of a single principal in a single local protocol session. Other strands represent actions of an *adversary*, who may control the network and may carry out cryptographic operations using keys that are public or have become compromised. An *execution* (or *bundle*) involves any number of regular strands and adversary strands, with the proviso that any message that is received must previously have been sent.

A *protocol* Π is a finite set of strands called the *roles* $\rho \in \Pi$. The roles contain *parameters*, and the *instances* of ρ are the strands that result from ρ

by plugging in values for these parameters. This set of instances—obtained from Π's roles by plugging in values for parameters—are the *regular strands* of Π.

Figures 1 and 3 show roles. We write roles and other strands either vertically or horizontally with double arrows $\bullet \Rightarrow \bullet$ connecting successive nodes. Single arrows $\bullet \rightarrow m$ and $\bullet \leftarrow m$ indicate that message m is being transmitted or received at the node (resp.).

A strand may contain only an initial segment of the nodes of a role. For instance, at a particular time, a local run of the *local-quote* role (Fig. 1) may have received a message, but given as yet no response. We say that this strand has *height* 1, rather than the height 2 it would have if the next step had occurred. For more information on strands as a basis for protocol analysis, see [18].

2   Attestation in SGX

Intel's SGX attestation mechanism involves four elements.

First, a *local quote* about a *subject enclave* σ can be verified by a *target enclave* τ resident on the same processor. The local quote is a Message Authentication Code (MAC) prepared keyed with a secret $\#(mdk, \tau)$ hashed from τ plus a unique secret mdk permanently protected within each processor (the Master Derivation Key, in SGX-speak). The content of the MAC is the *Enclave Record* (ER) for σ. The ER includes a hash of the code controlling σ and other data. The EREPORT instruction creates a local quote.

To check a local quote, τ executes instruction EGETKEY to obtain the MAC key $\#(mdk, \tau)$, and recomputes the MAC value. Enclave τ must be resident on the same processor, because mdk is used in the key $\#(mdk, \tau)$. A misbehaving τ cannot use this to forge local quotes targeted at a compliant τ', since τ', obtaining a different key $\#(mdk, \tau')$, will reject the forged MAC.

Second, to obtain attestations for entities on other devices, a *remote quote* is made by a particular enclave, the *quoting enclave* τ_q. It receives a claimed ER and a local quote q. It checks ER and q via EGETKEY. On success, it generates a digital signature on ER using the group signature scheme EPID [6].

Third, Intel's *attestation server* validates remote quotes. A client connects via TLS, provides a claimed digital signature and ER, and receives an answer within the TLS connection. The attestation server vouches that some signing key provisioned by Intel created the digital signature on ER. The EPID group signature scheme prevents Intel from knowing which processor it was; the quoting enclaves they provision generate valid, but indistinguishable, EPID signatures.

Fourth, the *attestation client* queries the server over TLS.

We eliminate TLS's complexities, replacing it with a simple confirmation via public key encryption. This does not affect anything that matters to attestation. Any version of TLS that ensures integrity will lead to the same conclusions.

2.1   The Core SGX Protocol

The four roles of the manufacturer's mechanisms are shown in Fig. 1. The local-quote role does not run on every value er, but only on values that are in fact the

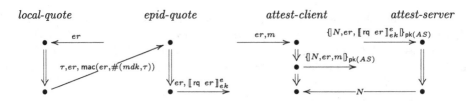

Fig. 1. SGX core roles

enclave record of some enclave executing on the processor with secret mdk. In the EPID-quote role, the quoting enclave makes sure that its initial input has the form shown by executing EGETKEY on mdk. In the attestation-server role, the server receives a message encrypted with its public encryption key. Inside that message is a nonce N, which it will release just in case the remaining components er, $[\![\mathsf{rq}\ er]\!]^e_{ek}$ form a valid digital signature on er, formed using an EPID key ek generated in a protocol with the manufacturer as processors are prepared [6]. It thus provides a supply chain guarantee that the processor is genuine.

The attestation client's role corresponds, except that the client cannot directly determine that its input is of the form er, $[\![\mathsf{rq}\ er]\!]^e_{ek}$; it needs the attestation server precisely for this. Thus, the client may possibly submit any message m. If the client successfully receives N, then in fact $m = [\![\mathsf{rq}\ er]\!]^e_{ek}$ for some EPID key ek. The attestation client chooses N randomly.

2.2   Rules for the SGX Protocol

Analyzing the manufacturer's protocol uses three rules. Each one codifies what follows when a role in Fig. 1 occurs. To express them, we use predicates that say when a strand is an instance of the roles, and to at least what height (number of steps). When a strand z engages in at least the first i transmissions and receptions of a role ρ, we write:

$\mathsf{LocQt}(z, i)$ if ρ is the *local-quote* role;
$\mathsf{EpidQt}(z, i)$ if ρ is the *epid-quote* role; and
$\mathsf{AttServ}(z, i)$ if ρ is the *attestation server* role;

To refer to the values selected for role parameters, we write:

$\mathsf{LocQtER}(z, er)$ if er is the enclave record value for *local-quote* instance z;
$\mathsf{LocQtPr}(z, mdk)$ if mdk is the processor secret;
$\mathsf{EpidQtKey}(z, ek)$ if ek is the signing EPID key of *epid-quote* instance z;
$\mathsf{EpidQtProc}(z, mdk)$ if z runs on the processor with secret mdk; and
$\mathsf{ASQtKey}(z, ek)$ if *attestation server* run z validates a quote signed with ek.

The rules also use uninterpreted predicate symbols. Their formal significance comes from the rules, which allow us to infer them, or infer further consequences from them. Their informal English descriptions relate them to the actual properties of the components they constrain.

Content of the Rules. The *local-quote* role executes on a valid SGX processor only if there is an SGX-protected enclave with the given enclave record *er*. It should be a sequence that starts with the enclave *id* number, the hash of its controlling code, and a public key, and may contain other entries subsequently. Writing :: for the list-construction operation, we thus have $er = eid :: ch :: k :: rest$.

The processor secret *mdk* can "name" the processor. Even if no one knows *mdk*, we can still reason about whether $mdk = mdk'$, etc. A run of the *local-quote* role on a processor with non-compromised *mdk* ensures there is an enclave with the parameters eid, ch, k, mdk, which we will write $\texttt{EnclCodeKey}(eid, ch, k, mdk)$:

Rule 1. Quote guarantees enclave

$\forall z : \textsc{strd}, \ eid, ch, rest : \textsc{mesg}, \ k : \textsc{akey}, \ mdk : \textsc{skey} . \ \texttt{LocQt}(z, 2) \wedge$
$\quad \texttt{LocQtER}(z, eid :: ch :: k :: rest) \wedge \texttt{LocQtPr}(z, mdk) \wedge \texttt{Non}(mdk)$
$\quad \implies \texttt{EnclCodeKey}(eid, ch, k, mdk).$

This straightforwardly states what a compliant processor's local quoting is supposed to tell us: It accurately reports some enclave running on that processor.

When the Attestation Server completes a run, what must hold? It has checked that the purported EPID signature was genuine, and the signing key *ek* generated interactively with the manufacturer's EPID master secret. It also vouches that the enclave mechanism can preserve the secrecy of *ek* within the EPID quoting enclave.[1] Hence:

Rule 2. AS says EPID key is manufacturer-made and non-compromised

$\forall z : \textsc{strd}, \ ek : \textsc{akey} . \ \texttt{AttServ}(z, 2) \wedge \texttt{ASQtKey}(z, ek)$
$\quad \implies \texttt{ManuMadeEpid}(ek) \wedge \texttt{Non}(ek).$

The conclusion $\texttt{Non}(ek)$ feeds back into the protocol analysis: a non-compromised key often requires compliant local sessions to have occurred. The conclusion $\texttt{ManuMadeEpid}(ek)$ will also be used as a premise in the next rule.

The third rule applies when the *epid-quote* role executes a complete strand z with a valid EPID key. This is a supply chain property. It ensures that the processor is in fact manufactured by Intel, which also generated a non-compromised processor secret *mdk*. Moreover, the processor is capable of preserving the secrecy of *mdk* and ensuring that it is used only in accordance with the roles shown in Fig. 1. The conclusion is simply $\texttt{Non}(mdk)$, stating that *mdk* is non-compromised, again enabling further protocol analysis.

Rule 3. Manufacturer-made EPID on non-compromised processor

$\forall z : \textsc{strd}, \ ek : \textsc{akey}, \ mdk : \textsc{skey} . \ \texttt{EpidQt}(z, 2) \wedge$
$\quad \texttt{EpidQtKey}(z, ek) \wedge \texttt{EpidQtProc}(z, mdk) \wedge \texttt{ManuMadeEpid}(ek)$
$\quad \implies \texttt{Non}(mdk).$

---

[1] Since an out-of-order execution attack falsifies this claim [7], the current SGX does not satisfy our axioms.

2.3   Protocol Analysis with CPSA

Suppose that an *attestation client* has a run, following its role defined in the lower right of Fig. 1. We assume that it queries an attestation server AS with $\mathtt{Non}(\mathtt{dk}(AS))$, and uses a fresh, unguessable nonce N. We also assume the purported enclave record to be of the form $er = eid :: ch :: k :: rest$. What else must then have happened, given the protocol of Fig. 1?

What CPSA Does. A CPSA run starts with a scenario, in which some protocol activity is assumed to have occurred, which in this case is a regular *attestation client* strand. Moreover, additional facts may be included, such as $\mathtt{Non}(\mathtt{dk}(AS))$ and $\mathtt{Unique}(N)$. The latter asserts that N was freshly generated and unguessable ("uniquely originating").

CPSA's job is then to find all minimal, essentially different executions that enrich the initial scenario [18]. To find them, CPSA explores increasingly detailed scenarios—often with additional regular strands—until it finds some that are sufficiently rich. "Sufficiently rich" means:

1. Whenever a regular strand receives a message, the adversary can supply that message, possibly using messages transmitted previously by regular strands. The adversary has the usual, Dolev-Yao derivations [12], starting with initial values compatible with assumptions such as $\mathtt{Non}(\mathtt{dk}(AS))$ and $\mathtt{Unique}(N)$.
2. Suppose η instantiates the variables of a rule R to make the hypothesis of R true. Then η yields a true instantiation of the conclusion of R.

CPSA uses *authentication tests* [18] to find a small set of enrichments to explain a message reception that does not yet satisfy Clause 1. CPSA considers how to add new regular strands and new hypotheses about compromised keys. Alternative possible explanations cause branching in the search.

When R and η are a counterexample to Clause 2, CPSA adds information to make the conclusion hold. When the conclusion is an equation $s = t$, CPSA equates the values $\eta(s)$ and $\eta(t)$. When the conclusion is an atomic formula $P(t_1, \ldots, t_k)$, it adds its instance $P(\eta(t_1), \ldots, \eta(t_k))$ to the scenario.

The approach accommodates additional forms of conclusion, containing *conjunctions*, *existentially quantifiers* $\exists x \,.\, \phi$, and *disjunctions* (logical *ors*, although not in this paper). These syntactic forms are preserved by all homomorphisms [19], and the rules are *geometric sequents* [14]. This yields scenarios that cover all possible executions that homomorphically enrich the initial scenario [13,18,36].

CPSA is implemented in Haskell, and the core program takes input in s-expression format, and gives its output as s-expressions. This is then converted by several supplementary tools to other forms, especially `xhtml` to be displayed in a browser.

CPSA's Input and Output. Given a protocol and rules, CPSA's input is a scenario consisting of some strands of regular participants, together with assumptions such as $\mathtt{Non}(\mathtt{dk}(AS))$ and $\mathtt{Unique}(N)$ or other facts (closed atomic formulas). The starting scenario and similar structures are called *skeletons*.

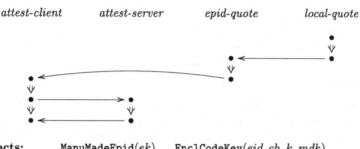

Facts: ManuMadeEpid(ek),   EnclCodeKey(eid, ch, k, mdk)
***Non* keys:**   Non(mdk),   Non(ek),   Non(dk(AS))

Fig. 2. Consequences of an attestation client success

CPSA returns skeletons representing all minimal, essentially different executions enriching the initial skeleton. This is the empty set when the initial skeleton cannot occur; e.g. it hypothesizes some security disclosure that cannot occur. Very often, this set is small, containing only one or a few possibilities.

CPSA presents its results by diagrams like those in Figs. 2, 4, etc., in xhtml. Each diagram shows some strands, presented as vertical columns of transmissions and receptions, together with arrows summarizing ordering information among the events. Each skeleton also shows the parameter values of the different strands, and the other facts that hold in this skeleton.

2.4   Applying CPSA to the SGX Protocols

In our case study, an *attestation client* has a run, following its role defined in Fig. 1. We assume it queries an attestation server AS such that Non(dk(AS)), and uses a fresh, unguessable nonce N. We also assume the purported enclave record to have the form $er = eid :: ch :: k :: rest$. What else must have happened, given the remainder of the protocol contained in Fig. 1?

We ask CPSA this question, subject to Rules 1–3. CPSA answers by computing the result shown in Fig. 2. The assumed attestation client run is shown as the leftmost column in Fig. 2. The keys ek and mdk are new, implicitly existentially quantified values. The client does not find out what they are, but knows they exist. CPSA computes this in three steps.

1. The first step introduces the attestation server run shown immediately to the right. CPSA infers this as a consequence of the protocol definition. Only an attestation server run can extract the nonce N from the encryption inside which the client transmits it. Rule 2 now applies to the new strand, introducing the facts ManuMadeEpid(ek) and Non(ek).
2. Since CPSA now knows that the client run started by receiving a valid EPID-signed remote quote, CPSA explains it by a matching run of the *epid-quote* role. Its mdk parameter was previously unknown. By Rule 3, we infer Non(mdk).

3. How was the local quote $\mathsf{mac}(er, \#(mdk, \tau))$ generated? CPSA infers it can come only from a run of the *local-quote* role with matching parameters. Applying Rule 1, it adds the fact that the enclave record describes an enclave running on mdk. This fact is expressed by $\mathsf{EnclCodeKey}(eid, ch, k, mdk)$. The analysis is now complete.

Omitting Rules. Omitting Rule 1 does not change the diagram, but the fact $\mathsf{EnclCodeKey}(eid, ch, k, mdk)$ is lost. We no longer know that there is an enclave controlled by the code with hash ch and public key k running on processor mdk.

Omitting Rule 3 omits this fact, as well as the (rightmost) *local-quote* strand. The key mdk is no longer known to be Non. Finally, omitting Rule 2 means that only the *attest-server* strand is available. Each rule has a predictable effect on how much of the analysis goes through.

Attestation Consequence. We have now identified the exact consequences that follow from a successful attestation client run with fresh N and non-compromised $\mathsf{dk}(AS)$: A processor with *confirmed supply chain* generated a local quote for the enclave record er. On that same processor, a remote quote was created from the local quote. Finally, on that processor there is an *enclave* under control of the *known code* ch with associated key k.

These conclusions depend on the rules: SGX hardware should ensure that a local quote on a processor with non-compromised mdk ensures a corresponding enclave (Rule 1); the attestation server succeeds only when the remote quote was generated with a properly provisioned, non-compromised EPID key (Rule 2); and the EPID key provisioning should ensure that a processor with an acceptable EPID key can keep its mdk non-compromised (Rule 3).

Making the three rules hold requires challenging—not yet fully achieved—engineering [7]. However, the rules summarize the requirements succinctly, transparently, and usefully for mechanized analysis.

3   An Application Protocol Using Quotes

Section 2 shows how to use SGX attestation. To learn $\mathsf{EnclCodeKey}(eid, ch, k, mdk)$, we attempt a Attestation Client local run with $er = eid :: ch :: k :: rest$. If we succeed with fresh nonce N and non-compromised peer key $\mathsf{Non}(\mathsf{dk}(AS))$, then $\mathsf{EnclCodeKey}(eid, ch, k, mdk)$ holds for some mdk with $\mathsf{Non}(mdk)$.

Suppose software analysis of the code with hash ch shows this code will:

1. generate a fresh key pair k, k^{-1};
2. place the public value k into the its enclave record, while protecting the private value k^{-1}; and
3. use k^{-1} only for the cryptographic operations required by certain roles of Π, and only under the control structure required by those roles.

Hence $\mathsf{Non}(k^{-1})$; so we can use k to contact enclave eid for those roles of Π. In this section, we work out an example protocol, using a rule that summarizes the software analysis (1)–(3), plus a rule that expresses the client's policy of checking an attestation before engaging in the application level protocol Π.

As an example application level protocol, consider the *Yes-or-No* protocol, as shown in Fig. 3. In this protocol, the client P (a.k.a. the *poser*) sends a yes/no question Q together with two nonces Y and N encrypted with $\mathsf{pk}(A)$. The job of the compliant answerer A is to release either the first nonce Y in case the answer is *yes* or else the second nonce N in case the answer is *no*. If P completes the branch receiving Y, P learns one answer, and P learns the other answer by completing the other branch. Before asking its question, the poser obtains a valid enclave record of the form $eid :: ch :: \mathsf{pk}(as) :: rest$, abbreviated er in Fig. 3.

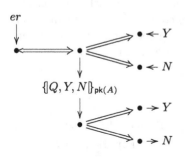

Fig. 3. The Yes-or-No protocol

Our CPSA analysis concentrates on the authentication property, which is that when P completes along either branch, the answerer must in fact have executed the corresponding branch. If the poser thinks the answer was *yes*, then the answerer really committed to *yes*; and likewise for *no*. There is an additional secrecy goal, to ensure that even an adversary that can guess what question Q will be asked cannot determine what the answer is. The adversary cannot distinguish

Run 1 in which the answer was *yes*; v_0 was chosen as the value of the parameter Y; and v_1 was chosen as the value of the parameter N; from

Run 2 in which the answer was *no*; v_1 was chosen as the value of the parameter Y; and v_0 was chosen as the value of the parameter N.

Distinguishing these two runs would require distinguishing $\{\!|Q, v_0, v_1|\!\}_{\mathsf{pk}(A)}$ from $\{\!|Q, v_1, v_0|\!\}_{\mathsf{pk}(A)}$. With a semantically secure encryption, this is intractable.

An Attestation Rule for the Peer. Suppose the predicate $\mathsf{AnsCode}(ch)$ holds true only of bitstrings that result by compiling and hashing source code that we have analyzed. Suppose, moreover, that our analysis indicates this code satisfies properties (1)–(3), specifically when "certain roles of Π" means the two answerer roles of the Yes-or-No protocol. Unless other entities discover its private key k^{-1}, k^{-1} will be non-compromised, i.e. known only to a principal that will use it only in accordance with the protocol. Moreover, the processor prevents other entities from discovering k^{-1} from an enclave, as it encrypts evicted memory. This justifies a rule:

Rule 4. (Answerer attestation) $\forall\, eid, ch : \mathrm{MESG}\,.$

$$\mathsf{EnclCodeKey}(eid, ch, k, mdk) \land \mathsf{AnsCode}(ch) \quad\Longrightarrow\quad \mathsf{Non}(k^{-1}).$$

Client Rule: Obtain Quote First. Suppose parties executing the poser roles in the Yes-or-No protocol obtains an attestation for its peer before starting the run. Perhaps its code ensures a control flow in which the code implementing the poser roles cannot be reached until after an attestation is complete. We can express this via a pair of rules, using the predicates $\text{PoseY}(s, i)$ and $\text{PoseN}(s, i)$ to mean that strand s is an instance of the poser affirmative or negative role, up to height (step) i. The parameter predicates $\text{Eid}(s, eid)$, $\text{Ch}(s, ch)$, $\text{Ans}(s, a)$, and $\text{Rest}(s, rest)$ to indicate strand s is given an enclave record with components (respectively) eid for the EID; ch for the controlling code hash; a for the answerer peer; and $rest$ for the remainder. The following rule asserts that the start of an affirmative poser strand must be preceded by a successful attestation client run with suitable er:

Rule 5. (Client gets quote) $\forall\, s \colon$ STRD, $eid, ch, rest \colon$ MESG, $a \colon$ NAME.

$$
\begin{aligned}
&\text{PoseY}(s, 1) \quad \wedge \text{Eid}(s, eid) \wedge \text{Ch}(s, ch) \wedge \text{Ans}(s, a) \wedge \text{Rest}(s, rest) \\
\implies \quad &\exists\, z \colon \text{STRD}, n \colon \text{TEXT}, as \colon \text{NAME}.\, \text{AttCl}(z, 3) \wedge \text{AttClN}(z, n) \wedge \\
&\text{AttClAs}(z, as) \wedge \text{AttClEr}(z, eid :: ch :: \text{pk}(as) :: rest) \wedge \\
&(z, 2) \prec (s, 0) \wedge \text{Non}(\text{pk}(as)) \wedge \text{Unique}(n)
\end{aligned}
$$

A symmetric rule—about a negative poser strand $\text{PoseN}(s_{no}, 1)$ of height at least 1—is not needed, since any negative poser strand agrees with a positive strand up to height 1 (and 2). Thus, Rule 5 applies to s_{no} also.

Protocol Analysis: Application Level. Suppose now a poser runs the *yes* branch to completion, with challenge nonce Y, code hash ch, and peer public key $\text{pk}(as)$. Moreover, assume:

Fact: $\text{AnsCode}(ch)$ **Keys:** $\text{Unique}(Y)$.

Now CPSA constructs the diagram shown in Fig. 4. The leftmost strand starts by receiving the enclave record. Rule 5 ensures that there is a *attest-client* run that precedes it, indicated by the dotted arrow. The middle reconstructs the consequences in Fig. 2. Using $\text{EnclCodeKey}(eid, ch, \text{pk}(as), mdk)$, which Fig. 2 implies, and the assumption $\text{AnsCode}(ch)$, CPSA applies Rule 4, inferring $\text{Non}(\text{dk}(as))$.

Hence, only an answerer strand can extract Y from $\{\!|Q, Y, N|\!\}_{\text{pk}(as)}$; the adversary does not have the decryption key. Thus, CPSA infers the rightmost strand.

The analysis in the *client-no* case corresponds exactly.

Omitting Rules. Omitting Rule 4 has the expected effect: Without it, CPSA has no grounds to infer $\text{Non}(\text{dk}(as))$. If the key $\text{Non}(\text{dk}(as))$ is compromised, perhaps the adversary has used it to decrypt $\{\!|Q, Y, N|\!\}_k$, and the adversary can transmit Y back to the poser P. Thus, the rightmost strand in Fig. 4, the *ans-yes* strand, will not be added. The poser has no evidence of the authenticity of the answer.

Omitting Rule 5 means that no other strands need to be added. Without an attestation, nothing is known about $\text{Non}(\text{dk}(as))$.

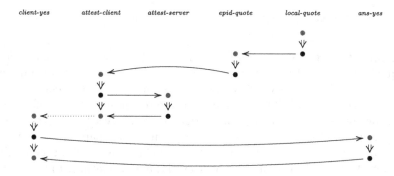

client-yes   attest-client   attest-server   epid-quote   local-quote   ans-yes

Fig. 4. CPSA output for client protocol, *yes* branch.

4   Types of Rules

We first categorize Rules 1–3 from Sect. 2 and Rules 4–5 from Sect. 4. We divide them into three types: *hardware* rules, *trust* rules, and *attestation* rules.

Hardware Rules. Rule 1 stipulates a *hardware* property, namely when the processor generates a local quote on *er*, there is an enclave with record *er*. Rule 3 is also, at least partly, a hardware requirement: a processor with a manufacturer-made EPID key protects *mdk*, and uses it only to generate and check local quotes. There is also a *trust* aspect: the manufacturer should not install a manufacturer-made key *ek* unless the processor can protect its secret *mdk*.

These rules define the hardware requirements. Naturally, the hardware's enclave support must also justify the code analysis leading to the attestation rules.

Trust Rules. Rules 2 and 5 are trust rules. Rule 2 expresses our trust that the manufacturer will operate a reliable Attestation Server, and it defines what we need from the AS, namely confirmation of the origin of *ek* and of its protection from compromise. However, there is no attestation here, since there is no evidence that particular code is in control of the AS. Hence there is no direct evidence the code will ensure the conclusions we care about.

Rule 5 expresses the client's policy of always checking the remote attestation for *er* before asking a question Q. Again, there is no attestation here, since there is no evidence that particular code is in control of the client.

Attestation Rules. Rule 4 is an attestation rule. It applies only when its premise EnclCodeKey(eid, ch, k, mdk) is known to hold, i.e,. other evidence has already established the existence of an enclave *eid* with code (hashing to) *ch*.

A rational process—analyzing the behaviors of the code with known hash *ch*—governs proposed enclave rules. Does it randomly generate its keypair k, k^{-1} and install k in the enclave record? Does it protect the private k^{-1}, using it only in secure cryptographic algorithms? What holds (empirically or by code analysis) about side channels? Does the code respect the control flow of the specific roles in which this key is expected to engage? In attestation rules, we always know what code is in control of an enclave.

Developing the Rules. CPSA is an excellent assistant for developing rules. It gives quick interactive feedback when rules are too weak. This allows a designer to balance out the security goals she expects the system to achieve against the requirements she is willing to impose on the remaining components. CPSA's graphic output makes the effects of particular choices very clear. Its speed is very helpful; no individual run in the development of this paper took more than a few seconds on a standard laptop. CPSA is competitive with other symbolic protocol protocol analysis tools (e.g. Scyther [11] and Tamarin [29]) for a variety of examples [28], and seems much faster than some (e.g. Maude-NPA [15]).

The rules we have developed are modeled on the intent of the SGX mechanisms. However, we expect that other attestation mechanisms, based on different hardware primitives, will lead to alternative sets of rules. The use of those rules for protocol analysis, however, will be very similar in cases that we can envisage.

The Danger of Unsound Rules. What prevents an analyst from writing wishful-thinking rules rather than accurate descriptions of the intended system?

Nothing, in fact. The rules require scrutiny, to determine whether they are reasonable specifications of the system ingredients. We recommend that rules be reused whenever possible, so that when reusing components in a new design one should reuse the rules that have already passed scrutiny as specifying it. We offered our taxonomy of rules into hardware, trust, and attestation rules as a way to focus attention on the main jobs that rules fulfill in this application area. This is meant to encourage rule specifiers to write rules that have a clear, simple explanation. If they are wrong, there is more likely to be a well-known property of the system, or a way to test the system, to expose the error.

Uses of the Rules. The rules provide *specifications* of the relevant components. Hardware rules make clear what we need from SGX. Trust rules provide guidelines for organizations' public attestation server and client code. Attestation rules specify what behavior to permit from the attested code *ch*. Hence, the rules provide *guidance to an implementer* about how to build the components correctly, or whether to adopt existing components. *Testing* gets improved focus from these succinct, intuitive rules. The testers should especially attempt to identify whether these rules could be wrong.

They also help the *red team* that would like to find out how the mechanism can fail. It says which misbehaviors in the pieces would lead to a jackpot for the red team, namely the failure of the mechanism.

Alternate Protocols and Rules. We have considered a variety of different protocols, including Intel's newer, EPID-free ECDSA protocol [23], our own mechanism which uses standard signatures on top of EPID, and simplifications of the protocols that omit tags such as rq in Fig. 1. Additional rules are required in these cases, but they reuse the same ideas we have presented already.

A small change to the application-level protocol also assures the client that the attestation occurred recently.

5   Related Work and Conclusion

Security protocol analysis is a very well-developed field, with numerous sophisticated tools for trace properties (e.g. [4,15,29,33]), and some for determining indistinguishability properties also (e.g. [5,8]). In many cases, our work is compatible with other approaches rather than in competition with it. For instance, tamarin [29] has a notion of *restriction* used to restrict the traces of interest. This increases the value of using rules to formalize the context in which protocols run: Multiple tools can shed light on the consequences.

Enrich-by-need, which is specific to CPSA, is useful in development. It provides an overview of all minimal, essentially different possibilities.

Connecting security protocols to context has been less studied than one would expect. Protocol failures such as the renegotiation attacks on TLS [34] arise because the protocol does not provide enough information to its context when the authenticated identity of the peer changed.

Some papers a decade ago generated application-specific protocols for specific tasks, expressed in a session notation, and implementations for them [2,3], improving on a compiler for application-specific protocols [20]. More recently, a study of protocols and the goals they meet showed how application-level goals may be expressed in an extension of a language for protocol goals [35].

Rigorous reasoning about the behavior of TEEs is a recognized need [37]. Sihna et al.'s Moat proved confidentiality properties of the code in an enclave [39]. [38] provided a much easier way to prove a much narrower property: Separate the code of an enclave into a fixed library and user code. And automated control flow check on the user code ensures it does not abuse the library. The library can be subjected to a one-time code verification. Thus, many enclaves can be proved to interact with the external world only through properly encrypted I/O. A more general model may now be found in [40]; it uses a clean state machine transition model to formalize core integrity, confidentiality, and attestation properties that SGX and other TEE models such as Sanctum [10].

Gollamudi and Chong [17] produce code for enclaves that respect information flow properties, although at the cost of a larger trusted computing base.

Barbosa et al. [1] develop cryptographic-style definitions for core functionalities within TEEs including key exchange, attested and outsourced computation. They prove that specific schemes, in standard crypto-style pseudocode, achieve these functionalities. Their fine-grained results come at the cost of mechanized support and clean construction of protocols and rules. In particular, they do not identify anything similar to the contrast of hardware, trust, and attestation, as their goals are more aligned with cryptographic mechanisms.

Much of the recent work complements ours, which provides proof goals for enclave code. If the local code meets these derived goals, our analysis shows that protocols and code will cooperate to achieve our overall application goals.

Conclusion. We have illustrated, by means of example, how to combine reasoning about protocols with reasoning about their context of execution. All of our reasoning is mechanized, with a visualization of the executions for each scenario.

For attestation protocols, the rules may be divided into hardware rules, trust rules, and attestation rules. This provides an objective set of requirements for the supporting mechanisms, based in hardware for attestation or in trust anchors or trust between organizations. Modular layers provide a repeatable way to ensure user-level protocols are crafted to their trust and attestation context.

References

1. Barbosa, M., Portela, B., Scerri, G., Warinschi, B.: Foundations of hardware-based attested computation and application to SGX. In: IEEE EuroS&P, pp. 245–260 (2016)
2. Bhargavan, K., Corin, R., Deniélou, P.-M., Fournet, C., Leifer, J.J.: Cryptographic protocol synthesis and verification for multiparty sessions. In: IEEE Computer Security Foundations Symposium (2009)
3. Bhargavan, K., Corin, R., Fournet, C., Gordon, A.D.: Secure sessions for web services. ACM Trans. Inf. Syst. Secur. **10**(2), 8 (2007)
4. Blanchet, B.: An efficient protocol verifier based on prolog rules. In: IEEE CSFW, pp. 82–96. IEEE CS Press, June 2001
5. Blanchet, B., Pointcheval, D.: Automated security proofs with sequences of games. In: Dwork, C. (ed.) CRYPTO 2006. LNCS, vol. 4117, pp. 537–554. Springer, Heidelberg (2006). https://doi.org/10.1007/11818175_32
6. Brickell, E., Li, J.: Enhanced privacy ID: a direct anonymous attestation scheme with enhanced revocation capabilities. In: ACM Workshop on Privacy in the Electronic Society, pp. 21–30. ACM (2007)
7. Van Bulck, J., et al.: Foreshadow: extracting the keys to the intel SGX kingdom with transient out-of-order execution. In: USENIX Security, pp. 991–1008 (2018)
8. Chadha, R., Cheval, V., Ciobâc, Ş., Kremer, S.: Automated verification of equivalence properties of cryptographic protocols. ACM Trans. Comput. Log. **17**(4), 23:1–23:32 (2016)
9. Coker, G., et al.: Principles of remote attestation. IJIS **10**(2), 63–81 (2011)
10. Costan, V., Lebedev, I.A., Devadas, S.: Sanctum: minimal hardware extensions for strong software isolation. In: USENIX Security Symposium, pp. 857–874 (2016)
11. Cremers, C., Mauw, S.: Operational Semantics and Verification of Security Protocols. Springer, Heidelberg (2012). https://doi.org/10.1007/978-3-540-78636-8
12. Dolev, D., Yao, A.: On the security of public-key protocols. IEEE Trans. Inf. Theory **29**, 198–208 (1983)
13. Dougherty, D.J., Guttman, J.D., Ramsdell, J.D.: Security protocol analysis in context: computing minimal executions using SMT and CPSA. In: Furia, C.A., Winter, K. (eds.) IFM 2018. LNCS, vol. 11023, pp. 130–150. Springer, Cham (2018). https://doi.org/10.1007/978-3-319-98938-9_8
14. Dyckhoff, R., Negri, S.: Geometrisation of first-order logic. Bull. Symb. Logic **21**(2), 123–163 (2015)
15. Escobar, S., Meadows, C., Meseguer, J.: Maude-NPA: cryptographic protocol analysis modulo equational properties. In: Aldini, A., Barthe, G., Gorrieri, R. (eds.) FOSAD 2007-2009. LNCS, vol. 5705, pp. 1–50. Springer, Heidelberg (2009). https://doi.org/10.1007/978-3-642-03829-7_1

16. Fournet, C., Gordon, A.D., Maffeis, S.: A type discipline for authorization policies. In: Sagiv, M. (ed.) ESOP 2005. LNCS, vol. 3444, pp. 141–156. Springer, Heidelberg (2005). https://doi.org/10.1007/978-3-540-31987-0_11
17. Gollamudi, A., Chong, S.: Automatic enforcement of expressive security policies using enclaves. In: OOPSLA, pp. 494–513 (2016)
18. Guttman, J.D.: Shapes: surveying crypto protocol runs. In: Cortier, V., Kremer, S. (eds.) Formal Models and Techniques for Analyzing Security Protocols, Cryptology and Information Security Series. IOS Press (2011)
19. Guttman, J.D.: Establishing and preserving protocol security goals. J. Comput. Secur. **22**(2), 201–267 (2014)
20. Guttman, J.D., Herzog, J.C., Ramsdell, J.D., Sniffen, B.T.: Programming cryptographic protocols. In: De Nicola, R., Sangiorgi, D. (eds.) TGC 2005. LNCS, vol. 3705, pp. 116–145. Springer, Heidelberg (2005). https://doi.org/10.1007/11580850_8
21. Guttman, J.D., Ramsdell, J.D.: CPSA inputs for understanding attestation, April 2019. https://web.cs.wpi.edu/~guttman/pubs/understanding_attestation_example/
22. Intel. Intel® Software Guard Extensions (Intel® SGX) (2016). https://software.intel.com/en-us/sgx
23. Intel. Intel® Software Guard Extensions (Intel® SGX) data center attestation primitives: ECDSA quote library API, November 2018. https://download.01.org/intel-sgx/dcap-1.0.1/docs/Intel_SGX_ECDSA_QuoteGenReference_DCAP_API_Linux_1.0.1.pdf
24. Kaplan, D., Powell, J., Woller, T.: AMD memory encryption, April 2016. https://developer.amd.com/wordpress/media/2013/12/AMD_Memory_Encryption_Whitepaper_v7-Public.pdf
25. Kremer, S., Künnemann, R.: Automated analysis of security protocols with global state. J. Comput. Secur. **24**(5), 583–616 (2016)
26. Lampson, B., Abadi, M., Burrows, M., Wobber, E.: Authentication in distributed systems: theory and practice. ACM Trans. Comput. Syst. **10**(4), 265–310 (1992)
27. Li, N., Mitchell, J.C., Winsborough, W.H.: Design of a role-based trust management framework. In: Proceedings, 2002 IEEE Symposium on Security and Privacy, pp. 114–130. IEEE CS Press, May 2002
28. Liskov, M.D., Guttman, J.D., Ramsdell, J.D., Rowe, P.D., Thayer, F.J.: Enrich-by-need protocol analysis for Diffie-Hellman. In: Guttman, J.D., Landwehr, C.E., Meseguer, J., Pavlovic, D. (eds.) Foundations of Security, Protocols, and Equational Reasoning. LNCS, vol. 11565, pp. 135–155. Springer, Cham (2019). https://doi.org/10.1007/978-3-030-19052-1_10
29. Meier, S., Schmidt, B., Cremers, C., Basin, D.: The TAMARIN prover for the symbolic analysis of security protocols. In: Sharygina, N., Veith, H. (eds.) CAV 2013. LNCS, vol. 8044, pp. 696–701. Springer, Heidelberg (2013). https://doi.org/10.1007/978-3-642-39799-8_48
30. Murray, T., van Oorschot, P.C.: Formal proofs, the fine print and side effects. In: IEEE SecDev, September 2018
31. Noorman, J., et al.: Sancus 2.0: a low-cost security architecture for IoT devices. ACM Trans. Priv. Secur. **20**(3), 7:1–7:33 (2017)
32. Ramsdell, J.D., Guttman, J.D.: CPSA4: a cryptographic protocol shapes analyzer with geometric rules. The MITRE Corporation (2018). https://github.com/ramsdell/cpsa
33. Ramsdell, J.D., Guttman, J.D., Liskov, M.: CPSA: A cryptographic protocol shapes analyzer (2016). http://hackage.haskell.org/package/cpsa

34. Rescorla, E., Ray, M., Dispensa, S., Oskov, N.: Transport Layer Security (TLS) Renegotiation Indication Extension. RFC 5746 (Proposed Standard) (2010)
35. Rowe, P.D., Guttman, J.D., Liskov, M.D.: Measuring protocol strength with security goals. Int. J. Inf. Secur. (2016). https://doi.org/10.1007/s10207-016-0319-z. http://web.cs.wpi.edu/~guttman/pubs/ijis_measuring-security.pdf
36. Saghafi, S., Danas, R., Dougherty, D.J.: Exploring theories with a model-finding assistant. In: Felty, A.P., Middeldorp, A. (eds.) CADE 2015. LNCS (LNAI), vol. 9195, pp. 434–449. Springer, Cham (2015). https://doi.org/10.1007/978-3-319-21401-6_30
37. Schuster, F., et al.: VC3: trustworthy data analytics in the cloud using SGX. In: 2015 IEEE S&P, pp. 38–54 (2015)
38. Sinha, R., et al.: A design and verification methodology for secure isolated regions. In: PLDI (2016)
39. Sinha, R., Rajamani, S., Seshia, S., Vaswani, K.: Moat: verifying confidentiality of enclave programs. In: ACM CCS, Moat (2015)
40. Subramanyan, P., Sinha, R., Lebedev, I.A. Devadas, S., Seshia, S.A.: A formal foundation for secure remote execution of enclaves. In: ACM CCS (2017)

Challenges of Using Trusted Computing for Collaborative Data Processing

Paul Georg Wagner[1]([✉]), Pascal Birnstill[2], and Jürgen Beyerer[1,2]

[1] Karlsruhe Institute of Technology, Karlsruhe, Germany
paul.wagner@kit.edu
[2] Fraunhofer Institute of Optronics, System Technologies and Image Exploitation
IOSB, Karlsruhe, Germany

Abstract. In recent years many business processes have become more interconnected than ever before. Driven by the advance of the Internet of Things, companies rely on complex data processing chains that span over many collaborating corporations and across different countries. As a result of this development, automated data acquisition and collaborative data usage is now a foundation of many innovative and successful business models. However, despite having a clear interest in sharing valuable data with other stakeholders, data owners simultaneously need to protect their assets against illegitimate use. In order to accommodate this requirement, existing data sharing solutions contain usage control systems capable of enforcing policies on data even after they have been shared. The integrity of these policy enforcement components is often monitored by a trusted platform module (TPM) on the data receiver's side. In this work we evaluate the adequacy of TPM-based remote attestation for protecting shared data on foreign systems. In order to do so we develop an attacker model that includes privileged system users and expose attack vectors on TPM-protected data sharing applications. We show that TPMs do not provide sufficient protection against malicious administrators from competing stakeholders. Finally, we describe the advantages of using Intel's Software Guard Extensions (SGX) to protect shared data in hostile environments and propose an enhanced system architecture that includes both SGX enclaves as well as a classical TPM.

Keywords: Trusted computing · Trusted platform modules ·
Software guard extensions · Usage control · Policy enforcement ·
Data sharing

1 Introduction

Ever since data have become invaluable assets in many modern business processes, preventing malicious attackers from accessing critical information is a major challenge. In the past, data protection efforts mostly consisted of securing internal information processing infrastructure, like corporate computer systems

© Springer Nature Switzerland AG 2019
S. Mauw and M. Conti (Eds.): STM 2019, LNCS 11738, pp. 107–123, 2019.
https://doi.org/10.1007/978-3-030-31511-5_7

and databases. Today, with complex data processing chains spanning over multiple collaborating corporations and across different countries, this isolated view on data security is not sufficient anymore. Especially many industrial use cases, such as the joint operation of production equipment and support of complex service agreements, require the flexible exchange of information between different stakeholders. Hence one of the most urgent security requirements in many modern applications is to monitor and control the usage of sensitive information, even after it has been transmitted to other stakeholders.

In general, data sharing solutions connect the databases of participating corporations and provide mechanisms to securely exchange data across corporate boundaries. While many of these systems are still heterogeneous in nature, there are ongoing attempts to consolidate common standards and governance models into a single trusted business ecosystem [9]. This results in a virtual data space that is responsible for controlling and securing the data sharing process across multiple participating corporations. Furthermore, data owners are often allowed to specify restrictions on how data receivers may use the disclosed information. In most cases this is achieved by distributing usage control policies alongside the original data. These usage rules are evaluated and applied by policy enforcement components that run on the data receiver's systems. Since the data receiver is motivated to bypass the imposed usage restrictions, it is necessary to remotely verify the integrity of these usage control components before transmitting sensitive information. Usually data owners rely on trusted platform modules (TPMs) [13] to establish a trusted software stack on the remote side. By executing the TPM-backed remote attestation protocol and thereby verifying the software stack of the target system, access to shared data can be limited to trustworthy (i.e. unmodified and sufficiently protected) data receivers.

In this work we evaluate the adequacy of TPM-based remote attestation for protecting shared data on foreign systems. We do this by assessing the current architecture of a particular data sharing solution, the Industrial Data Space, in this regard. Section 2 briefly describes how the Industrial Data Space architecture applies usage control components and TPMs in order to ensure data sovereignty across multiple corporations. In Sect. 3 we then develop an attacker model that includes privileged system users such as administrators and outline the problems that arise when TPMs are used to protect data on foreign systems. Finally, in Sect. 4 we propose an enhanced system architecture that uses the capabilities of Intel's Software Guard Extensions (SGX) alongside a TPM to protect cross-domain data flows even against malicious administrators. The identified security problems as well as the proposed architectural improvements apply for the specific case of the Industrial Data Space, as well as for any generic data sharing system that relies on TPMs to establish a trusted computing base.

2   Data Sovereignty in Collaborative Data Spaces

The *Industrial Data Space* [9] is a virtual data space intended to automate data sharing for smart business ecosystems while simultaneously preserving data sovereignty among its participants. In order to connect to the data space, participating corporations operate access points (called *connectors*) in their own respective IT infrastructure. Data space connectors can operate both as data provider and consumer, simultaneously sending and receiving information. They query remote data providers (i.e. other connectors) and are responsible for managing and conducting the subsequent data exchange. After processing the received information, the results are shared with neighboring connectors and serve as input for the next data processing step. That way complex data processing chains can be established across multiple collaborating corporations.

The data protection capability of the Industrial Data Space is based on a comprehensive usage control infrastructure that can monitor and govern shared data on foreign connectors. Unlike classical access control, usage control models focus on managing the future usage of data [10]. With usage control technology it is possible to restrict the processing and distribution of sensitive information even after it has been disclosed to other stakeholders. In the Industrial Data Space, data providers can define usage rules for their assets by specifying appropriate usage control policies. Whenever an outgoing data flow occurs, these policies are deployed on the receiving connector before transmitting any sensitive information. On the remote system a policy decision point (PDP) evaluates the received usage control policies and a policy enforcement point (PEP) enforces the specified rules on the shared data. Usually the PDP is included in the connector, while the PEPs are part of the data processing applications. Whenever sensitive information from another system is used by an application, its PEP generates an event that describes the specific data usage, sends it to the PDP and enforces the resulting decision. That way the usage control components on the data receiver's system ensure compliance with the usage restrictions specified by the data owner. Furthermore, the usage control components share data flow information across communicating connectors and hence constitute a distributed usage control infrastructure [7]. By specifying appropriate usage control policies, data providers can enforce complex usage strategies on their data, such as temporary or locally restricted access, even after they have been shared.

Any implementation of such a distributed usage control system has to make several assumptions. Most notably, the usage control components must not be maliciously manipulated or deactivated during their lifetime by either an internal or external attacker. Since it is the operating system's responsibility to protect the usage control components from any outside influence, we have to assume that it is implemented correctly and does not contain security-critical bugs. Furthermore, operating a distributed usage control system requires a mechanism to remotely verify the integrity of the remote protection components. In particular, the integrity of the remote connector, the data processing applications and the foreign usage control components has to be verified prior to a data flow. Additionally, transmitted data have to be encrypted in a way that only a trustworthy connector (and by extension trustworthy applications) can read them. Only if these requirements are fulfilled, the data provider can be sure that his usage control policies will be enforced correctly by the remote connector.

The connectors use trusted platform modules (TPMs) to establish a trusted computing base and meet these requirements. A TPM is a dedicated hardware chip that extends a computer with basic security related features [13]. It uses volatile platform configuration registers (PCRs) to measure the current hardware and software configuration as an unforgeable hash. This allows the data provider to seal confidential information to a certain TPM state. Furthermore, the data provider can use a remote attestation protocol to verify that the target system is in a trustworthy state before transmitting sensitive information. When a data provider is requested to share assets, his connector initiates the execution of the remote attestation protocol by transmitting a randomly drawn nonce to the remote side. The requesting connector then uses his TPM to generate a quote that contains this nonce and the current PCR values of his system. The quote serves as proof of the current system state and has been signed by the TPM with an attestation identity key (AIK). The AIK is an asymmetric cryptographic key pair that has been created by the TPM during a prior enrollment phase. While the public part of the AIK is known to all involved parties (usually it is certified by a CA), the private key never leaves the TPM. The signed quote is then transmitted back to the data provider, who verifies both nonce and signature, before confirming that the included PCR values belong to the expected, unmodified connector system. If these checks are successful, the data provider is convinced that the remote connector is in a trustworthy state, since only the TPM of a correctly configured system could have generated such a signed quote. After the remote attestation protocol executed successfully, the data provider issues usage control policies to the attested data consumer and finally initiates the requested data flow. To prevent eavesdropping, the provider encrypts the transmitted data with the public part of an ephemeral key pair that has been generated by the trusted application during the remote attestation process. The trusted application authenticates the public key by including it in the signed quote as well. Figure 1 shows how a connector executes the remote attestation protocol and deploys necessary usage control policies before allowing data access. A trusted third party (TTP) is responsible for providing the known "good" PCR values that are compared to the values in the quote. Also, we assume the existence of a CA that certifies the public keys of all involved parties.

The remote attestation protocol enables data space connectors to establish trust in systems that are operated by competing corporations. In combination with a distributed usage control model, the Industrial Data Space architecture allows corporations to safeguard their assets across data processing chains that leave their own IT infrastructure. In the following section we base our analysis on the presented reference architecture. However, the identified problems are applicable to any generic data sharing system that uses TPM-based remote attestation to protect transmitted information on possibly hostile systems.

3   Attack Vectors

The advantage of using TPMs to establish a trusted computing base lies in their low cost, widespread availability and uncomplicated application to many prob-

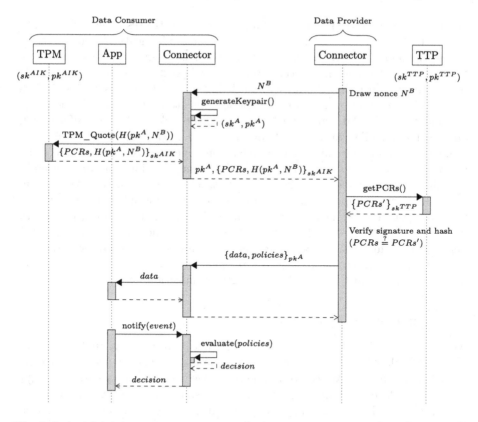

Fig. 1. Industrial data space connectors conduct remote attestation, data sharing and policy enforcement. N^B is a randomly drawn nonce. H is a hash function.

lems in the realm of trusted computing. However, there are drawbacks when using TPMs to protect sensitive information in foreign organizations. For example, distributed usage control systems can become insecure when the attacker model includes valid users of the attested system itself [14]. This is because malicious users have physical access to the TPM and can use it to decrypt previously intercepted data, as long as the PCR values do not change. Similar problems also occur in our use case. In order to point out the existing attack vectors regarding the use of TPMs, we first define a suitable security model by specifying the main attacker faced in the described scenario. Then we identify three different attack vectors on TPM-based data space architectures in general.

3.1 Security Model

The primary objective of a virtual data space is to secure the confidentiality of data that have been shared by a data provider. However, in our case the actual protection level that should be reached is specified by the deployed usage control policies. Depending on the implementation of the decision point, data providers can specify with fine granularity what constitutes as legitimate data usage. Hence the main security goal is to protect the integrity of policies across connectors and enforce them remotely on data consumers.

The main attacker in our scenario is a malicious data consumer who wants to illegitimately use shared data without being subject to any usage restrictions imposed by the data owner. An example for this attacker is a corporation that participates in the data space with the intent to resell the received information outside the controlled data space. In order to do so, the attacker has to bypass his own connector's usage control enforcement components and extract the received information from the virtual data space. Since the malicious corporation operates the attacked connector in its own infrastructure, it can instruct the system administrator to tamper with the installed protection mechanisms. As a result, the strongest attacker faced in this scenario is an administrator who tries to bypass the TPM-based protection mechanisms that the data provider verifies before sharing his data. While companies must always trust their own administrators with regard to the managed systems, in this case the administrator acts as an attacker against the interests of other organizations.

3.2   Manipulating Connectors

An obvious way for attackers to extract information from the virtual data space is to manipulate the connectors that are running in their own infrastructure. For example, the attacker could disable the usage control components or disrupt the policy enforcement mechanisms. However, since the connector systems are measured by a TPM, these modifications will manifest themselves in changed PCR values. Hence the data provider is able to identify tampered systems by executing the remote attestation protocol. A successful attacker would have to either forge the PCR values on his connector (which he has physical access to), forge a quote signature, or exploit a vulnerability in the remote attestation protocol to convince the data provider, even though the PCR values are bad.

Due to the nature of the TPM as a hardware based trust anchor, these attacks are infeasible. The TPM is designed to only extend PCRs with new measurements, it is not possible to set them to a desired value [13]. Furthermore, the security of the TCG specification has been evaluated thoroughly [3, 6, 12]. Assuming that the attacker cannot break commonly used digital signature algorithms, forging a quote requires the attacker to obtain the private part of the attestation identity key. However, this key is generated and managed by the TPM, which does not reveal the private key to the outside world. Nonetheless it is important for the attesting party to include and verify randomly drawn nonces in the quote (c.f. Fig. 1). Otherwise the attacker can intercept a correct quote and replay it later, instead of forging a quote signature. In general, the TPM-based remote attestation secures the integrity of data space connectors and prevents attackers from gaining illegitimate data access by directly manipulating them.

3.3 Duplicating Attested Connections

Since the TPM protects the connector software against tampering, a successful attacker has to extract data without previous manipulation. As described before, in our scenario the attacker operates and controls the connector system. Hence the attacker can use that system to establish additional attested connections to data providers, unbeknownst to the still running and unmodified connector software. For this attack, the adversary first launches a legitimate connector system. Since the connector software is not manipulated, the subsequently conducted remote attestations will be successful. However, no useful information can be intercepted because any transmitted data are encrypted with an ephemeral key unknown to the attacker (c.f. Fig. 1). At this point the attacker launches a separate process that itself initiates the remote attestation protocol and establishes another connection with the data provider. This new instance of the attestation protocol will also succeed, since the PCRs of the targeted connector are still correct. However, this time the attacker controls the connection (i.e. chooses the ephemeral session key) and may receive sensitive information from the unsuspecting data provider, without being subject to usage control enforcement. This attack succeeds because in general data providers cannot distinguish establishing a connection with the legitimate software from communicating with an attacker-controlled process on an otherwise unmodified connector system. If the attacker simultaneously blocks the network traffic of the legitimate connector process, the data providers do not even notice any additional connection attempts. As a result, attackers with access to an unmodified connector system can bypass all protection mechanisms by impersonating a data consumer and requesting information from data providers.

A possible solution is to regard the connector system as untrustworthy as soon as any process other than the connector software initiates an attested connection. On a technical level this would require that creating a new attested connection to a remote connector invariably triggers a measurement and extends the PCRs. In that case the additional attestation fails and the additional connection would not be established. Even though a trusted operating system could accomplish this by monitoring the network interfaces, consequently there would be a very large set of constantly changing, yet valid PCR values to verify. From an architectural point of view, this attack is possible because the used attestation protocol can only identify the whole attested system as an endpoint for the communication, but not single processes or users on that system. In other words, by using the TPM-based remote attestation, data providers can only make sure that their data is transmitted to a remote system that is in a specific state (i.e. has a certain TPM with certain PCR values), but they have no means of verifying who receives the information on the attested system. This problem cannot entirely be avoided by relying solely on TPM technology.

3.4 In-memory Tampering

As presented earlier, the TPM is responsible for protecting the connector against outside manipulation. This mechanism works by making malicious modifications of the connector implementation transparent to the data provider. When the connector system boots up, the TPM constructs a chain of trust that begins at the Core Root of Trust for Measurement (CRTM) and includes the BIOS as well as parts of the operating system. Ultimately, the connector's executable and configuration files are also measured and extended to the PCRs. During the subsequent remote attestation, the data provider precludes manipulations by verifying the PCR values. However, this procedure can only reveal connector modifications that occur before or during its launch. Once the connector is running, no more measurements are conducted and the PCRs do not change anymore. Since our attacker has administrative rights on the connector system, he can attach a debugger instance to the connector process and access its memory layout without changing the verifiable state of the system (i.e. the PCR values). Even simple tools from the GNU Compiler Collection like gdb and dump suffice for carrying out this attack. By directly accessing the connector's memory, an attacker can read out and manipulate confidential data that should be subject to usage restrictions enforced by the connector. The attacker can also tamper with the loaded code of both the connector and the data processing applications.

In order to address these types of attacks and allow the attestation of remote systems to be more flexible, measurements of executed applications can be automatically triggered during runtime. OS-based integrity measurement mechanisms, like the *Integrity Measurement Architecture* (IMA) on Linux, can appraise the integrity of data and executable files by comparing their hashes against prepared lists. Furthermore, the IMA can trigger TPM measurements while the system is running. For example, it is possible to measure the content of opened files as well as the memory image of every starting application and extend the PCRs accordingly. This allows to attest a system very precisely. In our case, a correctly configured IMA could detect the launch of a debugging tool and announce it to verifying parties by conducting an appropriate TPM measurement. However, this can lead to considerable side effects when operating connectors. For instance, when using the IMA in that manner, every starting application inevitably changes the PCR values. As a result there is a very large set of trustworthy PCR values, and validating them during remote attestation can be cumbersome. Furthermore, the IMA only measures the initial memory image of the loaded application. It is still possible to retrospectively modify memory regions of a running application without influencing the PCRs. As Sparks shows, this can be done by carefully manipulating the page tables of a running process [12]. D'Cunha proposes a countermeasure against this attack by continuously measuring the virtual address space of individual processes with each write access [2]. Nevertheless, continuously measuring a complete memory dump of a complex application is hardly feasible in practice. Apart from that, the data provider would also have to continuously keep probing the consumer's systems in order to re-verify the PCRs and detect any wrongdoing. In addition, this countermeasure only prevents an attacker from manipulating the connector's main memory without also influencing the PCRs. It is still possible for the attacker to simply read out sensitive information directly from memory without the original data provider noticing. Afterwards the attacker can use and redistribute the stolen data without any usage control policies being enforced on them.

In summary, there are strong attack vectors on systems that use TPM-based remote attestation to protect data sharing applications. The main cause of the described problems is that on the data consumer's side the operating system is still responsible for protecting transmitted information. However, privileged users who act as an attacker can evade many OS-level protection mechanisms such as address space isolation. Usually administrators are not viewed as attackers in many scenarios, because in general they have to be fully trusted with regard to their employer's systems. But as soon as distributed use cases are considered, for example in the context of the Industrial Data Space, administrators have to be viewed as attackers who try to evade usage restrictions that are imposed by competing companies. Since TPMs cannot sufficiently protect against this type of attack, other technologies have to be considered as well.

4   SGX in Collaborative Data Spaces

Intel's Software Guard Extensions (SGX) consist of a set of processor instructions extending the x86 architecture, along with hardware security modules that are included in newer Intel CPUs. SGX can provide a trusted execution environment for security critical applications, even if privileged software such as the operating system or a hypervisor is malicious. This is achieved by executing code as a protected container called *enclave*, which cannot be accessed by other processes, administrators, or even by the operating system itself. The enclave is protected by trusted hardware and is isolated from the rest of the system (reverse sandboxing). SGX allows to encapsulate critical software, for example cryptographic libraries or key management services, in protected shells that will behave in expected ways. Architectural details of SGX and a thorough analysis of its security are provided in [1]. Since then several attacks on some parts of the comprehensive SGX architecture have been revealed, including side-channel attacks [4] and a vulnerability related to Spectre [8]. However, countermeasures against these attacks have also been proposed [5]. Overall SGX is still regarded as secure and is being used in an increasing number of projects.

Whenever an SGX enclave is launched, its code and initial data are cryptographically hashed. This hash is called the enclave's *measurement*. A remote third party can verify the state of a running enclave by requesting a signed quote that includes the enclave's measurement. The quote can be verified by contacting the Intel Attestation Service (IAS) and comparing the attested measurement to a desired value. This ensures that the loaded enclave code has not been manipulated before execution, and hence establishes trust in the remotely running enclave. Furthermore, this attestation mechanism establishes a secure channel between the verifying party and the enclave using a modified Sigma protocol that includes a Diffie-Hellman key exchange. If the quote verifies correctly, the remote party is convinced that he communicates with the right enclave (measurement is correct) and that only this enclave instance knows the established shared secret.

Both parties can then derive a symmetric secret from the Diffie-Hellman key and use it to encrypt their further communication. In [1] the remote attestation protocol is explained in greater detail. A similar protocol is also possible between two enclaves that reside on one SGX platform. This is called *local attestation*. It can be used to locally verify the integrity of another enclave and establish a secure channel between them.

Regarding our scenario, the main advantage of using SGX technology over TPMs is that the attestation protocol can establish a shared secret between the data provider and an isolated enclave, which cannot be influenced or observed even by malicious administrators. On the other hand, using SGX requires an expansion of the trust model. Since so far only the Intel Attestation Service can verify the quotes generated by enclaves, it has to be fully trusted. However, Intel recently announced the upcoming support of third-party remote attestation infrastructures [11]. In the remainder of this section we describe how to use SGX technology for securing usage control infrastructures in our data sharing scenario.

4.1 SGX-Based Data Space Connectors

In order to benefit from the advantages of SGX technology in a collaborative data space, security critical modules have to be encapsulated in enclaves. This includes the usage control components as well as any software that is acquiring and processing sensitive information. On the data consumer's side, a connector enclave conducts remote attestations with the data providers, before collecting the requested data and associated usage control policies. The policies are forwarded to a dedicated PDP enclave, which determines usage control decisions by evaluating them. As before, the data processing applications contain PEPs that generate events for any attempted data usage and subsequently enforce the PDP's decisions. However, now the applications are realized as SGX enclaves and are locally attested by the connector enclave before they receive any sensitive data. The necessary communication between the data consumer's enclaves and the data provider is shown in Fig. 2. Immediately after launch the connector enclave verifies the integrity of the PDP enclave by locally attesting to its measurement value (called MRENCLAVE). Only if this local attestation is successful, the connector enclave executes the remote attestation protocol and establishes a shared secret with the data provider. If the remote attestation has been completed successfully as well, the data provider transmits the requested data along with usage control policies to the connector enclave. The connector enclave then acts as a trusted intermediary and shares the received data with each eligible application according to the specified usage rules. More concretely, the connector enclave first locally attests the active data processing applications, thereby verifying that the applications are legitimate and contain PEPs that enforce usage control decisions. Since the connector enclave does not know beforehand which data processing applications will be requesting data, a trusted third party (TTP) provides the expected enclave measurements. A secure channel to the TTP can be established by adding the TTP's public key to the code of the connector enclave. The integrity of this key is implicitly verified by the

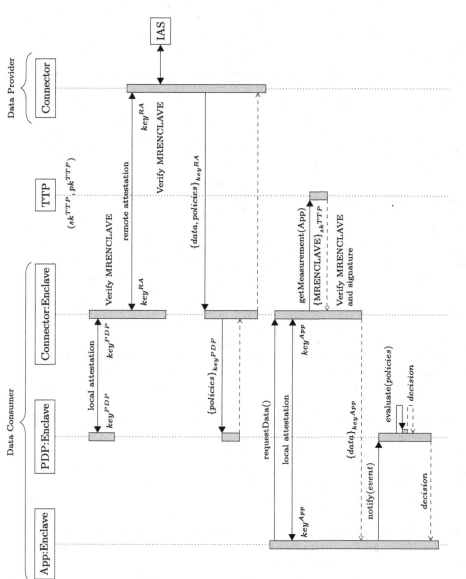

Fig. 2. A data space connector architecture based on SGX technology. Attestation messages are not shown.

data provider during the remote attestation. This process of locally attesting application enclaves avoids conducting separate remote attestations for every data processing application. If the local attestation of the application is successful, the connector releases the data to the application enclave. Afterwards the application's PEP contacts the PDP enclave for each attempted data access and enforces the resulting decision. For the sake of simplicity, Fig. 2 does not show the messages sent during the attestation procedures. In general, both the local and the remote attestation protocol establish a shared secret, which is then used to derive a symmetric session key for the attested connection. Further details of the attestation process are given in [1].

The security analysis of the SGX-backed connector solution is based on the same attacker model as before. We view the attacker as a malicious administrator of the data consuming connector system, who tries to intercept information and use it outside the usage restrictions imposed by the original data provider. Unlike with the previous TPM-based approach to data sovereignty, this solution shields shared data inside protected SGX enclaves from outside influence at all times. As a result, even malicious administrators cannot directly access or manipulate critical data and the in-memory tampering attack presented in the last section is not possible anymore. Another attack vector is the manipulation of enclave code before launching it on the data consumer's system. An attacker could try to tamper with the implementation of usage control components or modify the connector enclave in order to leak received data. However, tampering with enclave code is prevented by properly attesting the relevant enclaves before any data is released. Also, stealing sensitive data by duplicating attested connections is not possible anymore, because the attacker cannot successfully execute the remote attestation protocol with the data provider. Neither can the attacker pose as a data processing application and request data from the connector enclave, because the application is locally attested as well. By using SGX enclaves instead of TPMs to handle attestation, secure communication and data processing, the previously identified attack vectors have been resolved.

The proposed SGX-based architecture enables data providers to securely share information with collaborating data consumers. In addition to that, the architecture depicted in Fig. 2 also includes a usage control system that enforces usage restrictions on the shared data even after they have been transmitted. This makes it possible to realize flexible use cases where data from various sources have to be merged while simultaneously preserving data sovereignty. The architecture allows data providers to verify the trustworthiness of remote systems, and even malicious administrators cannot illegitimately access sensitive data. However, there are shortcomings with regard to the complexity of the data processing chains that can be constructed. Most importantly, the proposed architecture only supports internal usage control enforcement. This means that policy enforcement points can only be implemented as part of enclave applications. As a result the deployed usage rules can only control the usage of data that are processed by an application inside an enclave. Outside trusted enclaves the usage restrictions are no longer enforceable, which is why shared data must never leave the enclaves.

Since SGX-enabled processors only provide limited resources for enclaves, data processing applications cannot be very comprehensive. Typically only 128 MB encrypted memory (Enclave Page Cache, EPC) is available, which limits the size of applications that can run efficiently as enclaves. Furthermore, isolating the enclaves from the rest of the system – especially the operating system – has a considerable impact on the implementation of trusted applications. SGX enclaves have to link a specially modified system library, which re-implements numerous system operations that cannot be regularly executed by enclaves due to their independence from the operating system. This includes accessing memory and files, as well as inter process communication. Since applications running inside an enclave in general cannot depend on standard libraries, implementing complex data processing applications for the proposed architecture can be cumbersome or even impossible.

4.2   Joint TPM/SGX Architecture

Only by supporting the execution of data processing applications as normal, non-enclave processes, the disadvantages of an SGX-only solution can be overcome. However, data that are released outside enclaves into normal system processes still need to be protected. Due to the isolation from the rest of the system, usage control components that are realized as SGX enclaves cannot monitor normal system processes. In order to comprehensively enforce usage restrictions on non-enclave data processing applications, we need to support a powerful usage control system that can intercept data access on a kernel level (e.g. by hooking system calls). The integrity of such usage control components can be protected by including their code in a TPM-based chain of trust. However, as described previously, in our use case TPMs cannot sufficiently protect shared data against malicious administrators. In order to combine the flexibility of TPMs with the security of an SGX-based solution, a joint approach can be taken.

To achieve this we introduce a dedicated PEP that is responsible for intercepting data accesses and enforcing decisions across all data processing applications. In order to allow for complex data processing chains, this component does not run as an enclave and is instead implemented as a kernel module. As before, a PDP enclave receives usage control policies from the data provider and evaluates them for each intercepted event. The sequence of attestations that is necessary to securely share data using this architecture is illustrated in Fig. 3. During launch the TPM builds a chain of trust and measures both the PEP and all external data processing applications. Afterwards the connector enclave verifies the other enclaves (mainly the PDP, but also applications running as enclaves) by performing local attestations. Then the connector retrieves a TPM quote, queries the desired PCR values from the TTP and verifies all information. This step replaces the previously used TPM-based remote attestation. Instead of sending the quote to the data provider, the trusted connector enclave verifies the PCR values locally. Finally, the connector enclave performs the familiar remote attestation protocol with the data provider, thereby establishing a secure channel and announcing the integrity of the enclaves, the PEP and the outside applications. After the data provider trusts the data consumer's system, he uses the established key to transmit data and usage control policies to the connector enclave. Since the external enforcement point has been attested, data may now leave the enclave into external data processing applications, if the policies allow it. The external PEP is then responsible for enforcing the usage restrictions even outside the enclaves.

The proposed system architecture combines the advantages of TPMs and SGX enclaves. While an SGX enclave is responsible for establishing the communication with data providers, the TPM safeguards the received data when they leave the enclaves for processing. The connector enclave is remotely verified by the data provider and receives the sensitive data along with their protection policies using the established secure channel. As described in the previous section, an attacker cannot intercept this communication or manipulate the transmitted information in memory, unlike when using only a TPM for attestation. Furthermore, attackers have no opportunity to impersonate a connector enclave and execute the remote attestation protocol with the data provider in order to steal sensitive data. Hence the previously described attack by duplicating attested connections is not possible with the joint architecture. On the other hand, by using an additional TPM to verify the integrity of the external system, data can be securely shared with processes outside the realm of SGX. Operating the enforcement point as a kernel module, which supervises the data usage of all running system processes, allows the execution of complex data processing applications as normal non-enclave processes. After receiving data and policies from the remote data provider, it is the responsibility of the connector enclave to issue the policy deployment and ensure that sensitive information is released outside the protected enclave only if it continues to be protected by the usage control system. For this, the connector enclave verifies the integrity of the external enforcement point by comparing the PCRs of the TPM to desired values. If an attacker tampers with the PEP in order to maliciously influence policy enforcement, the measurements will inevitably change and the PCR verification fails. In that case the connector enclave will not release any sensitive data to the outside world.

Despite the advantages of a combined approach, including a TPM brings back some of the problems that have been avoided in the SGX-only architecture. Most importantly, the TPM cannot prevent malicious administrators from accessing the unencrypted main memory of running data processing applications. However, this attack vector is only applicable for data that are in fact being processed by non-enclave applications. Given a policy scheme that is capable of describing data flows outside enclaves, the joint architecture allows original data owners to specify protection policies that prevent highly confidential information from leaving the trusted enclaves. In that case the data are safe from malicious administrators, but the complexity of supported data processing applications is limited. Furthermore, using a TPM always adds parts of the operating system to the chain of trust. This means that we have to assume the OS to be implemented correctly and free of security-critical bugs. Otherwise an attacker could

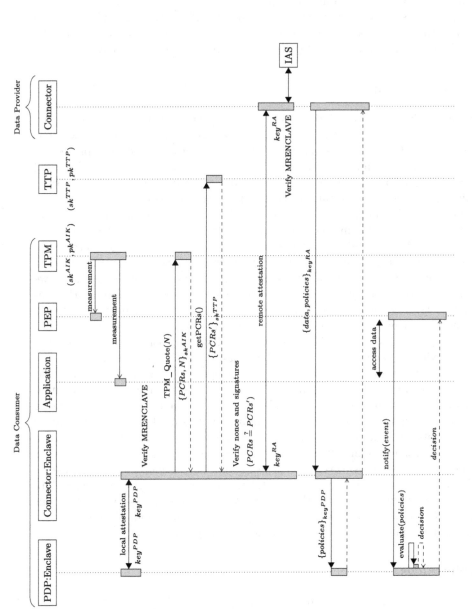

Fig. 3. A data space connector architecture based on TPMs and SGX technology. Attestation messages are not shown.

influence the enforcement point and bypass the protection mechanisms during runtime. While it is not necessary to trust the OS with the proposed SGX-only architecture, it is still a common requirement for many usage control systems. All in all, a system architecture that uses both SGX enclaves and a TPM resolves most of the attack vectors present with TPM-only solutions, while keeping the possibility of processing shared data in standard non-enclave applications.

5   Conclusion

In this work we evaluated the level of data sovereignty that can be reached by using TPMs to verify the integrity of data consumers. We have shown that especially in data sharing scenarios TPMs do not provide sufficient protection against malicious administrators from competing companies. Since TPM-based remote attestation can only identify the whole attested system as a trustworthy endpoint for the communication instead of a single process, sensitive data may be illegitimately intercepted. Furthermore, TPM-based attestation cannot adequately protect against in-memory tampering. In order to resolve these issues, we proposed an SGX-based connector architecture that enforces usage control policies even on malicious administrators. However, using SGX enclaves to process shared data considerably limits the scope of the data processing chains. Hence we proposed a joint connector architecture combining the advantages of both technologies. By including a TPM as well as SGX enclaves, this architecture supports powerful data processing applications while simultaneously preventing attacks that TPM-based systems suffer from. On the downside, using both technologies at once yields weaker security guarantees than the SGX-only solution.

Necessary future work includes the development of a policy scheme that makes it possible to distinguish data flows into enclaves from data flows into non-enclave applications. Due to the weaker security guarantees of data processing applications running outside enclaves, data providers need to be able to specify usage control policies that restrict the way their data may be processed. If multiple applications are involved in a data processing chain, this requirement needs to be enforceable across several enclaves as well. Furthermore, applying existing SGX development frameworks like SCONE[1] or Google's Asylo[2] to virtual data space architectures may ease the development of data processing applications in an SGX environment. However, the presented constraints of running data processing applications as SGX enclaves still remain problematic.

References

1. Costan, V., Devadas, S.: Intel SGX explained. IACR Cryptology Archive, p. 86 (2016)
2. D'Cunha, N.A.: Exploring the integration of memory management and trusted computing. Ph.D. thesis, Dartmouth College (2007)

---

[1] https://sconedocs.github.io/.
[2] https://asylo.dev/.

3. Delaune, S., Kremer, S., Ryan, M.D., Steel, G.: Formal analysis of protocols based on TPM state registers. In: 24th IEEE Computer Security Foundations Symposium (CSF 2011), pp. 66–80. IEEE (2011)
4. Götzfried, J., Eckert, M., Schinzel, S., Müller, T.: Cache attacks on Intel SGX. In: Proceedings of the 10th European Workshop on Systems Security, p. 2. ACM (2017)
5. Gruss, D., Lettner, J., Schuster, F., Ohrimenko, O., Haller, I., Costa, M.: Strong and efficient cache side-channel protection using hardware transactional memory. In: USENIX Security Symposium, pp. 217–233 (2017)
6. Gürgens, S., Rudolph, C., Scheuermann, D., Atts, M., Plaga, R.: Security evaluation of scenarios based on the TCG's TPM specification. In: Biskup, J., López, J. (eds.) ESORICS 2007. LNCS, vol. 4734, pp. 438–453. Springer, Heidelberg (2007). https://doi.org/10.1007/978-3-540-74835-9_29
7. Kelbert, F., Pretschner, A.: Data usage control enforcement in distributed systems. In: Proceedings of the Third ACM Conference on Data and Application Security and Privacy, pp. 71–82. ACM (2013)
8. Kocher, P., et al.: Spectre attacks: exploiting speculative execution. arXiv preprint arXiv:1801.01203 (2018)
9. Otto, B., Lohmann, S., Steinbuß, S., Teuscher, A.: IDS reference architecture model. Technical report, International Data Spaces Association (2018)
10. Park, J., Sandhu, R.: The ucon abc usage control model. ACM Trans. Inf. Syst. Secur. (TISSEC) 7(1), 128–174 (2004)
11. Scarlata, V., Johnson, S., Beaney, J., Zmijewski, P.: Supporting third party attestation for Intel SGX with Intel data center attestation primitives (2018)
12. Sparks, E.R.: A security assessment of trusted platform modules computer science. Department of Computer Science, Dartmouth College, USA, Technical report, TR2007-597 (2007)
13. TCG: Architecture overview. Specification Revision 1 (2007)
14. Wagner, P.G., Birnstill, P., Beyerer, J.: Distributed usage control enforcement through trusted platform modules and SGX enclaves. In: Proceedings of the 23rd ACM on Symposium on Access Control Models and Technologies, pp. 85–91. ACM (2018)

Secure Trust Evaluation Using Multipath and Referral Chain Methods

Mohammad G. Raeini[✉] and Mehrdad Nojoumian

Department of Computer and Electrical Engineering and Computer Science,
Florida Atlantic University, Boca Raton, FL 33431, USA
{mghasemineja2017,mnojoumian}@fau.edu

Abstract. The notions of trust and reputation have been well studied and integrated into computer networks and internet-based services, e.g., Amazon and eBay websites. Using trust and reputation as social mechanisms can enhance the quality, reliability and trustworthiness of networks or services. These social mechanisms can also be used to provide better security measures. Indeed, trust and reputation can be considered as soft security methods that compliment hard security techniques. However, data security and privacy are among the primary challenges in trust and reputation systems. We therefore propose a secure trust evaluation (STE) method in which privacy of trust values and corresponding weights are preserved. Our proposed method is constructed based on an information theoretic framework for modeling trust and two approaches that propagate trust in a network, i.e., multipath and referral chain techniques. In other words, we utilize secure multiparty computation to provide protocols by which the nodes in a network will be able to evaluate their trust values in a secure fashion. We also provide a fascinating application of our STE method in the context of network routing protocols.

Keywords: Secure trust evaluation · Secure trust measurement · Secure multiparty computation · Secure function evaluation

1 Introduction

Trust and reputation are common social mechanisms that have been used in different contexts including in human interactions, economics, multiagent systems and computer networks, among others. These social mechanisms are now well-studied and have been integrated into electronic applications and services, e.g., Amazon and eBay websites, search engines such as Google's PageRank algorithm, and social networks. These social mechanisms can also be utilized in any collaborative environments such as mining paradigms of digital currencies [19] as well as cryptographic protocols [21] to provide more trustworthy outcomes.

Trust and reputation are sometimes considered as soft security measures that compliment hard security measures such as cryptographic protocols. It is worth mentioning that, using soft security measures alongside hard security measures,

© Springer Nature Switzerland AG 2019
S. Mauw and M. Conti (Eds.): STM 2019, LNCS 11738, pp. 124–139, 2019.
https://doi.org/10.1007/978-3-030-31511-5_8

can provide more secure and trustworthy systems and networks [28,35]. In other words, integrating these social concepts into data and computation infrastructures can provide more reliable, secure and trustworthy platforms [11]. In fact, trusted computing is a term that refers to this idea and has been used in the IT security [11,37]. However, there exist many challenges in modeling and utilizing these social concepts.

First, these concepts are highly subjective in the sense that different people have different impressions about them. It should also be mentioned that these concepts are very contextual-based and time-dependent [8]. Fortunately, there has been significant attempts for modeling and measuring trust and reputation. In the computer science literature, Marsh [15] is among the first researchers who tried to provide a computational model for trust. Thereafter, other models, methods and metrics have been defined for measuring trust and reputation quantitatively. In a nutshell, there are different theories/approaches for modeling and evaluating trust and reputation concepts. Some of the well-known approaches for measuring trust include subjective logic [9,10], fuzzy logic [14], entropy-based models [32], and Demster-Shafer theory [33]. Reputation is usually evaluated based on the trust values. Some of the well-known reputation systems use simple summation, average and weighted average of trust values [11]. Other reputation systems utilize the Beta probability density function and Bayesian networks [11].

Second, there are studies [29] discussing that users are usually unwilling to provide honest feedback (ratings) in trust and reputation systems mainly due to fear of retaliation for negative ratings. As such, to have proper trust and reputation systems, it is important that such systems preserve the privacy of users' data while allowing them to perform the desired computations on their private values, e.g., trust values/rating scores of users in one another. There are different approaches for providing such systems. One approach is to use decentralized systems. Such reputation systems do not rely on any centralized authority, and thus, they are more reliable [5]. Another approach is to use cryptographic techniques, e.g., secure multiparty computation (MPC).

1.1   Our Contribution

This paper aims at addressing data security and privacy issues in trust and reputation systems. We use secure multiparty computation to provide a secure trust evaluation method. Our proposed method is based on the information theoretic framework [32] for modeling trust and two approaches that propagate trust in a network. These two approaches are referral chains in social networks and multipath trust propagation in a network. We provide two protocols that enable the nodes in a network to securely evaluate their trust values in one another. As an application, we use our proposed STE method to provide a secure network routing protocol. Our protocols can be based on any secret sharing scheme, e.g., the Shaimr's (t, n)-threshold secret sharing scheme [30]. We would like to emphasize that our protocols do not rely on any trusted third parties. In other words, the nodes in a network can perform the required computations for measuring their trust values securely. Using secure trust evaluation methods will result in more secure and trustworthy network-based systems and services.

The paper is organized as follows. In Sect. 2, we review existing works related to secure trust and reputation models. In Sect. 3, we provide the necessary preliminaries for our secure trust evaluation method. These include secure MPC based on secret sharing and an encoding approach that allows performing secure computations on real numbers. We use the floating-point representation of real numbers to perform secure computations on such numbers [1]. Note that, in our model, trust values are real numbers in $[-1, 1]$ interval. In Sect. 4, we provide our main contribution. We propose two secure protocols that are the building blocks of our STE method. We also provide a secure network routing protocol as an appealing application of the proposed STE method. Our technical discussion is presented in Sect. 5. The paper is concluded in Sect. 6.

2   Related Works

Data security and privacy are important issues in trust and reputation systems. Different approaches have been used to address such issues. Among others, we can point out approaches based on secure MPC techniques and those based on decentralized computation frameworks. In what follows, we review the previous works related to secure trust and reputation models. For comprehensive surveys related to trust and reputation systems, we refer the readers to [8,11].

In [33], two schemes for preserving the privacy of trust evidence providers were proposed. The proposed schemes use two non-colluding service parties, called authorized proxy and evaluation party, to manage the aggregated evidences and process the collected data in encrypted format. The proposed schemes are based on public key cryptography, e.g., RSA and additive homomorphic encryption such as Paillier scheme [24]. Centralized trust and reputation systems can take advantage of their users' data. To address such an issue, the authors in [2] proposed a privacy-preserving distributed reputation mechanism based on the notion of *mailboxes*. Malicious-k-shares protocol, a decentralized privacy-preserving reputation system, was proposed in [7]. Again, the protocol is based on the Paillier cryptosystem and uses source managers (e.g., the Chord distributed hash table [31]) to share the data among k agents and perform privacy-preserving distributed computations.

The privacy-preserving version of the P2PRep [3], called 3PRep, was proposed in [17]. The 3PRep enhances the P2PRep mechanism by adding two new protocols to preserve votes' privacy using semantically secure homomprphic encryption scheme. Three different schemes for privacy-preserving computations of reputation values were presented in [5]. Two of the proposed schemes use a trusted third party to calculate the reputation. The third scheme does not rely on any trusted third party. Pavlov et al. [25] argued that supporting perfect privacy in a decentralized reputation system is impossible. They then proposed three probabilistic schemes that are able to support partial privacy in decentralized additive reputation systems. The proposed schemes use secret splitting and secret sharing schemes, e.g., the Pederson secret sharing scheme [26].

There are other works related to privacy-preserving reputation systems. In [6], the authors provided the k-shares protocol, which was inspired by the protocol of [25]. The advantage of k-shares protocol is that it has a lower message complexity compared to the protocol proposed in [25], i.e., $O(n)$ versus $O(n^2)$. Finally, the authors of [4] introduced a dynamic privacy-preserving reputation system. This scheme is able to deal with the dynamic structure of some decentralized reputation systems wherein nodes (users) in the network leave and join the network constantly.

3 Preliminaries

3.1 Secure Multiparty Computation

Secure multiparty computation (MPC) is a computational model in which a group of parties can evaluate a public function on their private data without revealing their data. This idea was first introduced by Yao [34]. Secure MPC, a.k.a., secure function evaluation (SFE) [16], can be realized using cryptographic primitives such as secret sharing schemes, homomorphic encryption techniques and Yao's Garbled circuits. In secret sharing-based MPC, a secret sharing scheme, e.g., the Shamir's (t, n)-threshold secret sharing [30], is used to generate and distribute the shares of secrets (private data) among the participating parties. The computations are then carried out on the shares of those secrets. At the end of the computations, an appropriate technique, e.g., the Lagrange interpolation, is used to obtain the result of the computation.

Secure MPC Based on Secret Sharing. Secure MPC based on the Shamir's secret sharing scheme works as follows. First of all, it should be noted that in secure multiparty computation there are n parties where each has a private value, which can be considered as a secret. Moreover, the computations are performed in a finite field such as Z_p, where p is a prime number. In order to perform a computation (evaluate a function) using secure MPC, each party first selects a polynomial $f(x) \in Z_p[x]$ whose coefficient are random values in Z_p and its constant term is the party's secret/private value. Mathematically speaking, each party P_i selects a polynomial as follows:

$$f_i(x) = \alpha_i + a_{i,1}x + a_{i,2}x^2 + \cdots + a_{i,t-1}x^{t-1}.$$

where α_i is the secret of party P_i, for $i = 1, 2, \ldots, n$ and $a_{i,1}, a_{i,2} \ldots, a_{i,t-1}$ are random numbers in Z_p. Moreover, t is the threshold of the secret sharing scheme. Each party then evaluates its polynomial on n points, such as $1, 2, \ldots, n$, to generate the shares of its secret. The parties then distribute the shares of their secrets among each other. To evaluate a function securely, the parties perform the required computations on the shares of their data. They finally execute Lagrange interpolation on their updated shares to obtain/reconstruct the result of their computation, i.e., the function value. Secure MPC based on secret sharing is illustrated in Fig. 1.

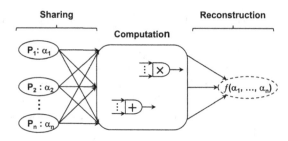

Fig. 1. Secure multiparty computation using secret sharing [18].

3.2   Floating-Point Representation of Real Numbers

Secure computation techniques primary work based on integer numbers, i.e., finite field elements. In our secure trust evaluation method, the trust values are rational numbers in $[-1, +1]$ interval. Therefore, we need to use secure MPC techniques on real numbers. There are different encoding approaches, e.g., floating-point representation that allows secure computation techniques to be used on real numbers. In this paper, we utilize the floating-point representation of real numbers, presented in [1], although other approaches can be used.

Floating-point representation is a method to represent real numbers using a fixed-precision significand v and an exponent p. The exponent p defines how the real number should be scaled in a given base. For instance, when the base is 2, the representation would be $v \cdot 2^p$. In order to have a proper representation, the authors in [1] used a 4-tuple (v, p, z, s) with base 2 to represent each real value u. In this representation, v is an l-bit significand and p is a k-bit exponent. Moreover, z is a binary value which is 1 if and only if $u = 0$, and s is the sign bit. The sign bit s is set when the value u is negative. For a real value u, the representation will be $u = (1 - 2s)(1 - z)v \cdot 2^p$.

4   Secure Trust Evaluation (STE)

4.1   Information Theoretic Framework for Modeling Trust

The concept of trust (in human interactions or social networks) is very related to the concept of uncertainty in information theory. This subtle connection was formalized in [32], wherein an information theoretic framework for modeling trust was introduced. Due to the similarity between trust and uncertainty, trust can be measured by entropy, which is a well-accepted concept in information theory. Having said that, two trust models were proposed in [32], an entropy-based trust model and a probability-based trust model. For the probability-based trust model, two approaches were studied, a Binomial distribution and a Bayesian approach. The authors then discussed that the Bayesian approach captures the concept of uncertainty more appropriately.

The information theoretic framework for modeling trust works based on the observations of nodes. In what follows, we briefly explain how trust is evaluated in this framework. Assume a network is given and node A in the network wants to evaluate its trust (for performing an action, e.g., packet forwarding) in another node, say node X. To do so, the past behaviors of node X regarding that specific action is considered. In the trust model based on the Bayesian approach, first the probability of node X performing that action is calculated. If node X has been asked to perform an action N times, and among them, node X has performed that action k times, the probability of performing that action in the next request, i.e., the $(N + 1)$-th request, is defined as follows [32]:

$$Pr(V(N + 1)) = \frac{k + 1}{N + 2} \tag{1}$$

wherein k is the number of times that node X has performed a specific action upon N total requests. In fact, $Pr(V(N + 1))$ is the probability that node X will perform that specific action in the $(N + 1)$-th request. Note that $V(i)$ is the random variable of performing an action at the i-th request [32]. In the information theoretic framework for modeling trust, trust can also be calculated as entropy, which in fact measures the uncertainty. Having a probabilistic trust value, the entropy-based trust value of node A in node X for performing an action is defined as follows [32]:

$$T(A : X, action) = \begin{cases} 1 - H(p), & \text{for } 0.5 \leq p \leq 1 \\ H(p) - 1, & \text{for } 0 \leq p < 0.5 \end{cases} \tag{2}$$

where $H(p) = -p \, \log_2(p) - (1 - p) \, \log_2(1 - p)$ and p is the probability as defined in Eq. 1. The information theoretic framework [32] is an elegant way of modeling the concept of trust. There are a few points that should be emphasized. The trust values in the information theoretic framework can be represented as probability-based values or entropy-based values. Equation 2 shows the relation between these two types of trust values and how they can be converted to each other. It is also important to note that probability-based trust values are in $[0, 1]$ interval, whereas entropy-based trust values vary within $[-1, 1]$ interval. In our STE method, the trust values are in $[-1, 1]$ interval.

4.2   Secure Trust Evaluation Using Multipath Trust Propagation

Trust in a network can propagate in different ways. In this section, we briefly discuss how a node can evaluate its trust in another node using the multipath trust propagation approach. In the multipath trust propagation, a node (say node A_1) wants to evaluate its trust in another node (say node B). To this end, node A_1 asks other nodes, say nodes A_2, A_3, ..., A_n, in the network to reveal their opinions about node B. Figure 2 shows a sample multipath trust propagation in a network.

After receiving the trust values (from other nodes, i.e., A_2, A_3, ..., A_n), node A_1 calculates its trust in node B as follows:

$$T_{A_1 B} = Trust(A_1 : B) = \sum_{i=1}^{n} w_i T_i \tag{3}$$

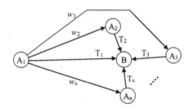

Fig. 2. Multipath trust propagation [32].

where T_1 is the trust value of node A_1 in node B (i.e., based on direct observation) and w_1 is the weight that node A_1 considers for its direct trust value in node B. Moreover, T_i, for $i = 2, \ldots, n$, is the trust value (opinion) of node A_i in node B, which is returned from node A_i to node A_1. Also, w_i is the weight that node A_1 considers for its trust in node A_i for $i = 2, \ldots, n$; see Fig. 2. Note that w_i-s are selected by node A_1 such that $0 \leq w_i \leq 1$ and $\sum_{i=1}^{n} w_i = 1$. Since $0 \leq w_i \leq 1$ and $-1 \leq T_i \leq 1$, we will have $-1 \leq T_{A_1 B} \leq 1$. The maximum value that $T_{A_1 B}$ can get is when $T_i = 1$. In that case, $T_{A_1 B} = \sum_{i=1}^{n} w_i T_i \leq \sum_{i=1}^{n} w_i = 1$. The minimum value that $T_{A_1 B}$ can get is when $T_i = -1$, where we have $T_{A_1 B} = \sum_{i=1}^{n} w_i T_i \geq \sum_{i=1}^{n} w_i(-1) = -1 \times \sum_{i=1}^{n} w_i = -1$. Note that it is assumed $\sum_{i=1}^{n} w_i = 1$.

We now propose a protocol that allows a node in a network, e.g., node A_1, to evaluate its trust in another node, e.g., node B, using the multipath trust propagation approach. In fact, the nodes on the multipath network perform their computations using secure multiparty computation. To this end, the nodes use the Shamir's secret sharing scheme to share their secrets (in this case, their trust values in each other) and perform computations in a secure fashion. Note that the nodes on the multipath, illustrated in Fig. 2, need to securely evaluate the function represented in Eq. 3. In this equation, w_i's are private values of A_1 while T_i is the private value of node A_i, for $i = 2, \ldots, n$. Protocol 1 shows our secure trust evaluation method using the multipath trust propagation approach.

4.3   Trust Evaluation Using Referral Chains

The idea of using referral chains (referral graphs) in trust and reputation systems was introduced in [35] and further studied in [20,36]. Yu and Singh [35] defined a referral chain as follows. Given the graph representation of a network (e.g., a social network), a referral chain from node A_0 to node A_n is basically a path between the two nodes. Such a referral chain is represented as $\chi = \langle A_0, A_1, \ldots, A_n \rangle$, where A_i is a neighbor of A_{i+1}.

The concept of referral chain in a network can capture the notion of trust propagation in a good way. In [35], the authors used this concept for estimating the quality of nodes in a trust network, in which the trust value of a node (say node A) in another node (say node B) is measured based on three factors [20,35]: A's direct observation of B, the B's neighbors opinion about B, and the A's opinion about the neighbors of B. Having the trust values of the nodes on

Protocol 1. Secure Trust Evaluation Using the Multipath Approach

Input: Trust values $\{T_1, T_2, \ldots, T_n\}$ and weights $\{w_1, w_2, \ldots, w_n\}$.

Output: Calculates $T_{A_1 B} = \sum_{i=1}^{n} w_i T_i$ using secure MPC.

1 Each party (node) A_i, for $i = 1, 2, \ldots, n$, uses floating-point representation to encode its input into a single finite field element.

2 Each party A_i uses the Shamir's secret sharing scheme to generate the shares of its input T_i. Party A_i selects a polynomial as follows:

$$f_i(x) = T_i + a_{i,1}x + a_{i,2}x^2 + \cdots + a_{i,t-1}x^{t-1}.$$

where T_i is the trust value of node A_i in node B.

3 Party A_1 uses the Shamir's secret sharing scheme to generate the shares of its weights, i.e., w_i's. A_1 selects a polynomial as follows:

$$g_i(x) = w_i + b_{i,1}x + b_{i,2}x^2 + \cdots + b_{i,t-1}x^{t-1}.$$

where w_i is the weight that party A_1 considers for node A_i.

4 Each party distributes the shares of its input among all parties. The share-exchange matrix [23] (wherein party A_i generates the i-th row and receives the i-th column) is as follows:

$$E_f = \begin{bmatrix} f_1(1) & f_1(2) & \ldots & f_1(n) \\ \vdots & \vdots & \ddots & \vdots \\ f_n(1) & f_n(2) & \ldots & f_n(n) \end{bmatrix} \begin{matrix} \leftarrow \text{Shares of } T_1 \text{ generated by } A_1 \text{ using } f_1(x) \\ \vdots \\ \leftarrow \text{Shares of } T_n \text{ generated by } A_n \text{ using } f_n(x) \end{matrix}$$

5 Party A_1 distributes the shares of its weights w_i's, for $i = 1, \ldots, n$. The share-exchange matrix is as follows:

$$E_g = \begin{bmatrix} g_1(1) & g_1(2) & \ldots & g_1(n) \\ \vdots & \vdots & \ddots & \vdots \\ g_n(1) & g_n(2) & \ldots & g_n(n) \end{bmatrix} \begin{matrix} \leftarrow \text{Shares of } w_1 \text{ generated by } A_1 \text{ using } g_1(x) \\ \vdots \\ \leftarrow \text{Shares of } w_n \text{ generated by } A_1 \text{ using } g_n(x) \end{matrix}$$

6 Party A_i, for $i = 1, 2, \ldots, n$, performs the following computation:

$$T^i_{A_1 B} = \sum_{k=1}^{n} g_k(i) \times f_k(i).$$

where $g_k(i)$ is the share of a weight that party A_i has received from party A_1 and $f_k(i)$ is the share of T_k that party A_i has received from party A_k. Moreover, $T^i_{A_1 B}$ means the share of party A_i of trust value $T_{A_1 B}$. Note that after each multiplication, $g_k(i) \times f_k(i)$, the participating parties must execute a degree reduction protocol, as explained in [22].

7 Each party A_i, for $i = 2, 3, \ldots, n$, sends the result of the computation, in the previous step, to party A_1.

8 A_1 uses Lagrange interpolation to obtain the final result, i.e., $T_{A_1 B}$, as follows:

$$T_{A_1 B} = \sum_{i=1}^{n} (\prod_{\substack{k=1 \\ k \neq i}}^{n} \frac{k}{k - i} \times T^i_{A_1 B})$$

a referral chain, the trust over the referral chain propagates according to the trust propagation operator; see Definitions 5 and 6 of [35]. In our secure trust evaluation method, we consider a general case of a referral chain consisting of n nodes as illustrated in Fig. 3:

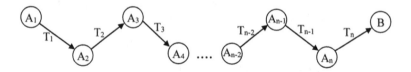

Fig. 3. A referral chain in a network [35].

The trust value of node A_1 in the last node on the referral chain, i.e., node B, is calculated as follows [35]:

$$T_{A_1 B} = T_{A_1 A_2} \otimes T_{A_2 A_3} \otimes \cdots \otimes T_{A_n B} \tag{4}$$

where $T_{A_i A_{i+1}}$, for $i = 1, 2, \ldots, n-1$, is the trust value of node A_i in node A_{i+1} and it is represented as T_i in Fig. 3. Moreover, $\otimes$ represents the trust propagation operator, which is defined as follows:

Definition 1. $x \otimes y :=$ if $(x \geq 0 \wedge y \geq 0)$ then $x \times y$; else $-|x \times y|$ [35].

The trust propagation on a referral chain is then defined as follows:

Definition 2. For any k, where $k \in \{1, 2, \ldots, n\}$, the trust of A_1 in A_k is defined as: $T_{A_1 A_k} = T_{A_1 A_2} \otimes \cdots \otimes T_{A_{k-1} A_k}$ [35].

In the following, we propose a protocol that enables a node in a network to evaluate its trust in another node through a referral chain. The main idea is that the nodes on the referral chain use secure MPC based on secret sharing to carry out the trust evaluation computations, i.e., to evaluate Eq. 4 in a secure fashion. The procedure of secure trust evaluation on a referral chain is described in Protocol 2. Note that, in Protocol 2, the trust value of node A_i in node A_{i+1} is represented as T_i, where $i = 1, \ldots, n$. That is, $T_i = T_{A_i A_{i+1}}$.

To execute the trust propagation operator, i.e., $\otimes$ in Definition 1 and Eq. 4, two trust values are compared with zero (i.e., if $x \geq 0 \wedge y \geq 0$) before the multiplication of each pair of trust values. Thus, in order to carry out the trust propagation operator in Protocol 2, each pair of trust values need to be securely compared with zero. This can be done in different ways. One solution is to use a secure comparison protocol, e.g., a protocol from Table IV of [27]. Another approach is to use secure MPC for determining the sign of the final trust value, i.e., $T_{A_1 B}$, as follows. Each party (node) A_i encodes and shares the sign of its trust value T_i: If A_i's trust value is positive (i.e., $0 \leq T_i < 1$), then A_i shares 0 among all parties. If A_i's trust value is negative (i.e., $-1 \leq T_i < 0$), then A_i shares 1 among all parties. Parties then exchange and add their shares and

---

Protocol 2. Secure Trust Evaluation Using the Referral Chain Approach

---

Input: Trust values $\{T_1, T_2, \ldots, T_n\}$, where $T_i = T_{A_i A_{i+1}}$,

Output: Calculates $T_{A_1 B} = T_1 \otimes \cdots \otimes T_n$ using secure MPC.

1 Each party A_i, i.e., each node on the referral chain, uses floating-point representation to encode its input T_i into a single finite field element.

2 Each party A_i uses the Shamir's secret sharing scheme to generate the shares of its trust value T_i. Party A_i selects a polynomial as follows:

$$f_i(x) = T_i + a_{i,1}x + a_{i,2}x^2 + \cdots + a_{i,t-1}x^{t-1}.$$

where T_i is the trust value of node A_i in node A_{i+1} on the chain.

3 Each party A_i distributes the shares of its trust value among all parties. The share-exchange matrix [23] (wherein party A_i generates the i-th row and receives the i-th column) is as follows:

$$E_f = \begin{bmatrix} f_1(1) & f_1(2) & \cdots & f_1(n) \\ \vdots & \vdots & \ddots & \vdots \\ f_n(1) & f_n(2) & \cdots & f_n(n) \end{bmatrix} \begin{matrix} \leftarrow \text{Shares of } T_1 \text{ generated by } A_1 \text{ using } f_1(x) \\ \\ \vdots \\ \leftarrow \text{Shares of } T_n \text{ generated by } A_n \text{ using } f_n(x) \end{matrix}$$

4 Each party A_i multiplies its received shares:

$$T^i_{A_1 B} = \prod_{k=1,\ldots,n} f_k(i)$$

where $f_k(i)$ is the share that party A_i has received from party A_k where $k = 1, 2, \ldots, n$. Moreover, $T^i_{A_1 B}$ means the share of party A_i of trust value $T_{A_1 B}$. Note that, after each multiplication, the participating parties must execute a degree reduction protocol as shown in [22].

5 Each party A_i for $i = 2, 3, \ldots, n$ sends its result of the multiplication, in the previous step, to party A_1.

6 Party A_1 uses Lagrange interpolation to obtain the final result, i.e., $T_{A_1 B}$:

$$T_{A_1 B} = \sum_{i=1}^{n} \left(\prod_{\substack{k=1 \\ k \neq i}}^{n} \frac{k}{k - i} \times T^i_{A_1 B} \right)$$

---

send the results to party A_1. By obtaining the final result (using the Lagrange interpolation), party A_1 can determine the sign of the final trust value as follows: If the final result is 0, the sign of the final trust value (i.e., $T_{A_1 B}$) is positive. Otherwise, it is negative.

It is worth mentioning that a disadvantage of the referral chain approach is that, on long chains, the trust propagation operator fades the trust value of node A_1 in node B [20]. An alternative solution for the referral chain approach is to use a weighted average of the trust values on the chain, where the weights decrease monotonically, i.e., $1 \geq w_1 > w_2 > \cdots > w_n \geq 0$. Note that w_i's are selected such that $\sum_{i=1}^{n} w_i = 1$. In such a monotonically-decreasing weighted referral chain, the trust value $T_{A_1 B}$ can be securely evaluated using Protocol 1.

4.4   Secure Network Routing

The concept of trust, as a soft security measure, can be used for improving the quality of network services in different ways. For instance, trust models can improve network routing protocols and provide malicious-node-detection capability [32]. An important thing in most networks is the security and privacy of the nodes' data. It is important for the nodes in a network to not reveal their private data, e.g., their trust values [29, 32]. This is because, if trust values are revealed, nodes with high trust values may be compromised by adversaries. This can reduce the trustworthiness of the whole network.

In this section, we use our proposed protocols to provide a secure network routing protocol. By using the secure network routing protocol, a node in a network can find a high quality route in a network while the nodes' private data is not revealed. Secure network routing protocols can provide a better networking platform in the sense that adversaries will not be able to figure out how an action, e.g., packet forwarding in a network, is carried out. We first need to define the quality of a route in a network.

The Quality of a Route in a Network. Assume a network is given and node A and node N_{dest} are two nodes in that network. Moreover, suppose node A intends to perform an action in the network, e.g., to forward a packet to node N_{dest}. There are usually different routes in the network for performing such an action. In order to execute the packet forwarding action with a higher chance of success, node A can determine the quality of each route prior to forwarding its packet to the destination. One approach for defining the quality of a route in a network is based on the trust values of nodes on that route [32]. Suppose R is a route in a network and $\{N_i\}$ represents the set of all nodes on route R. Similar to [32], we define and calculate the quality of route R as follows:

$$Quality(R) = \begin{cases} \prod_i T_i & \text{if } T_i > 0 \; \forall \text{ nodes } N_i \text{ on route } R \\ \min\{T_i\} & \text{otherwise} \end{cases} \tag{5}$$

where T_i is the trust value of node A in node N_i on route R. Equation 5 is basically multiplications of trust values on route R. In cases that there are nodes with negative trust values on the route, we define the quality of route as the minimum trust value, i.e., the smallest negative trust value.

We now propose a protocol that enables a node in a network to evaluate the quality of a route in a secure manner. Our proposed secure network routing protocol works as follows. Assume node A intends to evaluate the quality of route R. Node A evaluates the trust value of each node on the route using the secure trust evaluation protocols (Protocol 1 and Protocol 2). Then, node A calculates the quality of the route using Eq. 5. To find a high quality route, node A must calculate the quality of different possible routes (to its desired destination) and find the route with the highest quality. The secure network routing protocol is provided in Protocol 3. Note that we assumed each node, including node A, has a trust record on which the trust values are stored [32].

Protocol 3. Secure Network Routing Protocol

Input: Nodes' trust records, i.e., nodes observations or opinions.

Output: A high quality route in the network from node A to node N_{dest}.

1 Let $\{S_i\}$ denote the set of all nodes on all possible routes between node A and node N_{dest} in the network.

2 **for** *any node* S_i **do**

3   **if** *node A has a trust record about node S_i* **then** Node A uses that trust record.

4   **else** Node A sends trust recommendation request about node S_i to other nodes. Node A collaboratively with other nodes use Protocol 1 and Protocol 2 to securely evaluate its trust value in node S_i.

5 Let R denote a particular route in the network and let $\{N_i\}$ denote the set of all nodes on route R. Let T_i denote the trust value of node A in node N_i. Node A calculates the quality of route R as follows:

$$Quality(R) = \begin{cases} \prod_i T_i & \text{if } T_i > 0 \ \forall \text{ nodes } N_i \text{ on } R \\ \min\{T_i\} & \text{otherwise} \end{cases}$$

Note that the above multiplication is performed locally by node A. However, each T_i is computed securely when node A does not have a trust record about node N_i; see step 4.

6 Let $\{R_i\}$ denote the set of routes from node A to node N_{dest} in the network among which A wants to find a good quality route. Node A selects a route which has a good quality, e.g., larger than a threshold or the route with the maximum quality, as follows:

$$R^* = argmax_{R_i}\{Quality(R_i)\}$$

7 Node A updates its trust records using the recent observations and calculated trust values.

8 Node A initiates its desired action on the high quality route, i.e., route R^*.

---

5 Technical Discussion

In this paper, we introduced a secure trust evaluation (STE) method. Our proposed approach is based on the information theoretic framework for modeling trust and two approaches that propagate trust in a given network, i.e., multipath trust propagation and referral chains. The Beta reputation system [12] is a specific case of the information theoretic framework for modeling trust. Note that the trust value in the information theoretic framework is measured using

Eq. 1 in Sect. 4. In the Beta reputation system, the reputation of a user is calculated as $\frac{r+1}{r+s+2}$ (see [12] and [13]). The Beta reputation system is one of the commonly referred reputation systems in the literature. Thus, our secure trust evaluation method can be used wherever the Beta reputation system is applicable. For instance, our proposed protocols can be used in computer networks and Internet-based services that use the Beta reputation system.

It is worth mentioning that our proposed STE method is a decentralized trust evaluation system. This has its own advantages and makes a network more reliable and trustworthy because the nodes in a network do not reveal their private values to any third party or any other nodes. Recall that the secure protocols (Protocol 1 and Protocol 2) in our trust evaluation method use secure MPC and secret sharing schemes, e.g., the Shamir's (t, n)-threshold secret sharing scheme, which are powerful tools for secure function evaluation.

Another fact in many privacy-preserving trust and reputation systems is that, regardless of using the cryptographic primitives or any other privacy measures, a ratee in a reputation system can figure out the impact of a rater's feedback (rate) on its reputation [13]. This is because a feedback is usually provided after a transaction is completed. Therefore, the ratee knows when the rater has left his feedback. The ratee can then see the impact of that feedback on its reputation. Although the ratee might not be able to figure out the exact feedback rate, he will be able to figure out if the feedback is positive or negative.

Our proposed secure trust evaluation method addresses the aforementioned issue appropriately. In our model, when a node (say node A) in a network intends to evaluate its trust in another node (say node B), node A asks other nodes for their ratings about node B. The process of evaluating the trust value of node A in node B is carried out in such a way that node B may not even notice its reputation has been evaluated by other nodes. This makes sense because, in a decentralized trust and reputation system, the nodes are witnesses for each others' behavior. Recall that in our trust model, the trust value of a node is evaluated as a weighted average of other nodes' ratings; see Eq. 3.

Finally, the security analysis of our protocols is inherited from the security of the underlying secret sharing scheme, which is the Shamir's scheme. In our proposed protocols, the parties use this scheme to generate shares of their secrets, i.e., trust values. They then perform their computations on the shares of trust values rather than trust values themselves. Note that our protocols work in a semi-honest (passive) adversarial model. In other words, we assumed that the nodes in the network are honest-but-curious. In a passive adversarial model, the participating parties act honestly and follow the protocols' rules but they are curious to learn other parties' private data. It is worth mentioning that our protocols can deal with active adversaries if we utilize verifiable secret sharing.

6   Concluding Remarks

In this paper, we introduced a secure trust evaluation (STE) method. Our STE method consists of two protocols that allow the nodes in a network to securely evaluate their trust values in one another. The proposed protocols in our STE method use secure multiparty computation based on the Shamir's secret sharing scheme to guarantee the security and privacy of the parties' private data. As an application, we also proposed a secure network routing protocol that shows how our proposed STE method can be used for improving network routing protocols.

Furthermore, our proposed STE method can be used in different networks for providing more reliable and trustworthy services. Our STE method relies on the information theoretic framework for modeling trust, which is a powerful trust model. Besides, our STE method can be utilized in other trust and reputation systems, e.g., the Beta reputation system and the weighted average reputation model. As stated earlier, soft security measures such as trust and reputation mechanisms can compliment hard security measures to provide more reliable and trustworthy networks. Therefore, consideration should be given to further improve trust and reputation systems.

Acknowledgment. Research was sponsored by the Army Research Office and was accomplished under Grant Number W911NF-18-1-0483. The views and conclusions contained in this document are those of the authors and should not be interpreted as representing the official policies, either expressed or implied, of the Army Research Office or the U.S. Government. The U.S. Government is authorized to reproduce and distribute reprints for Government purposes notwithstanding any copyright notation herein.

References

1. Aliasgari, M., Blanton, M., Zhang, Y., Steele, A.: Secure computation on floating point numbers. In: NDSS (2013)
2. Anceaume, E., Guette, G., Lajoie-Mazenc, P., Prigent, N., Tong, V.V.T.: A privacy preserving distributed reputation mechanism. In: 2013 IEEE International Conference on Communications (ICC), pp. 1951–1956. IEEE (2013)
3. Aringhieri, R., Damiani, E., Di Vimercati, S.D.C., Paraboschi, S., Samarati, P.: Fuzzy techniques for trust and reputation management in anonymous peer-to-peer systems. J. Am. Soc. Inform. Sci. Technol. **57**(4), 528–537 (2006)
4. Clark, M.R., Stewart, K., Hopkinson, K.M.: Dynamic, privacy-preserving decentralized reputation systems. IEEE Trans. Mob. Comput. **16**(9), 2506–2517 (2017)
5. Gudes, E., Gal-Oz, N., Grubshtein, A.: Methods for computing trust and reputation while preserving privacy. In: Gudes, E., Vaidya, J. (eds.) DBSec 2009. LNCS, vol. 5645, pp. 291–298. Springer, Heidelberg (2009). https://doi.org/10.1007/978-3-642-03007-9_20
6. Hasan, O., Brunie, L., Bertino, E.: Preserving privacy of feedback providers in decentralized reputation systems. Comput. Secur. **31**(7), 816–826 (2012)
7. Hasan, O., Brunie, L., Bertino, E., Shang, N.: A decentralized privacy preserving reputation protocol for the malicious adversarial model. IEEE Trans. Inf. Forensics Secur. **8**(6), 949–962 (2013)
8. Hendrikx, F., Bubendorfer, K., Chard, R.: Reputation systems: a survey and taxonomy. J. Parallel Distrib. Comput. **75**, 184–197 (2015)
9. Josang, A.: An algebra for assessing trust in certification chains. In: Proceedings of the Network and Distributed Systems Security Symposium (NDSS 1999). The Internet Society (1999)

10. Jøsang, A.: A logic for uncertain probabilities. Int. J. Uncertain. Fuzziness Knowl.-Based Syst. **9**(03), 279–311 (2001)
11. Jøsang, A., Ismail, R., Boyd, C.: A survey of trust and reputation systems for online service provision. Decis. Support Syst. **43**(2), 618–644 (2007)
12. Jsang, A., Ismail, R.: The beta reputation system. In: Proceedings of the 15th Bled Electronic Commerce Conference, vol. 5, pp. 2502–2511 (2002)
13. Kerschbaum, F.: A verifiable, centralized, coercion-free reputation system. In: Proceedings of the 8th ACM Workshop on Privacy in the Electronic Society, pp. 61–70. ACM (2009)
14. Manchala, D.W.: Trust metrics, models and protocols for electronic commerce transactions. In: Proceedings of the 18th International Conference on Distributed Computing Systems (Cat. No. 98CB36183), pp. 312–321. IEEE (1998)
15. Marsh, S.P.: Formalising trust as a computational concept. Ph.D. thesis, University of Stirling (1994)
16. Micali, S., Rogaway, P.: Secure computation. In: Feigenbaum, J. (ed.) CRYPTO 1991. LNCS, vol. 576, pp. 392–404. Springer, Heidelberg (1992). https://doi.org/10.1007/3-540-46766-1_32
17. Nithyanand, R., Raman, K.: Fuzzy privacy preserving peer-to-peer reputation management. IACR Cryptology ePrint Archive 2009, 442 (2009)
18. Nojoumian, M.: Novel secret sharing and commitment schemes for cryptographic applications. Ph.D. thesis, Department of Computer Science, University of Waterloo, Canada (2012)
19. Nojoumian, M., Golchubian, A., Njilla, L., Kwiat, K., Kamhoua, C.: Incentivizing blockchain miners to avoid dishonest mining strategies by a reputation-based paradigm. In: Arai, K., Kapoor, S., Bhatia, R. (eds.) SAI 2018. AISC, vol. 857, pp. 1118–1134. Springer, Cham (2019). https://doi.org/10.1007/978-3-030-01177-2_81
20. Nojoumian, M., Lethbridge, T.C.: A new approach for the trust calculation in social networks. In: Filipe, J., Obaidat, M.S. (eds.) ICETE 2006. CCIS, vol. 9, pp. 64–77. Springer, Heidelberg (2008). https://doi.org/10.1007/978-3-540-70760-8_6
21. Nojoumian, M., Stinson, D.R.: Socio-rational secret sharing as a new direction in rational cryptography. In: Grossklags, J., Walrand, J. (eds.) GameSec 2012. LNCS, vol. 7638, pp. 18–37. Springer, Heidelberg (2012). https://doi.org/10.1007/978-3-642-34266-0_2
22. Nojoumian, M., Stinson, D.R.: On dealer-free dynamic threshold schemes. Adv. Math. Commun. (AMC) **7**(1), 39–56 (2013)
23. Nojoumian, M., Stinson, D.R., Grainger, M.: Unconditionally secure social secret sharing scheme. IET Inf. Secur. (IFS) Spec. Issue Multi-Agent Distrib. Inf. Secur. **4**(4), 202–211 (2010)
24. Paillier, P.: Public-key cryptosystems based on composite degree residuosity classes. In: Stern, J. (ed.) EUROCRYPT 1999. LNCS, vol. 1592, pp. 223–238. Springer, Heidelberg (1999). https://doi.org/10.1007/3-540-48910-X_16
25. Pavlov, E., Rosenschein, J.S., Topol, Z.: Supporting privacy in decentralized additive reputation systems. In: Jensen, C., Poslad, S., Dimitrakos, T. (eds.) iTrust 2004. LNCS, vol. 2995, pp. 108–119. Springer, Heidelberg (2004). https://doi.org/10.1007/978-3-540-24747-0_9
26. Pedersen, T.P.: Non-interactive and information-theoretic secure verifiable secret sharing. In: Feigenbaum, J. (ed.) CRYPTO 1991. LNCS, vol. 576, pp. 129–140. Springer, Heidelberg (1992). https://doi.org/10.1007/3-540-46766-1_9
27. Raeini, M.G., Nojoumian, M.: Comprehensive survey on secure comparison protocols. Tecnical report (2019)

28. Rasmusson, L., Jansson, S.: Simulated social control for secure internet commerce (position paper). In: Proceedings, New Security Paradigms Workshop, Lake Arrowhead (1996)
29. Resnick, P., Zeckhauser, R.: Trust among strangers in internet transactions: Empirical analysis of Ebay's reputation system. In: The Economics of the Internet and E-commerce, pp. 127–157. Emerald Group Publishing Limited (2002)
30. Shamir, A.: How to share a secret. Commun. ACM **22**(11), 612–613 (1979)
31. Stoica, I., Morris, R., Karger, D., Kaashoek, M.F., Balakrishnan, H.: Chord: a scalable peer-to-peer lookup service for internet applications. ACM SIGCOMM Comput. Commun. Rev. **31**(4), 149–160 (2001)
32. Sun, Y.L., Yu, W., Han, Z., Liu, K.R.: Information theoretic framework of trust modeling and evaluation for ad hoc networks. IEEE J. Sel. Areas Commun. **24**(2), 305–317 (2006)
33. Yan, Z., Ding, W., Niemi, V., Vasilakos, A.V.: Two schemes of privacy-preserving trust evaluation. Future Gener. Comput. Syst. **62**, 175–189 (2016)
34. Yao, A.C.: Protocols for secure computations. In: 23rd Annual Symposium on Foundations of Computer Science, SFCS 1908, pp. 160–164. IEEE (1982)
35. Yu, B., Singh, M.P.: A social mechanism of reputation management in electronic communities. In: Klusch, M., Kerschberg, L. (eds.) CIA 2000. LNCS (LNAI), vol. 1860, pp. 154–165. Springer, Heidelberg (2000). https://doi.org/10.1007/978-3-540-45012-2_15
36. Yu, B., Singh, M.P.: An evidential model of distributed reputation management. In: Proceedings of the First International Joint Conference on Autonomous Agents and Multiagent Systems: Part 1, pp. 294–301. ACM (2002)
37. Zyskind, G., Nathan, O., et al.: Decentralizing privacy: using blockchain to protect personal data. In: 2015 IEEE Security and Privacy Workshops (SPW), pp. 180–184. IEEE (2015)

Personal Cross-Platform Reputation

Johannes Blömer and Nils Löken[(✉)]

Paderborn University, Paderborn, Germany
{johannes.bloemer,nils.loeken}@uni-paderborn.de

Abstract. We propose a novel personal reputation system for cross-platform reputation. We observe that, in certain usage scenarios, e.g. crowd work, the rater anonymity property typically imposed on reputation systems is not necessary. Instead, we propose a relaxed notion of rater anonymity that is more applicable in the crowd work scenario. This allows us to construct a secure personal reputation system from simple cryptographic primitives.

1 Introduction

Crowd workers, who perform tasks of variable complexity in a range of fields, e.g. design things, develop software, visit places in their area to take photographs, or generally serve as a distributed workforce for solving simple tasks, often operate on multiple platforms when selling their services to requesters, who seek solutions to their tasks. Platforms serve the purpose of bringing crowd workers and requesters together, typically focussing on a particular type of task, i.e. there are platforms for designers, text creators, software developers, etc. These platforms organize their work force, handle workers' payments, and enable requesters to contact specific workers if necessary—this feature would be of particular interest for platforms specializing in creative tasks.

Typically, platforms operate reputation systems to gather and provide information on requester satisfaction, e.g. satisfaction with the solutions a crowd worker provided. Such information is then displayed to other potential requesters under the assumption that the potential customer or requester would be satisfied with buying from a particular crowd worker if previous requesters were satisfied [10]. Therefore, it is important for crowd workers to build and maintain a good reputation.

However, since reputation systems are presently operated by platforms, there is a legitimate threat of vendor lock-in, i.e. crowd workers cannot reasonably switch platforms without losing all of their reputation. On the other hand, crowd workers often operate on multiple platforms in order to compensate for low numbers of offered tasks on individual platforms. Workers operating on multiple platforms can be expected to have lower reputation scores than their counterparts

---

This work was partially supported by the Ministry of Culture and Science of the German State of North Rhine-Westphalia within research program "Digital Future".

S. Mauw and M. Conti (Eds.): STM 2019, LNCS 11738, pp. 140–157, 2019.
https://doi.org/10.1007/978-3-030-31511-5_9

only operating on a single platform—not because of lower total requester satisfaction, but because the scores are split and stored separately across platforms.

We propose a *personal reputation system* that enables crowd workers to maintain their reputation scores themselves, and without tying these scores to specific platforms. Thus, personal reputation systems mitigate vendor lock-in and negate the disadvantage of reputations scores distributed among various platforms.

Related Work. Reputation systems, in general, have been studied extensively [1–4,8,9,12], and in multiple disciplines. These systems are often restricted to single platforms or systems (such as peer-to-peer systems), but cross-platform reputation has also been considered.

As an example, Grinshpoun *et al.* [7] propose CCR, a model for cross-community reputation. Essentially, CCR allows online forums and similar communities to import reputation scores from other communities and to provide other communities with such scores. CCR mainly focuses on how to translate reputation scores, e.g. from a three-star scale to a five-star scale, while also considering differences in communities. As an example, consider a discussion forum on vehicle engines. In such a community, reputation may represent expertise in the topic discussed. The forum may allow new registrants to import reputation scores from an automobile discussion forum, but even if both communities use the same scale for their reputation scores, the engine discussion forum may not adopt the other community's scores on a one-to-one basis, because the automobile forum covers different topics, and an expert in automobiles is not necessarily an expert in engines. Hence, CCR weights reputation during translation.

While CCR considers the cross-community/platform aspect of our work, reputation scores are still stored at some platform; our personal reputation system goes as step further and the rated subjects store their reputation scores. However, concepts of CCR are applicable to our system when it comes to the interpretation of reputation, as the reputation has been obtained via different platforms.

Pingel *et al.* [14] implement a cross-platform reputation system for online forums. Their system is claimed to achieve several notions of security, anonymity, etc. The system assumes a centralized, but not necessarily trusted, service collecting reputation information from and distributing it to multiple communities. Since the reputation service is not trusted, and to grant users control over their data, users are to store their reputation scores themselves.

A drawback of Pingel *et al.*'s solution is the use of a centralized service to aggregate reputation scores; in contrast, our personal reputation system does not rely on centralized infrastructure.

As we see from the previous examples, reputation can be managed and stored in different ways, e.g. by centralized servers for individual or multiple communities or by the rated entities. Dennis *et al.* [5] discuss some (de-)centralized approaches to reputation storage and management in peer-to-peer networks, and then present decentralized storage of reputation via distributed ledgers, i.e. blockchain. While Dennis *et al.* consider the drawbacks of their approach in terms of limited throughput, they fail to mention the significant ecological impact of their proposal, particularly if implemented using proof-of-work blockchains.

While we use technologies similar to blockchains, we put away with proof-of-work and other consensus mechanisms. Still, our personal reputation system features some of the drawbacks of blockchains, e.g. in bandwidth consumption.

Impact of Usage Scenarios on Anonymity Guarantees for Raters. Reputation systems in the cryptographic literature typically provide rater anonymity unconditionally or at least as long as raters behave honestly. This level of rater anonymity is important, because it has been shown that raters are more honest in their feedback if they are anonymous, i.e. they do not have to fear backlashes from ratees.

However, in the crowd work scenario, and focussing particularly on creative tasks such as text creation, rated solutions are one of a kind products, tailored towards a single and specific requester/customer. Due to product specifics, the creator of the product can be assumed to know the requester, who is a future rater of the product's creator. Then, due to details of products mentioned in reviews, ratees are potentially able to connect a review they receive to one of their creations, and thus the rater. A ratee may also be able to use temporal closeness of a provided solution and a received rating to link a rating to a rater. On the other hand, in order for the ratee to improve their future work based on criticism expressed in reviews, the ratee should know what product the review refers to. In turn the ratee knows the rater. Both views imply that, in the crowd work scenario, it is unlikely and undesirable for raters to remain anonymous towards the rated entity.

On a related note, a rater generally cannot be anonymous towards a platform that has mediated between the rater and the ratee: the platform must know the rater and the ratee in order to pay the ratee for her solution and bill the rater in return. The platform can use details from observed solutions and reviews to link raters and reviews in the same manner ratees can. As a consequence, for our personal reputation system, we relax the notion of rater anonymity typically imposed on reputation systems. Instead, we aim for *rater anonymity towards the general public*, so, given a rating, the rater remains anonymous towards every party not involved in the transaction.

Our Contribution. Our personal reputation system combines concepts from previous work, such as decentralized storage of reputation and some technologies also used in blockchains with novel approaches to security. Our personal reputation system provides rater anonymity towards the general public, i.e. everyone except the rater, ratee and the platform. Adopting this weakened, yet sensible, notion of anonymity, we construct our personal reputation system from simple building blocks. Particularly, our construction uses hash functions, signatures, and commitment schemes.

Paper Organization. In Sect. 2, we present the formal definition of personal reputation systems, as well as the building blocks used in our construction of a personal reputation system. We present our personal reputation system in Sect. 3.

Finally, in Sect. 4, we discuss our design choices of our model of personal reputation systems, as well as our construction, and its limitations.

2 Preliminaries and Building Blocks

In this section, we first present our definition and security notions of personal reputation systems. We then proceed to present the building blocks used in our construction of a personal reputation system.

2.1 Personal Reputation Systems

On a formal level, a personal reputation system is a collection of algorithms and interactive protocols between the various entities involved, particularly platforms, raters, and ratees. In our example scenario from the introduction, crowd workers would take on the roles of ratees, while requesters would serve as raters.

After the system and some parties have been initialized, the raters can receive (PTRs). A PTR is issued by a platform to a rater, and certifies that the rater has bought a service from some ratee. Eventually, the ratee hands out a rating token to the rater. Using the PTR and the rating token, the rater can then submit her review. Afterwards, everyone can verify that the ratee has received a given rating, and that the rating originates from a rater who has bought a product or service from the ratee via a given platform.

Definition 1. *Formally, a* personal reputation system *consists of four probabilistic algorithms (GlobalSetup, RateeSetup, PlatformSetup, Verify) and three protocols (IssuePTR, IssueRT, Rate), and features five types of parties: a parameter generator, ratees, platforms, raters, and verifiers. An entity may play the roles of multiple types of parties.*

GlobalSetup *is executed by a parameter generator which takes in security parameter 1^Λ and outputs public parameters params.*

RateeSetup *is executed by a ratee who takes params as input and outputs a private key usk and corresponding verification key uvk.*

PlatformSetup *is executed by a platform which takes in params and outputs a private key psk and corresponding verification key pvk.*

IssuePTR *is executed between a rater and a platform who take params as input; the rater additionally takes in the platform's verification key pvk; the platform additionally takes in her secret key psk, a helper string tid,[1] and a ratee's verification key uvk. The rater outputs PTR ptr.*

IssueRT *is executed between a rater and a ratee who take params as input; the rater additionally takes in the ratee's verification key uvk and her PTR ptr; the ratee additionally takes in her secret key usk. The rater outputs a rating token rt.*

---

[1] *tid* could be a transaction or billing number.

Rate *is executed between a rater and a ratee who take in params; the rater additionally takes in the ratee's verification key uvk, her rating token rt, and her (unprocessed) rating review; the ratee additionally takes in her secret key usk. Both parties output the (processed) rating r.*

Verify *is executed by a verifier who takes in params, a ratee's and platform's verification keys uvk and pvk, respectively, and a (processed) rating r; the verifier outputs* valid *or* invalid.

For every security parameter Λ, helper string tid, and unprocessed rating review, we require

$$
\Pr \left[
\begin{array}{l}
params \leftarrow GlobalSetup(1^{\Lambda}), \\
(usk, uvk) \leftarrow RateeSetup(params), \\
(psk, pvk) \leftarrow PlatformSetup(params), \\
(ptr|\bot) \leftarrow IssuePTR(params, pvk|params, psk, tid, uvk), \\
(rt|\bot) \leftarrow IssueRT(params, uvk, ptr|params, usk), \\
(r|r) \leftarrow Rate(params, uvk, rt, review|params, usk): \\
Verify(params, uvk, pvk, r) = \mathsf{valid}
\end{array}
\right] \geq 1 - \mathsf{negl}(\Lambda),
$$

where the probability is over the random choices of the algorithms.

We stress that the non-global setups are independent of each other, so ratees can work with multiple platforms, and platforms can work with multiple ratees. We also point out that, although we have no enrollment operation for raters, raters establish a permanent identity with platforms. After all, platforms will naturally want to send invoices to raters for services provided by the platforms. However, these identities are not directly part of our system, but influence our system in the form of the helper strings *tid* used in PTR generation. PTR are tied to a single transaction. Given a rating, a platform should be able to identify the rater that has created the rating using a rating token generated from the PTR. Then, the platform should be able to identify *tid* based on the PTR.

For typical reputation systems, a couple of security properties have been proposed. Although there is no agreement in the literature on the exact formulation of these security notions, some security concepts show up time and again. Those notions are:

- binding of ratings to transactions,
- prevention of self-rating,
- linking of multiple ratings by the same rater for the same transaction,
- authenticity and integrity protection for ratings,
- rater anonymity, and
- traceability of misbehaving raters.

See [3] for a discussion and definition of these notions in the context of reputation systems. As a side note, it has recently been found that linkablility and traceability do not necessarily imply that two linked ratings can be traced to the same rater [11], but this does not pose a problem in the recent formulation of reputation systems in the universal composability framework [2], and it also does not pose a problem in our particular construction.

Our security notions for personal reputation systems are very similar to the ones proposed for reputation systems. Therefore, and we discuss our construction with respect to these notions on an intuitive level; this is feasible due to the simplicity of our construction. However, we formalize the notions of authenticity and integrity protection, i.e. rating unforgeability, and rater anonymity, specifically towards the general public.

The notion of rating unforgeability requires ratees to be unable to change ratings or to compute ratings themselves, without involvement of another party. The notion is defined relative to security experiment $\text{Exp}^{\text{forge}}$ shown in Fig. 1.

The experiment keeps track of honest platforms and raters via sets P and R, respectively. Set P contains the honest platforms' secret and verification keys. Set R contains for each honest rater an identifier, and over time, also transaction identifiers, PTR and rating tokens issued to the respective rater, as well as the rater's submitted rating. The goal is for the adversary to come up with a rating that Verify declares valid under a given ratee's verification key and any of the honest platforms' verification keys, while the rating has not been submitted by any of the honest raters.

In experiment $\text{Exp}^{\text{forge}}$, all ratees, as well as malicious raters and platforms, are played by the adversary. The adversary can set up new honest platforms and raters by calling the relevant oracles. Other oracles can be called for making honest platforms issue PTR to honest raters and to make honest raters request rating tokens from ratees or make them submit reviews. In the experiment, honest platforms and raters do not interact with corrupt raters and platforms, respectively.

Definition 2. *A personal reputation system is* secure against rating forgery *if for all probabilistic polynomial time adversaries $\mathcal{A}$ we have $\Pr[\text{Exp}^{forge}_{\mathcal{A}}(\Lambda) = 1] \leq \text{negl}(\Lambda)$, where the probability is over the random choices of the adversary and the experiment.*

We now turn toward the notion of rater anonymity. Based on our crowd work scenario, as described in the previous section, full rater anonymity is neither feasible nor desirable. Instead we settle for the weakened notion of rater anonymity towards the general public. The notion requires the general public to not learn who submitted a particular rating to a ratee, but the ratee and the platform that mediated the transaction between the rater and the ratee may learn the rater's identity. Rater anonymity towards the general public is still necessary as to protect trade secrets of the rater, the platform, and the ratee. These considerations leads us to adopt the notion of rater anonymity towards the general public as the anonymity notion of choice for our personal reputation system. The notion of rater anonymity towards the general public is formalized with respect to indistinguishability experiment Exp^{anon} as shown in Fig. 2.

In the experiment, as before, sets P and R are used to track honest platforms and raters played by the experiment. Additionally, the experiment plays an honest ratee identified by verification key uvk^*. In contrast to the unforgeability

$\underline{\text{Exp}_{\mathcal{A}}^{\text{forge}}(\Lambda)}$:

Setup: set $P \leftarrow \emptyset$, $R = \emptyset$, computes $params \leftarrow$ GlobalSetup(1^Λ), and give $params$ to $\mathcal{A}$.

Query: $\mathcal{A}$ adaptively queries oracles

- $\mathcal{O}_{\text{PCr}}() \rightarrow pvk$ for creating new platforms.
- $\mathcal{O}_{\text{RCr}}() \rightarrow id_R$ for creating new raters.
- $\mathcal{O}_{\text{PTR}}(pvk, id_R, uvk) \rightarrow tid$ for issuing PTRs to raters.
- $\mathcal{O}_{\text{RT}}(id_R) \rightarrow \{0,1\}$ for issuing rating tokens to raters.
- $\mathcal{O}_{\text{Rate}}(id_R, review) \rightarrow \{0, 1\}$ for making raters rate a ratee.

Responses: Upon query

- $\mathcal{O}_{\text{PCr}}()$:
  - $(psk, pvk) \leftarrow$ PlatformSetup($params$)
  - $P \leftarrow P \cup \{(psk, pvk)\}$
  - give pvk to $\mathcal{A}$.
- $\mathcal{O}_{\text{RCr}}()$:
  - $id_R \leftarrow |R|$, $R \leftarrow R \cup \{(id_R, \emptyset)\}$
  - give id_R to $\mathcal{A}$.
- $\mathcal{O}_{\text{PTR}}(pvk, id_R, uvk)$:
  - check $\exists (s, pvk) \in P$ for some s
  - check $\exists (id_R, X) \in R$ for some X
  - if checks succeed:
    * $tid \leftarrow_\$ \{0,1\}^\Lambda$
    * $(ptr|\perp) \leftarrow$ IssuePTR($params$, $pvk|params, s, tid, uvk$) playing the rater and the platform
    * if the protocol did not abort: $Y \leftarrow X \cup \{(tid, (uvk, pvk, ptr), \perp, 0, \perp)\}$
    * else: $Y \leftarrow X \cup \{(tid, \perp, \text{invalid}, 0, \perp)\}$
    * $R \leftarrow (R \backslash \{(id_R, X)\}) \cup \{(id_R, Y)\}$
    * give tid to $\mathcal{A}$

- otherwise: give $\perp$ to $\mathcal{A}$
- $\mathcal{O}_{\text{RT}}(id_R, tid)$:
  - check $\exists (id_R, X) \in R$ and $(tid, (u, v, p), \perp, 0, \perp) \in X$ for some u, v, and p
  - if checks succeed:
    * $rt \leftarrow$ IssueRT($params, u, p$) playing the rater while $\mathcal{A}$ plays the ratee
    * if the protocol did not abort: $Y \leftarrow (X \backslash \{(tid, (u, v, p), \perp, 0, \perp)\}) \cup \{(tid, (u, v, p), rt, 0, \perp)\}$
    * else: $Y \leftarrow (X \backslash \{(tid, (u, v, p), \perp, 0, \perp)\}) \cup \{(tid, (u, v, p), \text{invalid}, 0, \perp)\}$
    * $R \leftarrow (R \backslash \{(id_R, X)\}) \cup \{(id_R, Y)\}$
    * give 1 to $\mathcal{A}$
  - otherwise: give 0 to $\mathcal{A}$
- $\mathcal{O}_{\text{Rate}}(id_R, tid, review)$:
  - check $\exists (id_R, X) \in R$ and $(tid, (u, v, p), r', 0, \perp) \in X$ for some u, v, and p
  - check $r' \neq \text{invalid}$
  - if checks succeed:
    * $r \leftarrow$ Rate($params, u, r', review$) playing the rater while $\mathcal{A}$ plays the ratee
    * $Y \leftarrow (X \backslash \{(tid, (u, v, p), r', 0, \perp)\}) \cup \{(tid, (u, v, p), r', 1, r)\}$
    * $R \leftarrow (R \backslash \{(id_R, X)\}) \cup \{(id_R, Y)\}$
    * give 1 to $\mathcal{A}$
  - otherwise: give 0 to $\mathcal{A}$

Output: Eventually, $\mathcal{A}$ outputs a tuple (uvk^*, r^*). If for any $(psk, pvk) \in P$ Verify($params, uvk, pvk, r$) = valid, and for all tuples $(id_R, X) \in R$ and all $(tid, (uvk, pvk, p), \cdot, \cdot, r) \in R$ we have $r \neq r^*$, then experiment outputs 1. Otherwise, the experiment outputs 0.

Fig. 1. The rating forgery experiment for personal reputationsystems played with adversary $\mathcal{A}$

experiment, in the anonymity experiment honest entities can interact with corrupt entities. This is reflected in the various variants of oracles used for different constellations of honest and dishonest entities interacting. Particularly, oracles for issuing PTR, for issuing rating tokens and for submitting reviews exist in multiple variants. Variant C denotes the variants featuring honest raters, but says nothing about the honesty of ratees and platforms. Variant H denotes the variants featuring an honest non-rater, i.e. ratee or platform. Finally, Variant D, only present in the oracle for issuing PTR, features both, honest platforms and honest raters. The oracle variants not only differ in the honesty of parties, but, as a consequence, also in their input and output behavior.

Definition 3. *A personal reputation system provides rater anonymity towards the general public if for all probabilistic polynomial time adversaries $\mathcal{A}$ we have $|\Pr[\text{Exp}_{\mathcal{A}}^{anon}(\Lambda) = 1] - 1/2| \leq \text{negl}(\Lambda)$, where the probability is over the random choices of the adversary and the experiment.*

$\text{Exp}_{\mathcal{A}}^{\text{anon}}(\Lambda)$:

Setup: set $P \leftarrow \emptyset$, $R = \emptyset$, computes $params \leftarrow \text{GlobalSetup}(1^{\Lambda})$, $(usk^*, uvk^*) \leftarrow \text{RateeSetup}(params)$, and give $params$ and uvk^* to $\mathcal{A}$.

Query I: $\mathcal{A}$ adaptively queries oracles

- $\mathcal{O}_{\text{PCr}}() \rightarrow pvk$ for creating new platforms.
- $\mathcal{O}_{\text{RCr}}() \rightarrow id_R$ for creating new raters.
- $\mathcal{O}_{\text{PTR:C}}(pvk, uvk)$, $\mathcal{O}_{\text{PTR:D}}(pvk, id_R, uvk) \rightarrow tid$ and $\mathcal{O}_{\text{PTR:H}}(pvk, id_R, tid) \rightarrow \{0,1\}$ for issuing PTRs; Variant C: corrupt rater, honest platform; Variant D: honest rater and platform; Variant H: honest rater.
- $\mathcal{O}_{\text{RT:C}}()$ and $\mathcal{O}_{\text{RT:H}}(id_R, tid) \rightarrow \{0,1\}$ for issuing rating tokens; Variant C: corrupt rater, honest ratee; Variant H: honest rater.
- $\mathcal{O}_{\text{Rate:C}}()$ and $\mathcal{O}_{\text{Rate:H}}(id_R, tid, review) \rightarrow \{0,1\}$ for making raters rate a ratee; Variant C: corrupt rater, honest ratee; Variant H: honest rater.

Responses: Upon query

- $\mathcal{O}_{\text{PCr}}()$:
  - $(psk, pvk) \leftarrow \text{PlatformSetup}(params)$
  - $P \leftarrow P \cup \{(psk, pvk)\}$
  - return pvk
- $\mathcal{O}_{\text{RCr}}()$:
  - $id_R \leftarrow |R|$, $R \leftarrow R \cup \{(id_R, \emptyset)\}$
  - return id_R
- $\mathcal{O}_{\text{PTR:C}}(pvk, uvk)$:
  - $tid \leftarrow_{\$} \{0,1\}^{\Lambda}$
  - $\perp \leftarrow \text{IssuePTR}(params, s, tid, uvk)$ playing the platform; $\mathcal{A}$ plays the rater
- $\mathcal{O}_{\text{PTR:D}}(pvk, id_R, uvk)$:
  - if $\exists(s, pvk) \in P$ for some s and $\exists(id_R, X) \in R$ for some X:
    * $tid \leftarrow_{\$} \{0,1\}^{\Lambda}$
    * $(ptr|\perp) \leftarrow \text{IssuePTR}(params, pvk|params, s, tid, uvk)$ playing the platform and the rater
    * if the protocol did not abort: $Y \leftarrow X \cup \{(tid, (uvk, pvk, ptr), \perp, 0, \perp)\}$
    * else: $Y \leftarrow X \cup \{(tid, \perp, \text{invalid}, 0, \perp)\}$
    * $R \leftarrow (R \setminus \{(id_R, X)\}) \cup \{(id_R, Y)\}$
    * return tid
  - otherwise: return $\perp$
- $\mathcal{O}_{\text{PTR:H}}(pvk, id_R, tid, uvk)$:
  - if $\exists(id_R, X) \in R$ for some X and $\forall(t, \cdot, \cdot, \cdot, \cdot) \in X : t \neq tid$:
    * $ptr \leftarrow \text{IssuePTR}(params, pvk)$ playing the rater; $\mathcal{A}$ plays the platform
    * if the protocol did not abort: $Y \leftarrow X \cup \{(tid, (uvk, pvk, ptr), \perp, 0, \perp)\}$

- * else: $Y \leftarrow X \cup \{(tid, \perp, \text{invalid}, 0, \perp)\}$
  * $R \leftarrow (R \setminus \{(id_R, X)\}) \cup \{(id_R, Y)\}$
  * return 1
  - otherwise: return 0
- $\mathcal{O}_{\text{RT:C}}()$:
  - $\perp \leftarrow \text{IssueRT}(params, usk^*)$ playing the ratee while $\mathcal{A}$ plays the rater
- $\mathcal{O}_{\text{RT:H}}(id_R, tid)$:
  - if $\exists(id_R, X) \in R$ and $(tid, (u, v, p), \perp, 0, \perp) \in X$ for some u, v, and p:
    * $rt \leftarrow \text{IssueRT}(params, u, p)$ playing the rater; if $u = uvk^*$, the experiment also plays the ratee on input $(params, usk^*)$, otherwise $\mathcal{A}$ plays the ratee
    * if the protocol did not abort: $Y \leftarrow (X \setminus \{(tid, (u, v, p), \perp, 0, \perp)\}) \cup \{(tid, (u, v, p), rt, 0, \perp)\}$
    * else: $Y \leftarrow (X \setminus \{(tid, (u, v, p), \perp, 0, \perp)\}) \cup \{(tid, (u, v, p), \text{invalid}, 0, \perp)\}$
    * $R \leftarrow (R \setminus \{(id_R, X)\}) \cup \{(id_R, Y\}$
    * return 1
  - otherwise: return 0
- $\mathcal{O}_{\text{Rate:C}}()$:
  - $r \leftarrow \text{Rate}(params, usk^*)$ playing the ratee
- $\mathcal{O}_{\text{Rate:H}}(id_R, tid, review)$:
  - if $\exists(id_R, X) \in R$ and $(tid, (u, v, p), r', 0, \perp) \in X$ for some u, v and p, and check $r' \neq \text{invalid}$:
    * $r \leftarrow \text{Rate}(params, u, r', review)$ playing the rater; if $u = uvk^*$, the experiment also plays the ratee on input $(params, usk^*)$, otherwise $\mathcal{A}$ plays the ratee
    * $Y \leftarrow (X \setminus \{(tid, (u, v, p), r', 0, \perp)\}) \cup \{(tid, (u, v, p), r', 1, r)\}$
    * $R \leftarrow (R \setminus \{(id_R, X)\}) \cup \{(id_R, Y)\}$
    * return 1
  - otherwise: return 0

Challenge: Eventually, $\mathcal{A}$ outputs a two rater identifiers id_0, id_1 such that $(id_0, X), (id_1, Y) \in R$ for some X, Y, platform verification key pvk such that $(psk, pvk) \in P$ for some psk, and unprocessed rating $review$. Pick $b \leftarrow_{\$} \{0,1\}$, perform actions of oracle queries $tid \leftarrow \mathcal{O}_{\text{PTR:D}}(pvk, id_b, uvk^*)$, $\mathcal{O}_{\text{RT:H}}(id_b, tid)$ and $s \leftarrow \mathcal{O}_{\text{Rate:H}}(id_b, tid, review)$. If $s = 0$, the experiment outputs -1 and aborts.

Query II: Same as Query I.

Output: Eventually, $\mathcal{A}$ outputs a bit b'. The experiment outputs 1 if $b = b'$ and 0 otherwise.

Fig. 2. The rater anonymity experiment played with adversary $\mathcal{A}$

2.2 Building Blocks

We now present the building blocks that we use in our construction of a personal reputation system: commitment schemes, signature schemes and hash functions. In addition to these building blocks, we briefly introduce their security notions.

A *commitment scheme* can be likened to a sealed envelope. It allows a person to commit to a value without publishing the value, and later on publish the value and convince others that the published value is the value the person originally committed to; c.f. Ch. 5.6.5 of [13]. Commitment schemes are binding, i.e. the value committed to cannot be changed, and hiding, i.e. the value remains unknown to everyone except the person who has committed to the value.

A *signature scheme* is the cryptographer's equivalent to a handwritten signature. The signature is supposed to identify the signer in a way that the signer cannot feasible deny to have created the signature. In order to prevent adversaries from simply copying signatures, the signature must also consider the message that is being signed, as to make clear that the signer indeed intended to sign the given message; c.f. Ch. 12 of [13]. Signatures must be existentially unforgeable under adaptively chosen message attacks, i.e. it is hard to compute a signature under a message without knowledge of the signer's secret key, even if many signatures for other messages under the signer's secret key are known.

A family of *hash functions* is a keyed function used to compute short fingerprints or digests (hashes) of long messages; c.f. Ch. 5 of [13]. These functions are collision resistant, i.e. it is hard to find two distinct messages that result in the same digest.

3 Construction

In this section, we first review the hash chain principle that we use to construct a personal reputation system. From hash chains and the building blocks presented in the previous section, we then construct our personal reputation system.

3.1 Hash Chain Principle

Our personal reputation system makes use of the hash chain principle. We use two types of hash chain entries, namely self-signed certificates and data blocks. Hash chain entries are tied together ("chained") using a hash function.

Self-signed certificates can only occur as the initial entry of a hash chain. They are 2-tuples that consist of a signature verification key and a signature on the key. We call a self-signed certificate *valid* if the signature is a valid signature on the verification key under the verification key.

Data blocks are 3-tuples consisting of data, a hash, and a signature. Data blocks cannot occur at the start of a hash chain. The hash contained in a data block is a hash of another hash chain entry, called the predecessor; hence, the hash establishes a successor/predecessor relation between hash chain entries, and thus, the chain.

If the hash is generated using a collision resistant hash function family, for any given set of hash chain entries, the successor and predecessor relations partially order the set with overwhelming probability, where the probability is over the random choice of the hash function from its family.

Considering a partially ordered set of hash chain entries, we call a data block *valid* if (1) the block's signature is a valid signature on the block's data and predecessor hash, and (2) the signature verification key that makes the data block's signature valid also makes the data block's predecessor valid. We call a set of hash chain entries valid, if it is totally ordered by the predecessor relation, and every element from the set is valid. It is easy to see that a valid set of hash chain entries contains exactly one self-signed certificate.

In summary, a hash chain scheme consists of four probabilistic polynomial time algorithms Setup, Initialize, Append, and VerifyChain. Setup is a parameter generation algorithm that chooses a concrete hash function and publishes its choice. Initialize sets up a new instance of the hash chain by establishing its initial block. Append adds a new block to an existing hash chain. VerifyChain verifies an existing chain as described above.

The successor and predecessor relations on hash chain entries give rise to the notions of minimal and maximal blocks for a set of hash chain entries: the minimal block is the only block from the set that does not have a predecessor in the set, whereas the maximum block is the only block from the set that does not have a successor block in the set; we denote the minimal and maximal blocks of a set E of hash chain entries as $\min E$ and $\max E$, respectively. Hence, for valid hash chains, the minimal block is the self-signed certificate, and the maximal block is the block most recently appended to the chain. For practical purposes, we assume the set of hash chain entries to be stored as an ordered set (ordered according to the predecessor relation), so we do not need to sort entries in our algorithms.

We now construct a concrete hash chain scheme from a signature scheme $\Sigma = (\text{KeyGen}, \text{Sign}, \text{Verify})$, and a collision resistant hash function family $H = (\text{KeyGen}, \text{Eval})$. Our hash chains work as follows.

Setup (1^Λ): let $hfk \leftarrow \text{H.KeyGen}(1^\Lambda)$ and output hfk.

Initialize (hfk): let $(sk, vk) \leftarrow \Sigma.\text{KeyGen}(hfk)$, let $\sigma \leftarrow \Sigma.\text{Sign}(sk, \text{H.Eval}(hfk, vk))$, and output $(sk, E = \{(vk, \sigma)\})$ as the hash chains secret key and first block, i.e. self-signed certificate.

Append $(hfk, sk, data, E)$: let $e \leftarrow \max E$ be the latest hash chain entry, compute $h \leftarrow \text{H.Eval}(hfk, \langle e, data \rangle)$, compute $\sigma \leftarrow \Sigma.\text{Sign}(sk, h)$, and output $E = E \cup \{(data, h, \sigma)\}$ as the (extended) hash chain.

VerifyChain (hfk, E): let $c \leftarrow \min E$ be the oldest hash chain entry, and parse c as (v, s). If parsing fails or $\Sigma.\text{Verify}(v, \text{H.Eval}(hfk, v), s) \neq \text{valid}$, output invalid. Otherwise, for all $e \in E \setminus \{c\}$ in ascending order (according to the successor relation), parse e as (d, h, s), let $e' \in E$ be e's predecessor and check that $\text{H.Eval}(hfk, \langle e', d \rangle) = h$ and $\Sigma.\text{Verify}(v, h, s) = \text{valid}$. If either check fails for any $e \in E \setminus \{c\}$, output invalid; otherwise output valid.

Our construction of a personal reputation system uses the hash chain principle in a gray box manner, i.e. we rely on the primitive as described above, but use the keys computed during setup and initialization in other contexts, too. For example the hash function key is used for hash function evaluations not related to the hash chain. Similarly, the signing key sk may be used to sign messages unrelated to the hash chain.

We also do not have any particular security notions for hash chains that we rely on when proving our construction secure. It should be noted though, that hash chains are fork consistent and append-only authenticated data structures if they are built from a collision resistant hash function family [6].

3.2 Our Personal Reputation System

As described before, our personal reputation system is to enable the distributed storage of ratings, independent of platforms. As a means for ratees to maintain a reasonable degree of control over their data (e.g. in compliance with data privacy laws), we have ratees store the ratings they receive. However, we employ the hash chain principle and the other primitives presented in the previous section in order to prevent ratees from tampering with the ratings. Particularly, if ratees try to reject unfavorable reviews or delete old ratings, this can be detected.

In our personal reputation system, *every ratee operates her individual hash chain.* We call a ratee's hash chain her "E-Set," and every E-Set is complemented by an "R-Set". The E-Set is used to register events, such as the issuance of a rating token to a rater, or the receipt of a rating from a rater. In order to prevent a ratee from rejecting an unfavorable rating, a rater first commits to her review and sends the commitment to the ratee. The rater sends the actual rating, including a decommit value only after she has received confirmation that the commitment has been appended to the ratee's E-Set. The rating is then stored in an R-Set entry that corresponds to the commitment's E-Set entry.

The previously mentioned (PTRs) that platforms hand out to raters are certificates on a one-time identity established by a rater with the platform. The PTR certifies that the rater has bought a service from a rater. The platform that was involved in the transaction is also mentioned in the certificate, and the PTR is tied to the specific transaction. We use the term "one-time" loosely, because the same identity is used for multiple publicly observable interactions between a rater and a ratee, i.e. issuance of a rating token and submission of a review, but the identity is one-time in the sense that all these interactions are tied to a single transaction on the platform, i.e. if a rater happens to buy a service from the same ratee twice, the rater would use different identities. Although then the ratee may know that she interacted with the same rater multiple times, the general public does not learn this fact.

A rating token in our system is a certificate on a rater's one-time identity issued by a ratee, together with the ratee's PTR. Rating tokens are issued in order to publicly register a transaction and the rater's transaction-specific one-time identity in the ratee's E-Set.

We now present our personal reputation system. Let $\mathsf{CS} = (\mathsf{Setup}, \mathsf{Commit}, \mathsf{Verify})$ be a commitment scheme, and let HC be the hash chain constructed as in Sect. 3.1 that uses a collision resistant hash function family $\mathsf{H} = (\mathsf{Setup}, \mathsf{Eval})$ and a signature scheme $\Sigma = (\mathsf{KeyGen}, \mathsf{Sign}, \mathsf{Verify})$. Our personal reputation system is as described below.

GlobalSetup (1^Λ): compute $cpp \leftarrow \mathsf{CS.Setup}(1^\Lambda)$, $hfk \leftarrow \mathsf{HC.Setup}(1^\Lambda)$, and publish $params = (cpp, hfk)$.

RateeSetup $(params)$: let $(usk, E\text{-}Set_{uvk}) \leftarrow \mathsf{HC.Initialize}(hfk)$ (i.e. the ratee's signing key and her self-signed certificate for verification key uvk that corresponds to usk), let $R\text{-}Set_{uvk} \leftarrow \emptyset$, publish $(E\text{-}Set_{uvk}, R\text{-}Set_{uvk})$, and privately output usk.

PlatformSetup $(params)$: compute $(psk, pvk) \leftarrow \Sigma.\mathsf{KeyGen}(1^\Lambda)$, publish pvk, and privately output psk.

IssuePTR $(params, pvk | params, psk, tid, uvk)$: The rater computes $(rsk, rvk) \leftarrow \Sigma.\mathsf{KeyGen}(1^\Lambda)$, and sends her one-time identity rvk to the platform. The platform fetches the self-signed certificate $e_0 \leftarrow \min E\text{-}Set_{uvk}$ of ratee uvk's hash chain, computes signature $t \leftarrow \Sigma.\mathsf{Sign}(psk, \mathsf{H.Eval}(hfk, \langle tid, e_0, rvk \rangle)$, and sends $ptr' = (pvk, uvk, rvk, tid, t)$ to the rater.
The rater privately outputs $ptr = (rsk, ptr')$.

IssueRT $(params, uvk, ptr | params, usk)$: The rater sends rvk to the ratee. The ratee sends $crt \leftarrow \Sigma.\mathsf{Sign}(usk, \mathsf{H.Eval}(hfk, rvk))$ to the rater. The rater computes $rt \leftarrow (rsk, ptr', crt)$, and engages in an execution of protocol Rate with the ratee: the rater's input is $(params, uvk, pvk, rt, \perp)$, i.e. an empty review; the ratee's input is $(params, usk)$. Finally, the rater outputs rt.

Rate $(params, uvk, rt, review)(params, usk)$: The rater verifies ratee uvk's hash chain $E\text{-}Set_{uvk}$ via $\mathsf{HC.VerifyChain}$ and aborts the protocol if verification fails. Otherwise, the rater identifies the most recent block $e \leftarrow \max E\text{-}Set_{uvk}$ of the hash chain, computes $(c, d) \leftarrow \mathsf{CS.Commit}(cpp, review)$, computes $data \leftarrow (rvk, ptr', crt, c)$ (where crt and ptr' are from rt and ptr, respectively), computes $h \leftarrow \mathsf{H.Eval}(hfk, \langle e, data \rangle)$, computes $\sigma \leftarrow \Sigma.\mathsf{Sign}(rsk, h)$, and sends $(data, h, \sigma)$ to the ratee.
The ratee computes $data' \leftarrow (rvk, crt, ptr', c, h, \sigma)$, executes $\mathsf{HC.Append}(hfk, usk, data', E\text{-}Set_{uvk})$ to obtain a new (publicly observable) E-Set entry, and sends the ratee's signature from the new E-Set entry to the rater.
The rater computes $r = (ptr', d, review)$, privately outputs r, and sends r to the ratee.
The ratee (re-)publishes $R\text{-}Set_{uvk} \leftarrow R\text{-}Set_{uvk} \cup \{r\}$, and privately outputs r.

Verify $(params, uvk, pvk, r)$: Fetch the self-signed certificate $e_0 \leftarrow \min E\text{-}Set_{uvk}$ of ratee uvk's hash chain, verify the hash chain $E\text{-}Set_{uvk}$ via $\mathsf{HC.VerifyChain}$, check $r \in R\text{-}Set_{uvk}$, check $\Sigma.\mathsf{Verify}(pvk, \mathsf{H.Eval}(hfk, \langle tid, e_0, rvk \rangle), t)$ (where tid, rvk, and t are from ptr' from r), check that arguments uvk and pvk match components uvk and pvk from r's ptr', and check that at most two entries $((rvk, crt, p, c, h, \sigma), h', \sigma') \in E\text{-}Set_{uvk}$ satisfy $p = ptr'$. If either check fails, output invalid. Otherwise, let $((rvk, crt, p, c, h, \sigma), h', \sigma')$ with $p = ptr'$ be maximal in $E\text{-}Set_{uvk}$ with respect to the successor relation. Check $\Sigma.\mathsf{Verify}(uvk, \mathsf{H.Eval}(hfk, rvk), crt) = \mathsf{valid}$, check $h = \mathsf{H.Eval}(hfk, \langle rvk, crt, ptr', c \rangle)$, check $\Sigma.\mathsf{Verify}(rvk, h, \sigma) = \mathsf{valid}$, and check $\mathsf{CS.Verify}(cpp, (review, d), c) = \mathsf{valid}$. If either check fails, output invalid; otherwise output valid.

Of course, parties do not trust each other, and thus do not trust the data sent by other parties. Therefore, all received data is recomputed and signatures are verified at the receiving end of communication. We have omitted such checks and computations to not clutter our presentation.

Efficiency. Unfortunately, the simplicity of the primitives used in our construction necessitates the whole hash chain to be requested, transmitted, and verified whenever someone wants to rate a ratee or verify a rating. Thus, both computation and bandwidth usage of these operations linearly depends on the number of previously issued rating tokens and the number of ratings. The inefficiency is caused by the need to verify ratees' hash chains ($E\text{-}Sets$) as part of these operations.

Mitigating Efficiency Bottlenecks. It stands to reason that replacing the hash chain in our construction by a more efficient fork consistent, append-only authenticated data structure, particularly, one with concise proofs, may make our construction more efficient. However, we expect that exchanging hash chains for a more efficient data structure does not provide significant new insights. We also expect that changes to our construction due to incorporating a different data structure would be relatively minor and would not affect our construction's security.

Security. We now consider the security of our personal reputation system. To that end, we first discuss our construction's security against rating forgery in a formal manner. Afterwards, we discuss our system's other security properties.

Theorem 1. *If HC is instantiated using a collision resistant hash function family H and a signature scheme Σ that is existentially unforgeable under adaptively chosen message attacks, and CS is a computationally binding commitment scheme, then our personal reputation system is secure against rating forgery.*

Proof. We remind the reader about the hash-then-sign principle. That is, hashing a message with a collision resistant hash function and then singing the hash using a signature scheme that is existentially unforgeable under adaptively chosen message attacks (euf-cma secure) results in an euf-cma secure signature. A similar result holds for combining a binding commitment scheme and an euf-cma secure signature scheme in a commit-then-sign fashion, resulting in an euf-cma secure signature. This can be proven by adapting the proof for the hash-then-sign case, exchanging collision resistance for the binding property.

We now prove that every adversary that breaks our personal reputation system's security against rating forgery must break the security of at least one of the underlying primitives. To that end, we split the set of successful adversaries (adversaries that make experiment $\text{Exp}^{\text{forge}}$ output 1 with non-negligible probability) into two categories, depending on what part of our reputation system is successfully attacked. Type A adversaries forge signatures under a platform's signature verification key. Type B adversaries forge signatures under a rater's signature verification key.

However, we first have to argue that every successful attack falls into one of these categories. For that, we observe that a successful adversary outputs a tuple (uvk^*, r^*), such that, for one of the honest platforms set up over the course of the experiment, the platform's signature verification key satisfies $\text{Verify}(params, uvk^*, pvk, r^*) = \text{valid}$. Reviewing the rating verification algorithm of our scheme, we find that only two of the components considered by Verify are not under control of the adversary, namely, the tuple $ptr' = (pvk, rvk, tid, t)$, and the tuple $rgs = (crt, p, c, h, \sigma)$, where $p = ptr'$, ptr' is part of r^*, and $r^* \in R\text{-}Set_{uvk}$. All other components are controlled by the adversary, particularly the ratees' $E\text{-}Set_{uvk}$ and $R\text{-}Set_{uvk}$ and their properties, as well as the signatures σ' contained in hash chain entries.

The public part of the PTR, ptr', is, among other things, a certificate on a rater's signature verification key rvk, which is used in the verification of signature σ. The certificate property of ptr' is verified under verification key pvk. From the fact that rating verification evaluates to valid under an honest platform's verification key and the fact that in experiment $\text{Exp}^{\text{forge}}$ honest platforms only hand out PTR to honest raters, we know that a successful adversary must have come up with an honest platform's PTR for a rater controlled by the adversary (type A adversary), or relies on PTR given to an honest rater, but changes/replaces that rater's review (type B adversary).

In either case, the adversary has to forge a signature that is created in accordance with the provably secure commit-then-sign and hash-then-sign principles, using primitives that are assumed secure.   □

Impracticability of Rating Removal. It is noteworthy that our notion of personal reputation systems, and particularly, our scheme, allow for the removal of ratings. In order to remove ratings, a ratee has to de-publish the ratings' $R\text{-}Set_{uvk}$ entries.

However, everyone can estimate whether a given ratee deletes ratings by comparing the cardinalities of the ratee's $R\text{-}Set_{uvk}$ and $E\text{-}Set_{uvk}$. These cardinalities should be roughly the same (allowing for transmission errors and connection time outs for ongoing rating procedures, etc.). Large discrepancies should raise alarms. In order to avoid discrepancies in set cardinalities, the $E\text{-}Set_{uvk}$ entry that corresponds to the deleted $R\text{-}Set_{uvk}$ entry needs to be deleted as well. However, deleting an entry from $E\text{-}Set_{uvk}$ comes with a host of problems on its own.

Deleting a single old entry from $E\text{-}Set_{uvk}$, i.e. any block other than the most recent one, can be detected by everyone, because the deletion of the single entry results in the new $E\text{-}Set_{uvk}$ not being totally ordered, so every attempt at verifying the hash chain $E\text{-}Set_{uvk}$ will fail. The most recent entry from $E\text{-}Set_{uvk}$

may be deleted, but the deletion can be detected by the rater that created the corresponding rating, and the rater can even prove that fact via the signature from the deleted hash chain block: receipt of that signature is a condition for the rater to submit her rating to the ratee. Of course, $E\text{-}Set_{uvk}$ can also be truncated, i.e. all of the most recent entries are deleted, in which case the previous detection and proof method apply to each of the deleted blocks individually, and thus increase the probability of detection.

If a rater detects that one of her ratings has been deleted, she can take appropriate action outside the scope of our scheme. Potential actions include reporting the ratee who has deleted the rating to the platform that participated in creating the PTR used in the rating process, as well as suing the ratee.

Of course, in order for raters to detect rating deletion, they have to perform their checks repeatedly. This requirement of having raters occasionally check for rating deletion may seem to put an unnecessary burden on raters, especially in comparison to currently deployed reputation systems. However, the time intervals in between two checks can increase over time. For example, intervals could be doubled after each successful check. This is because we can expect new ratings to be added to an $E\text{-}Set_{uvk}$. At the same time, assuming a rational ratee, the benefit of removing one old rating may be offset by the cost of removing all of the old rating's successors (and thus the increased probability of rating deletion).

Note that the above discussion on rating removal is independent of our use of hash chains and applies to replacements as well, because a malicious ratee may simply roll back her $E\text{-}Set_{uvk}$ to an earlier state. However, as long as the authenticated data structure used to instantiate $E\text{-}Set_{uvk}$ is fork consistent and append-only, the above detection method will apply.

Further Security Properties. Now that we have discussed our scheme's protection of rating authenticity and integrity, and the threat of rating removal, we have a look at the other security notions for (personal) reputation systems listed in Sect. 2.1, and argue on an intuitive level that our personal reputation system satisfies these notions.

Regarding *identity management,* we see that all major parties, i.e. raters, ratees, and platforms, involved in our personal reputation system have certified identities, multiple of them in the case of raters. Platform and ratee identities are established by their respective public signature verification keys that may or may not be certified by a certification authority as part of a public key infrastructure; however, such a structure is beyond the scope of our system. Raters' one-time identities are certified by platforms and ratees via their respective signatures in PTR and rating tokens, as well as their agreement on these identities, i.e. raters' signature verification keys. In addition, as mentioned before, raters' permanent identities are established by platforms (e.g. for billing purposes) and tied to raters' one-time identities via the helper strings *tid* which are contained in the publicly observable parts of PTR, i.e. component ptr'.

Regarding *rater anonymity,* we note that our construction withholds rater's permanent identities from the public. This can be seen immediately from the fact that there is no public establishment of permanent rater identities in our construction. Instead one-time identities are established, one identity per transaction. Assuming the helper strings *tid* contained in PTR, and particularly their public component *ptr'* contained in ratings, do not provide any information on raters' permanent identities to the public, the one-time identities of raters are unlinkable by the public in an information theoretic sense, both among each other and to the raters' permanent identities.

Thus, in the Exp^{anon} experiment, no adversary can do better than guessing what rater has performed the challenge rating. This establishes the following theorem.

Theorem 2. *If helper strings tid contain no information on rater's permanent identities, our construction achieves rater anonymity towards the general public.*

Although the public is unable to link a rating to a rater's permanent identity, the same one-time identity is used for multiple interactions between raters and other parties involved in the same transaction. This is because one-time identities and transactions are tied together by PTR, and the same PTR is used for all interactions that are part of the respective transaction. Thus, PTR allow for linking multiple ratings for the same transaction. Due to the aforementioned necessity of platforms establishing a permanent identity of raters, even though outside the scope of our reputation system, misbehaving raters can be traced. Furthermore, all ratings for a transaction can be traced to the same permanent identity.

Prevention of self-rating is a consequence from our use of PTR. Particularly, ratees cannot forge PTR or copy PTR from another transaction, because this would require forging either raters' or platforms' signatures. However, ratees can legitimately obtain a PTR by buying a product or service from themselves (via an honest platform), or by setting up a dishonest platform themselves. In reputation systems that do not require raters, ratees, and platforms to be disjoint sets and do not enforce the use of a single (permanent) identity for all roles, such attacks are always possible. Our personal reputation system is an example of such a system.

However, in many practical scenarios, platforms require payment for their services; typically a percentage of per-transaction payments. Thus, ratees buying from themselves via an honest platform involves costs to the ratee. If the costs to the ratee are higher than the benefits from a rating, self-rating via honest platforms can be mitigated, at least as far as rational ratees are concerned.

On the other hand, since our personal reputation system explicitly allows ratees to work with multiple platforms, and platforms will have different types of reviews, e.g. 5-star scale or free text reviews, there is a need for reputation evaluation functions that help with interpreting ratees' reputation. Such reputation evaluation functions not only consider the actual review for a transaction, but also what platform has brokered that transaction. Platforms that nobody has ever heard of, e.g. platforms set up by dishonest ratees, will have effectively no influence when evaluating reputation. Thus, by using appropriate reputation evaluation functions, the benefits of maliciously set up platforms can be minimized, preventing rational ratees from obtaining PTR from dishonest platforms.

In this context, CCR [7], c.f. related work, comes in.CCR considers such things as the confidence in reputation from different communities/platforms and weighs them accordingly. It should also be noted that reputation evaluation functions are an active research topic in economics.

4   Discussion

From theory's point of view, one can ask whether the primitives we use in our construction of a personal reputation system are necessary, or whether weaker building blocks suffice. For example, the signature scheme may be replaced by a *one-time signature scheme*. This is applicable to raters' signatures, because each rater creates exactly two signatures (and could have two one-time keys certified by the platform and the ratee as part of the PTR and the rating token). In practice, however, one-time signature schemes are often less efficient than signature schemes.

Additionally, applying one-time signatures does not allow the system to *recover from concurrent rating*, i.e. if two raters rate the same ratee at the same time, and thus use the same hash chain block as a basis for their computation, only one of the ratings can occur in the hash chain, while the other one has to be discarded. Otherwise, a fork of the hash chain occurs or rating verification will eventually fail (particularly, verification of the rater's signature inside a hash chain entry will fail). Hence, in order to recover from concurrent rating, one of the raters has to perform the rating process a second time, but based on the hash chain entry generated from the other rater's rating. While this is feasible with signature schemes, one-time signature schemes do not allow this (or rather: do not give any security guarantees in this situation).

From both, a theoretical and a practical point of view, one may criticise that our security model only considers security in the presence of malicious or rational ratees, but does not consider attacks by malicious platforms or raters, as well as collusion attacks. See [5] for discussions of some attacks of these types.

From a practical point of view, it is questionable whether platforms may actually be willing to participate in a personal reputation system, because personal reputation systems prevent vendor lock-in. After all, vendor lock-in may be a desirable feature from the vendor's perspective. However, our construction aims at minimizing the platform's involvement in the system.

A point of criticism with our system is that ratees have to be online constantly to accept new ratings or serve requests for their hash chains (E-Sets) and rating sets (R-Sets). We expect that specialized services will emerge to take on the roles of ratees.

Despite the potential benefits of such services, our reputation system provides the option for ratees to operate their own instance of the system, and thus, as long as ratees hold a copy of the singing key used for their hash chain, our proposal prevents vendor lock-in with respect to the service. The option for ratees to run their own instance of the reputation system also has the strong potential to prevent the formation of a single point of attack.

Services would also be helpful in normalizing reviews made on different scales, i.e. services that provide reputation evaluation functions mentioned at the end of the previous section. This type of service could re-use concepts from CCR [7], c.f. related work.   •

References

1. Androulaki, E., Choi, S.G., Bellovin, S.M., Malkin, T.: Reputation systems for anonymous networks. In: Borisov, N., Goldberg, I. (eds.) PETS 2008. LNCS, vol. 5134, pp. 202–218. Springer, Heidelberg (2008). https://doi.org/10.1007/978-3-540-70630-4_13

2. Blömer, J., Eidens, F., Juhnke, J.: Practical, anonymous, and publicly linkable universally-composable reputation systems. In: Smart, N.P. (ed.) CT-RSA 2018. LNCS, vol. 10808, pp. 470–490. Springer, Cham (2018). https://doi.org/10.1007/978-3-319-76953-0_25

3. Blömer, J., Juhnke, J., Kolb, C.: Anonymous and publicly linkable reputation systems. In: Böhme, R., Okamoto, T. (eds.) FC 2015. LNCS, vol. 8975, pp. 478–488. Springer, Heidelberg (2015). https://doi.org/10.1007/978-3-662-47854-7_29

4. Clauß, S., Schiffner, S., Kerschbaum, F.: k-anonymous reputation. In: ASIA CCS 2013, pp. 359–368. ACM (2013)

5. Dennis, R., Owen, G.: Rep on the block: a next generation reputation system based on the blockchain. In: ICITST 2015, pp. 131–138. IEEE (2015)

6. Feldman, A.J., Zeller, W.P., Freedman, M.J., Felten, E.W.: SPORC: group collaboration using untrusted cloud resources. In: OSDI 2010, pp. 337–350. USENIX Association (2010)

7. Grinshpoun, T., Gal-Oz, N., Meisels, A., Gudes, E.: CCR: a model for sharing reputation knowledge across virtual communities. In: WI 2009, pp. 34–41. IEEE Computer Society (2009)

8. Hendrikx, F., Bubendorfer, K., Chard, R.: Reputation systems: a survey and taxonomy. J. Parallel Distrib. Comput. **75**, 184–197 (2015)

9. Ismail, R., Jøsang, A.: The beta reputation system. In: 15th Bled eConference, p. 41 (2002)

10. Jøsang, A., Golbeck, J.: Challenges for robust trust and reputation systems. In: SMT 2009. Elsevier (2009)

11. Kaafarani, A.E., Katsumata, S., Solomon, R.: Anonymous reputation systems achieving full dynamicity from lattices. In: FC 2018 (2018). https://fc18.ifca.ai/preproceedings/87.pdf

12. Kamvar, S.D., Schlosser, M.T., Garcia-Molina, H.: The eigentrust algorithm for reputation management in P2P networks. In: WWW 2003, pp. 640–651. ACM (2003)

13. Katz, J., Lindell, Y.: Introduction to Modern Cryptography, 2nd edn. CRC Press, Boca Raton (2014)

14. Pingel, F., Steinbrecher, S.: Multilateral secure cross-community reputation systems for internet communities. In: Furnell, S., Katsikas, S.K., Lioy, A. (eds.) TrustBus 2008. LNCS, vol. 5185, pp. 69–78. Springer, Heidelberg (2008). https://doi.org/10.1007/978-3-540-85735-8_8

An OBDD-Based Technique
for the Efficient Synthesis
of Garbled Circuits

Stelvio Cimato[1(✉)], Valentina Ciriani[1], Ernesto Damiani[1,2],
and Maryam Ehsanpour[1]

[1] Dipartimento di Informatica, Università degli Studi di Milano, Milan, Italy
{stelvio.cimato,valentina.ciriani,maryam.ehsanpour}@unimi.it
ernesto.damiani@ku.ac.ae
[2] EBTIC - Khalifa University of Science and Technology, Abu Dhabi, UAE

Abstract. Secure Multi-party Computation (SMC) protocols are exploited to perform collaborative computation of a function between two or more parties while keeping the privacy of the private inputs and sharing the computed result only. The Garbled Circuit (GC) protocol, proposed by Yao, is one of the possible approaches to solve the SMC problem, based on the evaluation of the Boolean Circuit representing the given function.

Recently, the question to improve efficiency in secure multi-party computation has gained much interest. One of the proposed techniques to increase the efficiency of the GC protocol is based on the reduction of the number of non-XOR gates in the Boolean circuit, since the evaluation of XOR gates have no cost for the execution of the whole protocol.

The aim of this work is to define a post-processing procedure that, given an optimized GC, decreases the number of non-XOR gates by transforming some parts of the circuit. The strategy is based on the fact that some gates behave as XORs apart from one output and then, if that input never occurs, those gates can be replaced by a XOR without changing the output of the overall network. The technique we propose is based on the analysis of the GC by using *Ordered Binary Decision Diagrams (OBDD)* representation. We present the application of our technique to some standard circuits to show the effectiveness of our proposal.

1 Introduction

Outsourcing data for storage and/or processing poses a number of problems to users' privacy, especially when those data contain sensible information. Secure Multi-party Computation (SMC) protocols provide a way to perform privacy-preserving analysis of shared data, since they allow the computation of some function without revealing the private inputs. In general, a SMC protocol gives the possibility to two or more parties $P_1, P_2, \ldots, P_k$ with inputs $x_1, x_2, \ldots, x_k$ to compute a common function $f(x_1, x_2, \ldots, x_k)$ such that each party P_i can know only its own input x_i and the resulting value of the function f. The design

© Springer Nature Switzerland AG 2019
S. Mauw and M. Conti (Eds.): STM 2019, LNCS 11738, pp. 158–167, 2019.
https://doi.org/10.1007/978-3-030-31511-5_10

of efficient SMC protocols have been exploited for a variety of security-critical applications with sophisticated privacy and security requirements such as electronic voting, electronic auctions [10], electronic cash schemes, data mining [9], remote diagnostics [2,4], classification of medical data [2], or biometric recognition [1]. In addition the technology of secure multi-party computation has gained much interest recently in research community, governments and industry as a potential tool for performing benchmarking [7] and social analysis [3].

Yao proposed a first approach for addressing two-party SMC relying on the design of a Garbled Circuit (GC) [12], that allows the computation of a function represented as a normal Boolean circuit. In Yao's GC protocol the output of each gate in the GC is evaluated by exchanging some encrypted information between the two parties, so that only the output of the computation can be eventually revealed, while the disclosure of the inputs or of any intermediate value is avoided. Since the execution of this protocol requires interaction between the collaborating parties, the total cost and run-time interaction between parties increases linearly with the number of gates, and can be huge for complex functions. Therefore, reducing the circuit size and the number of gates is important to reduce the overall communication cost and the number of operations for the evaluation of GC.

In literature, different approaches and techniques have been presented for improving the efficiency of the evaluation of GC. The *Free-XOR* technique, proposed by Kolesnikov and Schneider [8], allows the evaluation of XOR gates without any communication between the parties and without performing any cryptographic operation. Therefore, a possible strategy to reduce the evaluation costs is to replace costly non-XOR gates with some *free*-XOR gates.

In this work, we propose a technique for reducing the number of non-XOR gates, and then reducing the number of interactions between the parties at run-time, during the evaluation of a GC. Previously, some attempts to improve the synthesis of GC have been presented relying on multiple valued logic [5], or exploiting quantum gates [6]. Standard logic synthesis methods rarely consider XOR gates, due to the high cost of XORs in the current CMOS technology. Therefore, the minimization methods exploited for optimizing garbled circuits use ad hoc strategies to introduce as more XORs as possible by technology mapping techniques or algebraic manipulation of the networks, e.g., transforming $(x \cdot \overline{y}) + (\overline{x} \cdot y)$ in $(x \oplus y)$.

In this paper we introduce a more sophisticated technique to "mine" hidden XORs in a circuit. The proposed method is Boolean since it is based on the subfunctions of the circuit, and it consists on a post-processing procedure, relying on Ordered Binary Decision Diagrams (OBDD). The representation using OBDDs helps us to find similarity among function representations and transform some non-XOR gates in XOR gates, preserving the overall computation of the circuit. In particular, the proposed strategy identifies some ad-hoc satisfiability don't cares in order to transform sub-circuits in EXORs.

We evaluate our technique applying the transformation to classical security circuits, such as an adder circuit, the circuit for the computation of Data Encryption Standard (DES) and MD5 cryptographic functions. In all cases, we compare the resulting circuits with the original Boolean circuits used in GC and show the improvements achieved in terms of reduced communication cost.

Contribution of the paper is twofold: (i) we introduce a new technique for improving the efficiency of the garbled circuit computing a given function, leveraging on OBDD representation; (ii) we propose new logic synthesis methods where the goal is different from traditional objectives, where circuit efficiency is usually evaluated in terms of space or component cost.

The rest of the paper is organized as follows: in Sect. 2 we present our post processing technique and the algorithm for computing the OBDD of the sub-functions of the circuit; in Sect. 3 we show the implementation of our algorithm and its application to some case studies, getting some experimental results; finally we draw some conclusions in Sect. 4.

2   Postprocessing Technique

In this section we propose and discuss a Boolean post-processing re-optimization strategy that decreases the number of non-XOR gates in a given circuit.

2.1   Swappable Gates

Let $f : \{0,1\}^n \to \{0,1\}$ be a Boolean function and C be a multilevel circuit corresponding to f. Recall that, in the Kolesnikov's protocol, any XOR gate, in C, costs 0. For this reason, in order to decrease the protocol cost, we are interested in transforming non-XOR gates into XORs. For simplicity, hereafter we will consider circuits containing two inputs Boolean gates only. The generalization to more-than-two-input gates is straightforward.

Definition 1. *Let $g : \{0,1\}^2 \to \{0,1\}$ be a two-input Boolean gate. A similar gate to g is a two-input Boolean gate $g_s : \{0,1\}^2 \to \{0,1\}$ such that $g(x,y) = g_s(x,y)$ for all $(x,y) \in \{0,1\} \times \{0,1\}$ but one. The input configuration (v_x, v_y) such that $g(v_x, v_y) \neq g_s(v_x, v_y)$ is the* distinct *input.*

For example, a XOR gate is similar to an OR gate since their output differs on the input $(1,1)$ only. We first note that there are four similar gates to XOR, which are depicted in Table 1.

Table 1. Truth table for gates similar to XOR.

A	B	A XOR B	A NAND B	A $\not\Rightarrow$ B	B $\not\Rightarrow$ A	A OR B
0	0	**0**	"1"	0	0	0
0	1	**1**	1	"0"	1	1
1	0	**1**	1	1	"0"	1
1	1	**0**	0	0	0	"1"

The main observation behind our result is that, in a multilevel circuit, it could happen that not all the possible couples of values in $\{0,1\} \times \{0,1\}$ appear in input to an internal gate (i.e., a gate that has, as input, at least an output of another gate of the circuit). For example, consider the simple function $f = (A \oplus B) + (A \cdot B)$, where $\oplus$ is the XOR gate, $+$ is the OR gate and $\cdot$ is the AND gate. We can simply note that the inputs to the OR gate never have the configuration $(1,1)$ (i.e., $A \oplus B$ and $A \cdot B$ cannot be equal to 1 at the same time, as shown in Table 2). For this reason, the functions $(A \oplus B) + (A \cdot B)$ and $(A \oplus B) \oplus (A \cdot B)$ are equivalent.

Definition 2. *A gate g_1 in a circuit C is swappable into a gate g_2, if g_1 is a similar gate to g_2 with distinct input (v_x, v_y), and the input configuration (v_x, v_y) never occurs as an input to g_1 in C.*

Our objective is then to identify gates that are swappable into XORs in an already minimized multilevel circuit. Observe that any inputs of a gate $g(x,y)$ in a multilevel circuit C is a primary input or the output of another gate of the circuit. In general, $x = f_x$ and $y = f_y$. For instance, considering the OR gate $g(x,y)$ in the circuit corresponding to the algebraic representation: $(A \oplus B) + (A \cdot B)$ we have that $x = A \oplus B$ and $y = A \cdot B$.

Let f be a Boolean function, we denote $f^1 = f$ and $f^0 = \overline{f}$. The following theorem shows an operative strategy for testing whether a gate g in C is swappable into a similar gate g_s.

Theorem 1. *Let C be a multilevel circuit with primary inputs $x_1, \ldots, x_n$ and $g(x,y)$ be a two-input gate in C such that $x = f_x(x_1, \ldots, x_n)$ and $y = f_y(x_1, \ldots, x_n)$. If $g_s(x,y)$ is a similar gate to g with distinct input (v_x, v_y), $g(x,y)$ is swappable into $g_s(x,y)$ iff*

$$f_x^{v_x} \cdot f_y^{v_y} = 0. \tag{1}$$

Table 2. Equivalent functions $(A \oplus B) + (A \cdot B)$ and $(A \oplus B) \oplus (A \cdot B)$.

A	B	$A \oplus B$	$A \cdot B$	$(A \oplus B) + (A \cdot B)$	$(A \oplus B) \oplus (A \cdot B)$
0	0	0	0	0	0
0	1	1	0	1	1
1	0	1	0	1	1
1	1	0	1	1	1

2.2   Post-processing Algorithm

By Theorem 1, it is possible to define a Boolean strategy for testing whether a gate g in C is swappable into a similar gate g_s (in particular a XOR gate). In order to compute the function in Eq. (1) for each gate g in a circuit C, starting

Algorithm 1. *Post-processing algorithm.*
swap2XOR
INPUT: *a circuit C*
OUTPUT: *an equivalent circuit C' where any swappable*
            gate g into XOR is changed with a XOR gate
NOTATION: *denote as op_g is the algebraic operator*
                corresponding to a gate g

compute the OBDD for each primary input $x_1, \ldots, x_n$;
forall *gate $g(x, y)$ where b_x (b_y) is the OBDD for f_x (f_y)*
  compute the OBDD for $(b_x \; op_g \; b_y)$;
    if *(g is a similar gate to XOR with distinct input (v_x, v_y))*
      if *$(v_x == 0)$ $b_x = NOT(b_x)$;*
      if *$(v_y == 0)$ $b_y = NOT(b_y)$;*
      $b = AND(b_x, b_y)$;
      if *$(b == 0)$ change g with a XOR;*

from the primary inputs, we compute the OBDDs of any sub-function and we test if gates, similar to XORs, are swappable.

Algorithm 1 computes an OBDD for each sub-function of the circuit, thus is polynomial on the OBDDs' size. Note that this strategy is, by nature, Boolean, since it requires the computation of the sub-functions of each gate. This implies that circuits with a high number of gates cannot be completely analyzed due to the complexity of the OBDDs. Nevertheless, the strategy is incremental starting from the primary inputs. Therefore, in case of complex circuits, we can analyze just an initial portion of the network, as shown in the next section. It is worth observing that the same holds for gates that are similar to the XNOR gate.

3   Implementation Details and Experimental Results

In this section we show the implementation of Algorithm 1 for the optimized INV-AND-XOR multi-level circuits (we refer to the circuits reported at https:// homes.esat.kuleuven.be/~nsmart/MPC, we denote as MPC-C). Note that the inverters can be replaced by (free) XOR gates. Therefore, the aim is to minimize the number of AND gates.

The circuits are minimized using Cadence Encounter RTL compiler in conjunction with the Faraday FSA0A C 0.18 mm ASIC Standard Cell Library. The hardware modules hierarchy was flattened and the allowed gates are INV1S, AN2, XOR2HS, TIE0, and TIE1. The obtained optimized circuits are finally processed with the strategy proposed in Sect. 2.

The circuits are represented by a list of the gates in the format:

1. number input wires in the gate,
2. number output wires in the gate,
3. list of input wires,
4. list of output wires,
5. gate operation (XOR, AND or INV).

In order to apply our strategy, we do not test just single gates, but small sub-circuits, as described below.

Considering the gates in Table 1, we can easily observe that:

1. the (x NAND y) gate is equivalent to the sub-circuit INV (x AND y),
2. the ($x \not\Rightarrow y$) gate is equivalent to the sub-circuit x AND (INV y),
3. the ($y \not\Rightarrow x$) gate is equivalent to the sub-circuit (INV x) AND y,
4. the (x OR y) gate is equivalent to the sub-circuit INV ((INV x) AND (INV y)).

Table 3. Truth table for gates swappable into XOR in a INV-AND-XOR multi-level circuit.

A	B	A XOR B	INV (A AND B)	A AND (INV B)	(INV A) AND B	INV((INV A) AND (INV B))
0	0	0	–	0	0	0
0	1	1	1	–	1	1
1	0	1	1	1	–	1
1	1	0	0	0	0	–

Thus, **swap2XOR** algorithm must consider the sub-graphs described in Table 3 and test the corresponding don't care conditions. Therefore, the overall strategy considers:

1. any inverter gate (INV w_i):
    (a) if $w_i = (w_j$ AND $w_h)$, then test whether INV (w_j AND w_h) is swappable into a XOR with distinct input (0,0);
    (b) if $w_i = $ (INV w_h) AND (INV w_k), then test whether INV ((INV w_h) AND (INV w_k)) is swappable into a XOR with distinct input (1,1);
2. any AND inverter gate (w_i AND w_j):
    (a) if $w_j = $ INV w_h, then test whether w_i AND (INV w_h) is swappable into a XOR with distinct input (0,1);
    (b) if $w_i = $ INV w_h, then test whether (INV w_h) AND w_j is swappable into a XOR with distinct input (1,0);

The OBDDs are computed and memorized in an array whose indexes correspond to the number of wires in the gate format. In particular, the first n elements of the array are initialized by the OBDDs containing the primary inputs. For example, let us consider the optimized circuit for a 32-bit adder that has 439 gates. The first 64 elements in the OBDDs' array consist of the primary inputs. From 64 to 405 we have OBDDs for the gates and the last 33 OBDDs (from 406 to 438) contain the output functions. To better describe the strategy, let us consider the sub-circuit containing the gates:

2 1 94 95 92 AND
1 1 92 89 INV

that correspond to: $w_{89} = $ NOT $(w_{94}$ AND $w_{95})$. In this circuit, the input combination $(0,0)$ never occurs for (w_{94}, w_{95}), thus we can replace the INV gate with the following:

2 1 94 95 89 XOR

and we can remove the AND gate if w_{92} is not an input to any other gate.

The post processing method has been implemented in C using the CUDD library for handling OBDDs. The experimental results have been performed on all the benchmarks proposed for MPC-C.

Tables 4 and 5 show the results for 32-bit and 64-bit adders. The first column describes the synthesis method (the original MPC-C, or MPC-C with the proposed post-processing phase). The second column describes the number of gates tested in the circuit (i.e., the number of cycles of the algorithm). The following three columns show the number of AND, XOR, and INV gates in the circuit. Finally, the last column reports the gain of our proposed method with respect to MPC-C without post-processing.

Table 4. Experimental results for 32-bit Adder.

Methods	32 - bit adder				
	#NCycle	#ANDs	#XORs	#INVs	# Gain
MPC-C	-	127	61	187	-
MPC-C + post-processing	**300**	125	63	187	**2**

Table 5. Experimental results for 64-bit Adder.

Methods	64 - bit adder				
	#NCycle	#ANDs	#XORs	#INVs	**#Gain**
MPC-C	-	265	115	379	-
MPC-C + post-processing	**500**	253	127	379	**12**

Data Encryption Standard (DES) [11] is a symmetric-key method of data encryption that was published by the National Institute of Standards and Technology (NIST) in the early 1970. Data Encryption Standard (DES) works by using the same key to encrypt and decrypt a message, so both the sender and the receiver should know and use the same private key. Cryptographic key and algorithm are applied to a block of data, which the block size in DES algorithm is 64 bits. DES takes a fixed-length block of the message (plaintext) and transforms it through a series of permutation and substitution into another bit-string (ciphertext) with same length. Encryption of a block of the message also takes place in 16 rounds.

Table 6. Experimental results for DES (Key Expanded).

Methods	#NCycle	#ANDs	#XORs	#INVs	#Gain
MPC-C	-	18175	1351	10875	-
MPC-C + post-processing	500	18170	1356	10875	5
MPC-C + post-processing	600	18148	1378	10875	27
MPC-C + post-processing	650	18125	1401	10875	50
MPC-C + post-processing	800	18048	1478	10875	127
MPC-C + post-processing	900	18021	1505	10875	154
MPC-C + post-processing	1000	17980	1546	10875	195
MPC-C + post-processing	1500	17861	1665	10875	314
MPC-C + post-processing	1700	17790	1736	10875	385
MPC-C + post-processing	1800	17751	1775	10875	424
MPC-C + post-processing	1900	17734	1792	10875	441

Table 7. Experimental results for DES (No Key Expanded).

Methods	#NCycle	#ANDs	#XORs	#INVs	#Gain
MPC-C	-	18124	1340	10849	-
MPC-C + post-processing	500	18122	1342	10849	2
MPC-C + post-processing	600	18108	1356	10849	16
MPC-C + post-processing	650	18086	1378	10849	50
MPC-C + post-processing	900	18021	1505	10875	154
MPC-C + post-processing	1000	17910	1554	10849	214
MPC-C + post-processing	1500	17799	1665	10849	325
MPC-C + post-processing	1600	17752	1712	10849	372
MPC-C + post-processing	1700	177170	1747	10849	407
MPC-C + post-processing	1800	17689	1775	10849	435
MPC-C + post-processing	1900	17680	1784	10849	444

DES uses a 64-bit key to customize the transformation; however, only 56 of these are actually used by the algorithm, but eight of those bits are used for parity checks. Decryption can performed by those who know the particular key used to encrypt.

Tables 6 and 7 show the experimental results for DES algorithms with key expanded and no key expansion in different time-cycles. the results show an interesting improvement in the number of non-XOR gates.

The MD5 algorithm is a one-way cryptographic function that accepts a message of any length as input and returns a fixed-length 128-bit digest value as output. The *message digest* output is sometimes also called the "hash" or "fingerprint" of the input. MD5 was designed by well-known cryptographer Ronald

Table 8. Experimental results for MD5.

Methods	#NCycle	#ANDs	#XORs	#INVs	# Gain
MPC-C	-	29084	14150	34627	-
MPC-C + post-processing	700	29083	14151	34627	1
MPC-C + post-processing	800	29079	14155	34627	5
MPC-C + post-processing	850	29078	14156	34627	6
MPC-C + post-processing	900	29077	14157	34627	7
MPC-C + post-processing	1000	29075	14159	34627	9
MPC-C + post-processing	1100	29072	14162	34627	12
MPC-C + post-processing	1200	29068	14166	34627	16
MPC-C + post-processing	1300	29067	14167	34627	17

Table 9. Comparison of our results in the number of non-XOR gates using BDDs method.

Methods	32-bit adder	64-bit adder	DES	MD5
MPC-C	127	265	18124	29084
MPC-C + post-processing	125	253	17680	29067
Gain	**2**	**12**	**444**	**17**

Rivest in 1991 used in many situations where a potentially long message needs to be processed. The most common application of MD5 is the creation and verification of digital signatures. Table 8 describes the experimental results for the MD5 function.

We recall that the complexity of the post-processing is polynomial in the OBDDs size. Several experiments have been stopped because of the huge dimension of OBDDs generated by the algorithm. It is important to note that even for stopped procedures we could find swappable XORs and transform the circuits as shown in the tables (Table 9).

4   Discussion and Conclusion

In this paper, we discussed about the idea of decreasing the communication complexity and computational cost of secure multi-party computation (SMC) by reducing the number of non-XOR gates since XOR gates have no cost for the execution of the secure computation protocol. We proposed OBDD-based function representation method to identify non-XOR gates that could be replaced by XORs. This approach is validated in the reported examples where adders, DES and MD5 function are considered. As shown in Table 8, we can conclude that we get a reduced number of non-XOR gates (AND gates) in *32-bit adder* of about 1.6%, in *64-bit adder* of about 4.6%, in *MD5* of about 0.05% and in *DES* of about 2.5%. We plan to extend both the technique and the experimentation by refining the application patterns and by considering more interesting use cases.

References

1. Barni, M., Droandi, G., Lazzeretti, R.: Privacy protection in biometric-based recognition systems: a marriage between cryptography and signal processing. IEEE Signal Process. Mag. **32**(5), 66–76 (2015)
2. Barni, M., Failla, P., Kolesnikov, V., Lazzeretti, R., Sadeghi, A.-R., Schneider, T.: Secure evaluation of private linear branching programs with medical applications. In: Backes, M., Ning, P. (eds.) ESORICS 2009. LNCS, vol. 5789, pp. 424–439. Springer, Heidelberg (2009). https://doi.org/10.1007/978-3-642-04444-1_26
3. Bogdanov, D., Kamm, L., Kubo, B., Rebane, R., Sokk, V., Talviste, R.: Students and taxes: a privacy-preserving study using secure computation. PoPETs **2016**(3), 117–135 (2016)
4. Brickell, J., Porter, D.E., Shmatikov, V., Witchel, E.: Privacy-preserving remote diagnostics. In: Proceedings of the 14th ACM Conference on Computer and Communications Security, pp. 498–507. ACM (2007)
5. Cimato, S., Ciriani, V., Damiani, E., Ehsanpour, M.: A multiple valued logic approach for the synthesis of garbled circuits. In: IFIP/IEEE 25th International Conference on Very Large Scale Integration, VLSI-SoC, pp. 232–236 (2017)
6. Ehsanpour, M., Cimato, S., Ciriani, V., Damiani, E.: Exploiting quantum gates in secure computation. In: Kubátová, H., Novotný, M., Skavhaug, A. (eds.) Euromicro Conference on Digital System Design, DSD 2017, Vienna, Austria, 30 August–1 September 2017, pp. 291–294. IEEE Computer Society (2017)
7. Kerschbaum, F., Strüker, J., Koslowski, T.G.: Confidential information-sharing for automated sustainability benchmarks. In: Galletta, D.F., Liang, T.-P. (eds.) Proceedings of the International Conference on Information Systems, ICIS 2011, Shanghai, China, 4–7 December 2011. Association for Information Systems (2011)
8. Kolesnikov, V., Schneider, T.: Improved garbled circuit: free XOR gates and applications. In: Automata, Languages and Programming, pp. 486–498 (2008)
9. Lindell, Y., Pinkas, B.: Secure multiparty computation for privacy-preserving data mining. J. Privacy Confid. **1**(1), 5 (2009)
10. Naor, M., Pinkas, B., Sumner, R.: Privacy preserving auctions and mechanism design. In: Proceedings of the 1st ACM Conference on Electronic Commerce, pp. 129–139. ACM (1999)
11. Tuchman, W.: A brief history of the data encryption standard. In: Internet Besieged, pp. 275–280. ACM Press/Addison-Wesley Publishing Co., New York (1998)
12. Yao, A.C.-C.: How to generate and exchange secrets. In: 27th Annual Symposium on Foundations of Computer Science, pp. 162–167. IEEE (1986)

Author Index

Printed in the United States
By Bookmasters